The Career Tool Kit

FOR HIGH SCHOOL STUDENTS

MAKING THE TRANSITION FROM SCHOOL TO WORK

Carol Carter

Gary Izumo

Sarah Lyman Kravits

Diane Lindsey Reeves

Prentice Hall

Upper Saddle River, NJ 07458

Library of Congress Cataloging-in-Publication Data

The career tool kit for high school students : making the transition from school to work /
Carol Carter . . . [et al.].
  p. cm.
  Includes index.
  ISBN 0-13-088417-0
  1. Vocational guidance—United States.   2. High school students—Employment—United
States.   3. School-to-work transition—United States.   I. Carter, Carol.

HF5381 .C2667 2001
650.14'0835—dc21

00-034669

Acquisitions Editor: Sande Johnson
Assistant Editor: Michelle Williams
Production Editor: Holcomb Hathaway
Director of Manufacturing and Production: Bruce Johnson
Managing Editor: Mary Carnis
Manufacturing Manager: Ed O'Dougherty
Art Director: Marianne Frasco
Marketing Manager: Jeff McIlroy
Marketing Assistant: Barbara Rosenberg
Cover Design: Joe Sengotta
Cover Art: Jude Maceren/Stock Illustration Source, Inc.
Composition: Aerocraft Charter Art Service
Printing and Binding:

Prentice-Hall International (UK) Limited, *London*
Prentice-Hall of Australia Pty. Limited, *Sydney*
Prentice-Hall Canada Inc., *Toronto*
Prentice-Hall Hispanoamericana, S.A., *Mexico*
Prentice-Hall of India Private Limited, *New Delhi*
Prentice-Hall of Japan, Inc., *Tokyo*
Pearson Education Singapore Pte. Ltd.
Editora Prentice-Hall do Brasil, Ltda., *Rio de Janeiro*

10 9 8 7 6
ISBN 0-13-088417-0

Contents

Preface

We Wrote with You in Mind

There are many useful and well-written books about success in school and in life. This one is special because it focuses on the skills needed for success in moving from school to work and is tailored for your particular experience and needs as a student in high school. We know that you have choices ahead about building a solid foundation for a successful career and a better life—that's what brought you to this educational experience. And we believe that the success of your career depends on certain basic skills we call "tools."

This book is entitled *The Career Tool Kit* because it contains information about the tools you need to build a long, happy, and successful working life, just as a metal tool box contains hand tools. These tools will also help you in successfully completing your educational program and transition into your career. In addition, just as a tool kit allows you to keep your tools together and carry them around, this book fits the information you need into one portable volume. This book, and the skills it describes, will fit easily into the demanding routine of your daily activities.

This Book Has Three Major Benefits

First, it will help you while you are in school. Many of the skills that you will use in your working life also apply to your student life: reading, writing, studying, listening, and so forth. Tools such as a positive attitude and self-image fuel your success both in and outside of school. The information on budgeting will help you organize your finances so that you can juggle your expenses. You want to come away from your educational experience with as many advantages as possible, including your diploma or certificate. Much of the advice in this book will help you stay in school and succeed at the tasks that you undertake there.

Second, it will help you identify and prepare for the job that you want. It helps you know yourself better so that you understand what kinds of jobs might best suit your unique talents and qualities. It provides information on the job search—where you find job listings, who can help you locate opportunities, and how to apply. It guides you through the application process and shows you how to present yourself in the best possible light on a resume as well as in an interview. And it helps you to handle both failure and success.

Third, it will continue to help you throughout your career. These pages contain important information about how to manage your time and money. There is valuable advice on workplace communication with bosses, coworkers, clients, and customers; a discussion of the qualities and skills that employers look for in their employees; information about your rights on the job; and a section on critical thinking at work (decision making and problem solving). Career success, as you seek to manage and balance the stresses of your working and personal lives, is affected by your physical and mental health. Through the chapters, hints on improving and maintaining your physical and mental health are provided. Advice about motivation, patience, listening, and other useful subjects will serve you well in the coming years.

The book's special features will help you make the most of your reading. We have broken up the material into bits and pieces that you can really chew on. If you flip through the book before you begin reading, you will see certain elements in each chapter:

NEW IN YOUR TOOL KIT. At the beginning of each chapter, this list summarizes the important topics that you will cover in the chapter.

SOUND BITES. Quotes from people who have made choices similar to yours, current students as well as graduates already in the workplace, appear throughout the text. These people are "in the trenches" and can give you an accurate, personal picture of what to expect as you move into the world of work.

REAL PEOPLE, REAL STORIES. This feature encourages you to get out into the real work world and talk with people. Making contacts and learning from them will be one of the most important benefits you get from this book.

FOOD FOR THOUGHT. These boxed passages give you examples to help explain concepts discussed in the text.

TECHNOLOGY AT WORK. These boxes, new to this edition, describe the many ways that new technologies shape our world, challenging you to learn more about technologies relevant to your life, school, and career.

YOUR TOOL KIT AT WORK. This section contains an assortment of applications at the end of each chapter that will help you put what you learn in the chapter into action. The applications relate to the specific chapter you have been reading and give you the chance to apply what you have just learned to specific questions and situations. You will strengthen your knowledge as you complete the questions and exercises.

Your education is what you make of it. Your school, your teachers, your classwork, and your reading combine to give you endless opportunities to learn and improve yourself in preparation for career success. They are some of the tools with which you will build your future. But you are responsible for picking up those tools and using them. When you use what you read in this book, you take advantage of the chance to clear your path toward success.

How strong a future you construct with your tools is up to you. But we feel confident that by choosing to pursue further knowledge, you have put yourself on the right road. Use *The Career Tool Kit* for help as you make your way to the job and career you want, from school to work, and keep it with you as you continue down the path, using your tools to mold your experiences into a long and successful life as a working citizen.

Acknowledgments

We need to thank many people who have helped to bring this book to life. Their advice, hard work, and information have been invaluable to us. We extend our heartfelt thanks to: Sande Johnson, Michelle Williams, Brian Hyland, Mary Carnis, Denise Brown, and Marianne Frasco of Prentice Hall.

We would also like to thank Gay Pauley at Holcomb Hathaway Production for her dedication and hard work.

Our teacher reviewers: Barbara H. Carter, Pasco-Hernando Community College; GeorgeAnn Drennan, University of New Mexico; Edye Garner, University of Wisconsin-Madison; Pamela Hoffman, Appalachian State University; Gary L. Kramer, Brigham Young University; Bob Nelson, Rutgers University; Robert C. Speirs, Jr., Hartnell College; Carolyn Curtis, Naugatuck Valley Community-Technical College; Linda Hjorth, DeVry Institute of Technology; Ziad Mubaslet, Advanced Career Training; John Schlenker, University of Maine; Phillip Sell, Highline Community College; Earl Wilkie, Pennsylvania Institute of Technology; and Monica Zeigler, Pace University. Special thanks to Pete Affeld, Dave Baker, and Dick Dormuth at Computer Learning Centers, Melissa Carrigan, for connecting us with TCI, Elaine Carroll at Katherine Gibbs, for help in tracking down interviewees, Judy Northrup, for financial advice, Ward Deutschman, for review and advice.

Interviewees who filled us in on the real world picture: Beverly Andre, Lisa Durden, Wray Gould, Lois Griffin, Catherine Hartlove, Daniel Hernandez, Alicia Jackson, Delores Lay, Noel Lee, Susan Lugay, Lisa Mercado, Karen Mitchell, Finus A. Rascoe, Jr., Aretha Thompson, and Jay Wade.

Fleet students who tested applications: John Isiah Allen, Lisa Bailey, Della Bankert, Levell Herbert, William Maurice Holland Jr., Jessica J. Lambert, Sean Miller, Jennifer Waters, Kevin Yearick, and Carolyn Elizabeth Zylka. Bob Giudice at Technology Career Institute (TCI), Scott Carter, for thinking of our name, Patricia Cuff and Patricia Spencer Vaughan for their contributions to the first edition that helped create a foundation for this edition.

Barbara Rudy Foti and Suzanne Weissinger for classroom suggestions.

Cynthia Nordberg and Kathleen Cole, for research and support.

Thank you, too, to all the others who have contributed their valuable energies to making this book a reality.

Finally, we'd like to thank teachers everywhere who continue to help students learn, grow, and improve their lives and the world. Your dedication, energy, and commitment to excel provide a model of leadership for students. We salute your inspired work.

About the Authors

Carol Carter is Vice President and Director of Student Programs and Faculty Development at Prentice Hall. She has written *Majoring in the Rest of Your Life: Career Secrets for College Students* and *Majoring in High School.* She has also co-authored *The Career Tool Kit, Keys to Career Success, Keys to Study Skills, Keys to Thinking and Learning,* and *Keys to Effective Learning.* She has taught welfare to work classes, team taught in the La Familia Scholars Program at Community College of Denver, and has conducted numerous workshops for students and faculty around the country. She is the host of the "Keys to Lifelong Learning Telecourse," a twenty-six episode telecourse to help students at a distance prepare for college, career, and life success. In addition to working with students of all ages, Carol thrives on foreign travel and culture; she has been fortunate enough to have been a guest in forty foreign countries.

Gary Izumo is a professor in business at Moorpark College and assists large businesses as a management consultant on issues ranging from corporate growth and organizational development, to operational effectiveness. In addition, he writes a monthly business column for the *Los Angeles Times,* Ventura County edition. Gary is an enthusiastic swimmer and reader, but most of all, he enjoys spending time with his family and friends. He believes in contributing to the community and he is an active volunteer to local schools on curriculum and technology matters. Gary is a graduate of Occidental College with a degree in economics and received his MBA from the University of California at Los Angeles.

Sarah Lyman Kravits is a student of life with a passion for learning. In her drive to help others discover their love for learning—and their essential selves—she has spent the last six years writing, researching, talking to students, and talking to teachers in pursuit of the best possible textbooks on student success. She has co-authored *The Career Tool Kit, Keys to Success, Keys to Effective Learning, Keys to Thinking and Learning,* and *Keys to Study Skills.* She originally hooked into the world of student success as Program Director for LifeSkills, Inc., a nonprofit organization that aims to further the career and personal development of high school students. Even earlier, being a Jefferson Scholar at the University of Virginia helped to bring her love of learning to new levels. She encourages readers to make the most of this time in school—it is an incredible gift.

Diane Lindsey Reeves is an author whose work focuses on helping people of all ages figure out what they want to be when they grow up. She enjoys sharing ideas about career exploration as a writer-in-residence in schools and in other types of programs for teachers and students. Reeves lives in Raleigh, North Carolina, where weekend jaunts are divided between the beach or the mountains. She is married and has two daughters. Reeves would love to hear from you via her website at www.careerideasforkids.com.

TAKING INVENTORY

I

It's all about feeling good about

yourself, knowing that you can

do whatever you want to do.

You have got to be positive—

strictly positive about yourself.

LEVELL HERBERT, COMPUTER STUDENT

1

Choosing Your Equipment

FINDING THE RIGHT MIND SET

NEW IN YOUR TOOL KIT

Positive self-image	Commitment
Positive self-talk	Patience
Good attitude	Integrity
Motivation	

Another class, another book.

You have probably been through a few of both in your time, and you deserve to know what is different and special about this one.

The Career Tool Kit will help you develop the skills you will need to succeed in your chosen career—whatever that may be. Whether doctor or plumber, there are a number of common skills that can virtually guarantee your success. Some of these skills will be new to you; some of them you've already been putting to good use for years. Used together, these skills will give you an edge in today's job market.

The title of the book, *The Career Tool Kit*, refers to these skills as tools. We like the metaphor of a tool kit because such a kit is portable and can carry a great number of tools for different purposes. The tools you stock in your tool kit are the skills you will use throughout your career—and your life. You can use these tools to paint a detailed picture of the successful career that you want.

In this chapter, you'll learn about:

- Using universal work skills
- Maintaining a positive self-image and good attitude
- Gathering five important basic tools:
  1. Motivation
  2. Commitment
  3. Habits
  4. Patience
  5. Integrity

Most important, you'll learn how to put these tools to work in your career plans.

Why You're Here

Have you ever sat through a class and wondered, "Why do I need to know this stuff?" or tried to imagine, "What does this have to do with real life?" This won't be a problem with the tool kit.

This book won't be teaching you how to create an Internet Web page or climate control or anything about a specific career opportunity or trade. There are other classes and books better suited for that job. Instead, this book will help you build a base of knowledge, a tool kit full of skills, that you can use with any vocation that you decide to study.

We call these skills "universal work skills," and we'll be talking about them on every page of this book. They're the skills you'll gather as you read. These skills apply to every vocation or job that you will ever study or have. They are universal—useful throughout the universe of careers. They act as a "bridge" between school success and work success (see Figure 1.1).

Learn them well and learn them now, and you'll an edge over others who wait until they become adults working in the workplace to learn them. That's often called learning things the hard way. It wastes time and energy. This approach is different because it gives you the opportunity to get these skills under your belt now so that when you are hired to do a job, you can focus on learning the job and doing your best instead of learning how to work.

That's why you are here reading this book and taking this course. In these pages, you will learn information about crucial

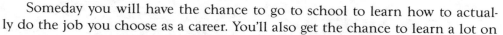

FIGURE 1.1

Universal skills are the foundation of success.

tools that will help you succeed on the job, now and down the road (see Figure 1.2). You will put all the skills into a tool kit that you will keep and use for a long time to come. As you work to master these skills, you will gain confidence in yourself and know that you and your work are worthwhile. Master these universal skills and, someday, someone will be very glad to have hired you.

"HERE" IS THE RIGHT CHOICE

Let's define what "here" means for you right now. You are in high school. You're working hard to make it through so you can graduate. Right? But then what?

Perhaps you've already started thinking about the kind of career you want to pursue. Many of you may be considering preparing for work in specific vocations or trades. You may be checking out various colleges or training programs. If so, you have already taken an important step—one that seems to cause many people a heap of trouble. You have already begun to focus your efforts; you are channeling your energy toward a goal. Be proud of yourself. You've done yourself a big favor. It will lead you on the path toward a better job and a better living.

Someday you will have the chance to go to school to learn how to actually do the job you choose as a career. You'll also get the chance to learn a lot on

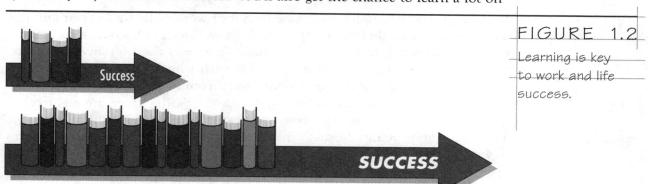

FIGURE 1.2

Learning is key to work and life success.

Food for Thought

Your skills and natural talents are like raw resources. They are like the nails, wood, and cement that you need to build a house. But something more is necessary. The *house plans* teach you to use those resources (how much of them to use, when to use them, and how to configure them) in order to come out with a well-made home at the end of the process. Everything working together helps you to arrive at your goal successfully. This book, along with the class you are taking (and other classes you have taken and will take in the future) are the building plans. What you will learn is how to develop and organize your mental, physical, social, and creative skills so that you can translate them into a successful career. We're here to help provide that tool kit and those house plans so that you can make success work for you!

the job. In fact, we believe that you should continue to learn on the job for the rest of your life. There is always more to learn. As long as you are learning, you will continue growing as a person and as a worker. It's a lifelong process.

That's what makes right here and right now the ideal time to start learning these basic skills. Many people don't give themselves time to learn them before going out into the world. They dive in without preparing themselves for what lies ahead. That won't be the case for you, however. You've had the good sense to give yourself the best possible chance to succeed. Even reading this book is an important decision. At this very moment, you are making a choice to make this book one of your tools. We, like your teachers, are entirely focused on your education and your future success in the workplace. You have made an excellent choice.

And, speaking of choices, you do realize, don't you, that a trained and educated employee has something the unprepared employee doesn't? Freedom of choice! Gaining skills like these and then getting the practical training that you need to do a job or pursue a career earn you the ability to make even more choices for yourself. Get some experience and even more training, and you continue to multiply your options. These choices give you more power to control your destiny. Believe us, that's a good thing!

Universal Work Skills

Let's get started with a look at those universal work skills we've been talking about. Remember, these aren't specific skills you need to become a computer expert or paralegal. Instead, they are basic skills you need for any career, no matter what you do, where you do it, and with whom you do it.

According to the experts on a government commission called SCANS (the Secretary's Commission on Achieving Necessary Skills), there are eight categories of skills that reflect the needs and experiences of real working people. These categories define the areas in which you need to be proficient in order to assure yourself of on-the-job success:

1. Interpersonal: Working with other people on the job
2. Information: Gathering and making use of information

3. **Systems:** Understanding interrelationships

4. **Technology:** Working with various technologies

5. **Basic skills:** Using the everyday skills that keep things moving

6. **Thinking skills:** Using your brain power to figure out your world

7. **Personal qualities:** Displaying traits that show you to be valuable and trust-worthy

8. **Resources:** Identifying, organizing, planning, and efficiently using available resources

Under each of these categories or "umbrellas" fall groups of topics. Look at Table 1.1 to see these topics. These topics are the skills—the tools—that you will learn throughout your reading.

When you complete this course, you will understand what it takes to be proficient in all these categories except technology, which you will cover in other classes as you start training for a specific type of job. Everything you will learn as you read falls under one of these umbrellas, but in a different order. That's because we wanted the chapters to progress in the way people actually experience the skills. As people, we move through these three steps:

1. Having self-knowledge and building personal skills

2. Developing interpersonal skills and preparing for the workforce

3. Entering the workforce and succeeding on the job

As you make your way through this book, you will see how the chapter topics and corresponding skills fit under each umbrella. When you have filled your tool kit, each category will be well represented inside. It's important that you give each category equal attention. Skills in only one or two areas won't give you the balance and well-rounded perspective you'll need to succeed on the job.

When you develop your tools in all areas and know how to use them well, you will build yourself a strong career foundation. These tools will be at the core of your successes. You will use them every day of your life. And you will never be able to say, "I can't think of how I can possibly use what I learned from reading that book!"

POP QUIZ!

Before we go any further, let's make sure you understand how these skills might work in an everyday, real-life situation. Match the following situation with the skill that it describes (use Table 1.1 for hints, if you need them):

1. You find information about careers at the library.
2. You talk to a friend's parent about an interesting project that he or she is managing at work.
3. You take notes at a seminar about how to apply for financial aid for college.
4. You volunteer at the local hospital to find out more about medical careers.
5. You get up an hour early to study for the SAT exam.
6. You use e-mail to request a catalog from a college you are interested in.
7. You make a flowchart showing the responsibilities of everyone on your sports team.
8. You decide that a two-year vocational school would best prepare you to meet your career goals.

A. Technology (using equipment and procedures properly)
B. Systems (human relationships)
C. Basic skills (listening/writing/taking notes)
D. Information (organizing/interpreting information)
E. Resources (managing time)
F. Thinking skills (decision-making, reasoning, visualizing)
G. Personal qualities (self-knowledge, responsibility and commitment)
H. Interpersonal (communication)

Correct answers (1-D; 2-H; 3-C; 4-G; 5-E; 6-A; 7-B; 8-F)

Positive Self-Image

Start filling your tool kit with how you look at yourself.

How you see yourself colors every corner of your life—your emotions, your relationships, and your level of success on your career path. We are powerful people. We control our thoughts, and we create ourselves in those thoughts. How we think of ourselves and the world becomes how we act in the world. Much of how we view ourselves comes from what we heard about ourselves as children, both from parents and other authority figures. For instance, someone who, as a child, gets in trouble a lot for spilling may grow up thinking of himself as clumsy.

Seeing one's self in a positive light is the first and most important task for each and every one of us. Each of us needs to be our own best cheerleader, our own best friend, and our own greatest resource. If we cannot count on ourselves for support, to whom else can we turn? A negative self-image not only paralyzes us, it sets us up for failure. But when we truly know and appreciate our own worth, we have the power to achieve success.

There are two parts to a positive self-image. One is called **self-esteem.** When you have good self-esteem, you perceive yourself to be of value. You respect yourself. You are satisfied that you are a capable and worthwhile

Self-image, noun.
One's conception or view of one's self ("self" includes one's own identity, abilities, and worth).

SKILL	WITHOUT KEY SKILLS
Interpersonal	
Communication, Cooperating as a team member, Working with clients/customers, Leadership, Managing workplace diversity, Negotiating and resolving conflict	You have difficulties in cooperating with coworkers to complete required tasks. Everyday conflicts that are part of work can't be resolved.
Information	
Evaluating information, Organizing/interpreting information, Communicating information verbally or in writing, Processing information (as on a computer)	You don't know where or how to find data critical for an assignment. Your boss doesn't understand your report and effort.
Systems	
Social systems (human relationships), Each company's organizational system, Systems of technology—how pieces of equipment work together	You make mistakes because you don't understand your role on your team. Work and communications occur mysteriously or in code . . . you feel left out.
Technology	
Choosing equipment and/or procedures to use in a given situation, Understanding how equipment and/or procedures work, Using equipment and procedures properly	Your boss is upset with your overtime; he doesn't know you are afraid to use the new equipment. You lose your job. You didn't upgrade your skills and they became obsolete.
Basic Skills	
Reading/proofreading/writing/taking notes, Listening, Speaking, Memory and concentration testing	You are confused and people don't understand you . . . everyone is frustrated. You have a difficult time getting, then keeping, a job.
Thinking Skills	
Creative thinking, Decision making, Problem solving, Knowing how to learn, Visualizing, Reasoning	It will be hard to grow as the job changes if you don't know how to continue to learn. Your career has stalled and you can't seem to move ahead despite how hard you try.
Personal Qualities	
Self-knowledge, Self-esteem, Integrity and honesty, Responsibility and commitment, Self-management (including self-assessment, goal-setting, motivation), Prioritizing	Despite the best technical skills, poor work habits cost you a great assignment. Your boss questions you endlessly about your work. Does she trust you?
Resources	
Managing time, Managing money, Managing material items, Managing people	Your personal financial blunders have hurt your attitude and work. You just can't seem to get to work or meetings on time. Your boss doesn't think you care.

TABLE 1.1

Key skills for school and work success.

human being. You know that your qualities and abilities can improve your life as well as the lives of other people. You see that your role in the future of the world, however large or small, makes a difference.

The other component is **self-confidence.** Self-confident people trust themselves. They believe in their ability to make positive changes in themselves and in the world. Self-confidence gives you belief in your power to act in helpful and important ways; it allows you to take your positive perceptions about yourself and turn them into action.

Put those two ideas together, and you have a solid base from which to go anywhere you desire. One saying conveniently combines both parts quite nicely: "If you perceive and you believe, then you can achieve." If you perceive your own abilities (self-esteem) and you believe in the worthiness of your abilities and actions (self-confidence), then you will achieve your goals and dreams.

If you sometimes get down on yourself or feel like a failure, you are in good company. Most people, even those who seem superconfident, struggle with those negative feelings from time to time. The difference between getting over them and letting them get to you is in how you look and think about those negative feelings. You *can* turn yourself around. How? With the power of your own vision and thoughts, for one.

Our thinking affects our behavior and our success, whether directly or indirectly. It's like hearing someone say "Great job" or "You messed up." Whether good or bad, we tend to believe what we hear about ourselves—whether the words come from someone else or from inside our own minds.

Use the technique of **positive thinking** as a way to "think yourself to success." If you hear yourself thinking "I am really stupid," stop yourself and change the thought to something like "I can do better next time and I will." Replace negative thoughts with positive ones—again and again and again—every time a negative thought tries to sneak its way into your mind. It will take a lot of practice over a lot of time to make progress. Just keep at it.

Another technique you can try is to make **positive statements** to yourself. In the morning when you look at yourself in the mirror (bed head and all) say things like "I am a terrific, valuable, and powerful person." Or get more specific: "I am going to complete that project today, and it will be wonderful." Be honest, sure, but be nice and give yourself a break!

One more idea is to replace have-to words, which take power from you, with **want-to words,** which enable you to have power and control. Take a look at Figure 1.3. The want-to words give us power because they imply a per-

Sound Bite

The courses help you feel better about yourself. If you have to take a test, or things like that, you always say to yourself, I don't think I'm going to be able to pass it. When you have that negative attitude about it, you're always going to do bad. You defeat yourself already from the start. If you have a positive attitude about it, you'll do well.

—J. Wade
technology student

FIGURE 1.3
Think empowerment.

Use		Avoid	
■ I want to	■ I promise to	■ I have to	■ I intend to
■ I choose to	■ I know I will	■ I should	■ I think I can
■ I will	■ I commit to	■ I'll try	■ I hope to

sonal decision to act. For example, when you say "I have to" or "I should," it appears that someone else had the power to tell you what you "had to" do. "I want to" and "I choose to" put you in the power seat—you have the desire and make the choice; you initiate the move and the decision.

Those three ideas—positive thinking, positive statements, and want-to words—will help you build your confidence. Each new skill, each school success, or each good grade is more proof that helps you believe in your own worth. Tell yourself about your accomplishments. Remind yourself of your successes and your steps in the right direction. Focus on your own potential. Most of all, don't ever forget how important you and your ideas are, no matter how many difficult spots you encounter in your life. Positive self-image will smooth your way more than any other tool.

Attitude

Pardon me, but your attitude is showing. Yes, your attitude shines through in everything you do—in good ways and in not so good ways.

Attitudes go with all kinds of feelings! You have probably heard someone say such things as, "She has a nasty attitude" or "He has a great attitude." These comments refer to the person's mental state. Or maybe you have heard, "Don't give me that kind of attitude!" The speaker means definition 2, or a way of acting that shows a disposition.

Your attitude affects everything that you do. It can help you immensely or trip you up and slow you down. It can open up opportunities for you, or it can push them away. It can hide them so you don't even know that they exist. Don't let your attitude be a stone in your shoe! Make it a tool. Tame it and put it into your tool kit to keep.

Attitude ties in with self-image, too. If you have a positive self-image, you will have an easier time projecting a good attitude. A negative self-image, though, will often result in a negative attitude that gets in your way. What you feel on the inside will shine through to the outside.

Attitude, *noun.*
1. One's disposition, opinion, mental set, etc.
2. A manner of acting, thinking, or feeling that shows one's disposition.

Food for Thought

People would rather be around a positive person than someone who is usually complaining or critical of others. How would you classify yourself? Do you tend to think positively? Do your conversations (attitude) reflect your image of yourself? You make a difference with yourself and others, positively or negatively, with how you think. Let's make our environment inviting and constructive with a positive attitude.

Here's how it works. First of all, you have the power to choose and change your attitude. You may think that you don't have a choice when it comes to attitude. That is a myth! You don't have to be a slave to your attitude. Tell it who's boss. Never let a bad attitude keep you from doing your best. Sure, you may fail sometimes. But when you do, learn what you can from the experience and move on. You don't have to make the same mistakes over and over again!

Your attitude colors everything you do, whether you see the glass half full or half empty. It can make or break some of the best opportunities in life. It is a tool that often makes the difference between success and failure. Get a grip on it!

Motivation

Working hard at developing a positive self-image and a positive attitude is just the beginning. Next in your tool kit is motivation.

Got goals? Then you need motivation. Motivation gives you the energy and the drive you need to dive in and work toward your goals. This tool keeps you moving when the going gets rough. And it can come from many different sources. For instance, did you ever wake up in the morning and not want to get out of bed? What motivated you when you finally got up? Did you remember that you had an important test in school? Did you want to avoid getting a detention for being late to school? Were you hungry for breakfast? These are all different kinds of motivation, and they all work!

Your motivation to pursue a particular career may run a little deeper. Maybe you want to make a lot of money. Maybe you want to spend your life helping others. Maybe you dream of being a big success in a particular field. Or, maybe you have something to prove to yourself or to others. It doesn't matter where it comes from; motivation is necessary to set your dreams in motion.

What happens if you have a good attitude but no motivation? Not much, we're afraid. You can have a good attitude and lots of other great skills, but if you don't have motivation, they won't do you much good. It's motivation that sets the wheels in motion and gets things going. Without it, you might as well live your whole life in bed! With a good attitude, of course.

Motivation, noun.
That which incites or impels, that which provides with a motive.

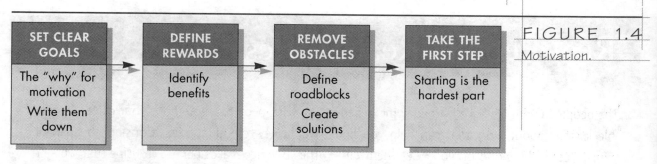

FIGURE 1.4
Motivation.

How can you get motivated? We're glad you asked. It's really not that hard if you take it step-by-step (see Figure 1.4). First, you set your goals—something as "small" as ace your next history exam or as "big" as graduate from high school with honors.

Next, define what your rewards may be. In the case of the exam, the reward may simply be the satisfaction of a job well done, or it may be the saving grace in bringing your semester grade up to par. In the case of graduating with honors, it may be just what you need to get accepted into the college of your choice.

The next step involves removing obstacles that stand in the way of your success. To get the A on the exam, you may have to miss out on going to a party with friends in order to stay home and study. For the graduation goal, you might have to take a summer course to keep on track. It all depends on your circumstances.

The last step is actually the taking first step toward reaching your goal. Watch out! That first step can be a doozy. But like they say, even a journey of a thousand miles starts with a single step. You won't get anywhere until you take the first step toward your destination. Just do it!

Food for Thought

If you have ever spent time exercising, you know that some days you feel psyched for it and some days you drag yourself to the gym (or the court or the track or the floor in front of your exercise video on television). Even when you feel unmotivated to work out, you usually have a surprise at the end—you're glad that you did it, and you feel good about what you accomplished! Sometimes you'll even feel more proud of yourself than you do when you are excited about working out, because you overcame your own lack of interest. That surprise feeling of pride and accomplishment can come from completing any other task that might seem bothersome when you start. It's the light at the end of the tunnel.

Commitment

Wow! Look at you! Great self-image, terrific attitude, motivated—you know your value in the world, and you have the drive to go out and prove it! You are well on your way. But, you're not quite there yet. Here's another tool to keep you moving in the right direction—commitment.

Real People, Real Stories

The people in your life have learned some incredible lessons about work that can help you find your place in the world of work. Get them talking, learn from their mistakes, and enjoy their successes. Listen to their stories. Experience is the best teacher—and you probably have more people than you realize who would be glad to do all they can to ensure your success.

In each chapter of this book, you will be asked to seek people out to talk with about various aspects of their work life. This process will serve two purposes. First, as we've just mentioned, is to learn from their adventures and misadventures in the workplace. Second is to develop your confidence (courage even!) in talking with people. Throughout your career, people will be key to your success. Consider this part of the "practice makes perfect" routine that will get you ready to take on the world of work!

First time out, let's stay pretty close to home. Cozy up with parents or grandparents, and ask them to tell you what they had wanted to do with their lives when they were your age. Get them to share how events and circumstances led them to be doing what they are doing now. And, in case you haven't a clue, ask them exactly what it is they do (or did) for a living. Use a separate sheet of paper to record your findings—in your best essay style, of course.

Anytime you make a promise to do something, whether it is to love someone for the rest of your life or to take out the trash after dinner, you have made a commitment. You have committed yourself to do something.

Even as a high school student, you make commitments all the time. Promising to get together with friends on Friday night, joining the basketball team, even taking a class like this are all commitments. You said you'd do something and you do it—that's commitment. You set a goal, and you do what it takes to achieve it—that's commitment. You are given an assignment and you do it—that's commitment.

Commitment implies vision and focus. It means that you focus your energies and attention on your commitment. When it's commitment to a goal you are talking about, you have to define the goal, figure out what it will take to achieve the goal, and then focus on achieving it. It's one thing to say something like "I've made a commitment to improve myself," and another thing to decide on a clear and specific course of action—by exercising regularly, for example, or by reading a book every week.

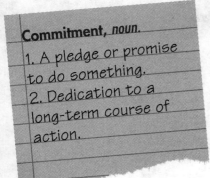

Commitment, *noun.*
1. A pledge or promise to do something.
2. Dedication to a long-term course of action.

Commitment is especially important when it comes to choosing a career. You may have good intentions (attitude) and plenty of energy (motivation), but without commitment you'd have no place to go. Without commitment, people tend to take the first thing that comes along—in relationships, in jobs, in anything—instead of working toward specific goals. It can be a real dead end.

Commitment gives you the clearest possible vision of where you want to go and how you want to get there. How can you become committed and then stay that way? Look at Figure 1.5. It identifies three key steps in making and keeping a commitment.

1. **Define your commitment.** Make a decision about something you want to do. How about "I want to read through this entire book with the rest of the class"? Be specific.

2. **Act on your commitment.** Don't just sit there; do something! Take the first step toward your goal. In this case, start reading the book!

3. **Stick to your commitment.** Renewing your commitment regularly will help you stay focused. Think about the goal you are trying to reach. Commitment is a vision (a view of your future), so staying committed means renewing that vision and keeping it as clear as possible.

When it comes to succeeding in the workplace, commitment gives you a valuable personal quality—responsibility. Commitment and responsibility are inseparable. When you act responsibly, you earn the respect and trust of others who see that you stick to your commitments and get the job done.

A commitment helps you define your goals and draw the line from yourself, here and now, to that dream of yours. It probably won't be a straight line because our lives are unpredictable. Things come up now and then that will cloud our vision. But if you commit to following the line with a good attitude and motivation, you will get there.

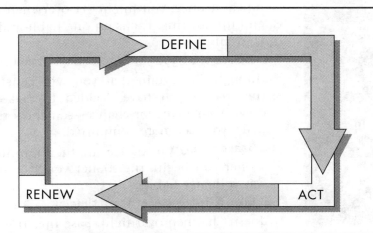

FIGURE 1.5

Commitment.

Habits

Yep, you've got them. So do we. Everyone has them—habits—good ones and not so good ones.

Habits belong in your tool kit because they affect so many of your activities. Habits are control freaks. They can control a lot of what you do, and they are stubborn about sticking around, whether you want them to or not! People hang on to habits of all kinds because they offer rewards. You get something in return for sticking to a habit. The worst habits sometimes bring the most immediate rewards; good habits tend to bring rewards over time. That's why it can be so tough to break bad habits and to stick with new ones.

> **Habit, noun.**
> A tendency to perform a certain action or behave in a certain way; a usual way of doing.

What do we mean by a bad habit? A bad habit is one that keeps you from pursuing your dreams, one that pulls you down into a rut and holds you there even if you want to get out.

Procrastination is an example of one of the most common bad habits. It constantly keeps people from moving ahead. Bad habits come in all shapes and sizes. People have bad habits at school, at home, with friends, with substances, and in their personal lives. Do you have any bad habits that keep you from reaching your goals? If so, it will take some strong, constant effort to beat your bad habits. How can you begin to break your not-so-helpful habits? Here are some helpful guidelines:

- **Recognize the habits that block your success.** Visualize where you want to be, and figure out the best way to get there. List the habits you want to break or change, with the most important ones at the top. Set a path for yourself.

- **Focus on one change at a time.** If you try too much at once, you might get overwhelmed and end up quitting. Focus on one habit and give it your all.

- **Believe that you want to change it now.** Think it through. Be certain that you will benefit from the change you have decided to make. Write down your plans for change—somehow that can make you feel more committed.

- **Start today.** Why waste another minute? The sooner you begin, the sooner you'll be on your way to better habits.

- **Take a little piece at a time.** Changing habits doesn't happen overnight. Ease into the change and be kind to yourself.

Food for Thought

Look at eating habits for an example. Say George has a bad habit of eating a lot of chocolates. That bad habit has an immediate reward because the chocolates taste immediately good as he eats them! Long term, the fat and sugar won't do much good. If he began eating more fruits and vegetables instead of chocolates, he would give up that immediate sugar high. The reward wouldn't come right away. After some time and some steady devotion to the new good habit, however, a more energetic, healthier body would begin to emerge—a much longer-lasting and valuable reward.

- **Reward yourself when you take a step in the right direction.** Give yourself credit where credit is due. Do something nice for yourself when you see that you've made progress. Be proud of yourself and confident that you are on the right track.

- *Give yourself time!* It generally takes twenty-one days to even start to change a habit. Use that time thinking about the change, trying it out, slipping back into the habit, and trying again. Hang in there! You can do it!

Patience

Another tool will come in handy while you're trying to break those bad habits, and that is patience. You've got to have it and you've got to have it NOW!

Building your career without patience is like building a house without a roof. Sure you save lots of time, but you may not like the results when you get through—especially when it rains!

Likewise, if you have a great attitude and are motivated, committed, and working to improve your habits, you still don't have it all. Sometimes it takes a long time—even years—to accomplish a goal. Without patience, you'll never make it to the finish line. And, you may end up settling for second best along the way.

Patience will serve you well. Success rarely happens overnight. The right opportunities will come your way, but often not right away. So remember, while you are patiently waiting for your ship to come in, use your other tools. Sitting around waiting for success to drop in your lap won't do you any good. Your positive self-image will keep your confidence up, attitude will keep you moving, motivation will keep you looking, commitment will keep you focused, and building good habits will increase your rate of success.

> **Patience,** *noun.*
>
> 1. The state of being able to endure pain, trouble, etc., without using self-control.
> 2. The will or ability to wait without complaint.

Integrity

Here's another personal quality worth adding to your tool kit—integrity. It's a quality that friend and foe alike will admire and respect.

The words in the definition on the following page—moral, principle, ethics, honesty, uprightness, sincerity—are probably familiar to you. But how do they translate into real life? How do you live at home, at school, and at work when you are a person of integrity? To give you an idea, here are four principles of integrity, each with an example of how they apply in daily living.

A person of integrity makes person, school, and work decisions based on admirable moral principles:

- You schedule time each day so that you have time to spend with family and friends and to complete all school, work, and sports obligations.
- You choose not to yell at your brother or sister when he or she does something to irritate you. Instead, you calmly work out the situation with him or her.
- You don't talk about your friends behind their backs.
- You admit to your teacher that you didn't finish the assignment on time.

A person of integrity deals with others honestly and tells the truth to self and to others:

- You tell your friend when he or she does something to upset you.
- You tell your parents when you make a mistake.
- You take the time to work out disagreements with friends and family members.
- You admit when you are wrong and take steps to correct your mistakes.

A person of integrity speaks and acts sincerely, voicing thoughts accurately and doing what feels right:

- You tell your mother that you will finish cleaning the house when she has to run errands, and you follow through by doing a good job.
- You praise your sister or brother for getting good grades on her or his report card.
- You use tact and kindness coupled with honestly and directness when you decide to break up with a partner.

Integrity, noun.

The quality or state of being of sound moral principle and ethics, honesty, uprightness, and sincerity.

A person of integrity considers the needs of others with his or her own needs when making the decisions that define the path through life:

- You offer to help however help is needed when your best friend has a family emergency.
- You volunteer to take care of your siblings so your parents can go out for dinner.
- You help shovel the walk or rake leaves for an elderly neighbor.

Integrity is a highly prized quality—in friends, in employees, and in spouses—because it means that people can trust you at the most basic level.

Whether the relationship is personal or professional, this trust brings freedom. If people trust how you think, work, and behave, they will allow you to make decisions and according to your own will.

Maybe you've already noticed this in your relationship with your parents. As a teenager, you want more freedom—to be with your friends, to go out and do things you enjoy, and just to do your own thing away from your family. Chances are that if you consistently do what you say you're going to do, come home when you are supposed to come home, and otherwise show yourself trustworthy, your parents will allow you more freedom. More freedom is one of the perks of acting with integrity.

Integrity isn't something that can be taught, however. Most of us learn something about right and wrong from parents, teachers, and our life experiences. But each of us makes our own choice about which path our lives will follow. Integrity isn't knowing the right way to behave; it's actually behaving that way. Right or wrong. Good or bad. Honest or dishonest. The choice is up to you.

You've Got the Basics

There you have it—the most basic foundation tools in your tool kit. New tools you should have in your tool kit include:

- Positive self-image
- Good attitude
- Motivation
- Commitment
- Good habits
- Patience
- Integrity

You won't go far without them. Make them a permanent part of your collection, and use them well. In the next chapters, we'll talk about other tools you'll want in your tool kit. But make sure you understand that the other tools won't work unless you have these first. This is the foundation for everything you need to be successful in life. Make sure it's strong and ready for whatever comes your way.

Your Tool Kit at Work

At the end of each chapter, you will find activities to help you apply what you've learned to your own situation. Following are some to help you think about the basic skills we've just covered and to give you a chance to think about their place in your life.

Just in case you are wondering, you will see these same skills mentioned in some of the other chapters, too. That's because these basic skills are closely related to and build on the workplace competencies we will be exploring later on in this book.

Give each activity your careful attention and fill up your career tool kit with all the right tools.

1.1 Universal Work Skills

Universal work skills are divided into basic skills and workplace competencies. The skills on the list add up to the knowledge you need in the workplace as well as how to put that knowledge to work. Both kinds of skills are necessary if you want to qualify for a good job, succeed on the job, and earn promotions as your career progresses.

The nine chapters in *The Career Tool Kit* are interrelated, which means that the basic skills and workplace competencies appear many times throughout this book, building upon each other and complementing one another. To give you a quick resource, skills are listed with numbers that indicate the chapter or chapters which focus on that skill. "A/C," which stands for "all chapters," means the skill is a basic theme that runs throughout the book.

Read the following list carefully. Check your current interest and skill level. Leave the last column unmarked for now.

UNIVERSAL WORK SKILL	MY SKILLS ARE:				I WOULD LIKE TO IMPROVE	I'M PROGRESSING
	EXCELLENT	GOOD	AVERAGE	POOR		
Basic Skills						
Thinking clearly and creatively (A/C)						
Making decisions (A/C)						
Solving problems (A/C)						
Positive self-image (A/C)						

(continued)

UNIVERSAL WORK SKILL	MY SKILLS ARE: EXCELLENT GOOD AVERAGE POOR				I WOULD LIKE TO IMPROVE	I'M PROGRESSING
Being responsible (A/C)						
Making choices based on values (A/C)						
Developing good habits (1)						
Basic Skills (continued)						
Working and living with integrity (A/C)						
Identifying goals (3, 7)						
Setting priorities (3, 7)						
Knowing how to learn (5)						
Reading (5)						
Writing (5)						
Listening (5, 6)						
Speaking (6)						
Demonstrating sociability (6, 7, 8)						
Workplace Competencies						
Communicating (A/C)						
Working in a diverse community (2)						
Managing time (3)						
Managing money (4)						
Participating in a team (6)						
Handling clients/ customers (6)						
Negotiating (6)						
Resolving conflicts (6, 9)						
Using resources (7, 8)						
Acquiring information (7, 9)						

Refer to your list as you go through the chapters. Note your progress in the last column.

Universal work skills can boost your success in school, on the job, and in life in general. Think about ways you may have used or are currently using these skills at school or in other ways right now:

_____

_____

_____

_____

_____

_____

_____

Name three universal work skills that you need to improve. Be specific and honest. The first step on your new career path depends on an honest assessment of yourself.

1. _____

2. _____

3. _____

1.2 Positive Attitude List—Your PAL

Because your attitude affects everything you do, positive attitudes are some of your most essential tools. They account for 80 percent of your success in your career and in your personal life.

You will build your positive attitude list (PAL) throughout this book. We will refer to the list as your PAL. A pal is a close friend who helps you and supports you, and that's the kind of effect your positive attitude can have on your future.

A new list will appear at the end of each chapter with related attitudes. You may find that an attitude will appear more than once if it applies to more than one chapter. We've included some attitudes frequently to highlight their importance in different situations.

Look over the following attitudes and circle the words that describe you best. Then select the one you want to improve first and write it in the space provided.

Ambitious. Actively seeks success.

Truthful. Is honest, sincere, and straightforward.

Tenacious. Holds firmly to ideals and strong values; never gives up.

Imaginative. Brings creativity to the job.

Thorough. Is complete and comprehensive in work.

Unique. Has special qualities and values them.

Dependable. Is reliable and trustworthy.

Enthusiastic. Shows a lively interest in the job and the people.

Self-confident. Has confidence in abilities.

I will develop my ability to be: _____

Here's a way to affirm your positive attitude. Write "I am" at the top of a 3 × 5 index card or Post-It® note. Below that, write the positive attitude that you want to develop:

I Am Dependable

Place the card where you will see it first thing in the morning. Your bathroom mirror or the refrigerator is a good spot. You can write your attitude on several cards or notes and put them in various places where you will see them. Recite, aloud if you can, your affirmation of your positive attitude many times each day. Always say it as if you already possess it: "I am dependable," rather than, "I will be dependable," or "I hope to be dependable." Remember, we choose our attitudes. Whatever the human mind can perceive and believe, it can achieve. Repeat your positive attitude affirmation, practice the attitude, and you acquire a new PAL.

The Habit Pledge

1.3

It's your turn to give your opinion. Is it more difficult for you to accept a new habit or to break an old one? Most people say it is getting rid of the old habit, not acquiring the new one, that causes trouble. You believe that

_____

_____

Analyze your habits. Which old one would you like to drop? What new habit would you like to adopt?

A new habit I'd like to develop is: _____

An old habit that gets in the way is: _____

Make the commitment—sign your name to the pledge and practice the Rule of 21.

I AM PRACTICING THE NEW HABIT FOR THE NEXT 21 DAYS.

_____

Name   *Date*

1.4 The 21-Day Habit Breaker

In the 21-day habit chart, list an old habit that interferes with your current life and goals. Then list a new habit you want to develop in its place. Put a check by, or circle, the date you practice the new habit. Avoid skipping days of practice. If you do skip a day, start the 21-day cycle over. Reward yourself when you succeed. As you can see from the example, you don't have to reward yourself every day—just enough that you show yourself some appreciation for your hard work.

OLD HABIT	NEW HABIT	DAY	MY REWARD
Ex: Watch television 9–10 P.M. weekdays	Study 9–10 P.M. weekdays	1	Watch television 9–10 P.M. weekends
		2	
		3	
		4	
		5	
		6	
		7	
		8	
		9	
		10	
		11	
		12	
		13	
		14	
		15	
		16	
		17	
		18	
		19	
		20	
		21	

1.5 Habits that Work

You probably already have habits that will help you achieve career success if you apply them to your working life. Do you get up on time in the morning? Perhaps you get to school ten minutes early, maybe you lay out clothes for the next day at night, or you help make dinner for your family.

On line 1 of the following chart, write a useful habit that you own and a corresponding situation where you want to apply it. For instance, perhaps you get to class early, but you always rush into soccer practice just after 3:30 P.M. You need to apply your school habit to your sports behavior. Extending the useful habit into the rest of your life takes a conscious decision and repetition. However, in twenty-one days you'll make strides. After all, you already own the habit that works. Fill the additional spaces with more habits as you think of them. Use tally marks to keep track of how many days you are able to extend your habit.

GOOD HABIT	WHERE/WHEN USED	WHERE/WHEN TO EXTEND	DAYS	REWARD
1.				
2.				
3.				
4.				

Take New Tools on the Road

1.6

Look over the "New in Your Tool Kit" list at the beginning of this chapter. Choose and write here your three most important tools you gained from reading this chapter.

1. _____
2. _____
3. _____

For each tool you just listed, write how you will apply that tool to achieve success in your work life. You can write about changes you might make as well as existing behaviors that you may reinforce and continue.

TOOL	HOW TO APPLY
1.	
2.	
3.	

Here's an example to get you thinking:

Tool: Positive self-talk

How to apply: I will put notes all around and talk to myself about my positive attributes because I tend to have low self-esteem. I will keep reminding myself that I am valuable and smart.

2

Today's World

THE DIVERSITY OF YOUR WORKPLACE

NEW IN YOUR TOOL KIT

Diversity

Tolerance

Acceptance

The Statue of Liberty, and the quote on this page, greeted thousands upon thousands of immigrants in the late 1800s and early 1900s as they sailed into the port of New York City to begin a new life in the United States. They came to try and make a better life for themselves. They were neither the first nor the last to make the trip. Immigrants—people of differing nationalities and races—are just one part of the diversity that marks the population of the United States.

Living in a country as increasingly diverse as this country, you can count on coming into contact with many different kinds of people as you continue your schooling and enter the workforce. This diversity will come in many forms—cultural-ethnic groups, age groups, stages of life or circumstances, the differently abled (sometimes referred to as individuals who are disabled or physically challenged), and value systems (such as religious affiliation and sexual orientation).

In this chapter, we'll take a look at how all this may affect you. We will talk about how to handle

Give me your tired, your poor, Your huddled masses yearning to breathe free, The wretched refuse of your teeming shore, Send these, the homeless, tempest-tossed to me, I lift my lamp beside the golden door.

—EMMA LAZARUS, INSCRIPTION BENEATH THE STATUE OF LIBERTY

any prejudice or discrimination that you may encounter, and we will introduce tools that will serve you well in this ever-diversifying world—your skills with languages, your ethnic-cultural identity, and tolerance and acceptance.

A Mosaic of Cultures

People have been immigrating to America since the 1400s. In the 1700s when the country was establishing its independence, immigrants were mainly from northern European countries and the British Isles. Then came the forced immigration of Africans, primarily as slaves. Later, in the 1800s came a large influx from southern and eastern Europe, mostly Italians, Greeks, Slavic peoples, Russians, and Poles, along with many Irish. In more recent times, many immigrating people have come from countries with primarily Asian and Hispanic populations—Japan, China, Korea, India, Mexico, South America, Central America, Caribbean nations such as Cuba and Haiti, and Philippines—as well as the Middle East.

And this is just a partial list! America is a land of many peoples who come from many different traditions. Except for Native Americans, everyone else, through either ancestry or their own efforts, has come from another part of the world. We are a jumble of cultures, but rather than melting in the style of the melting pot theory, we don't always give up our individuality. We are a mosaic of nationalities that sometimes mix and sometimes remain distinct.

Are you wondering yet what this has to do with you and your future career? It may seem strange to bring this subject up so early in the book. It may not seem practical or useful at the moment. But, believe us, the multicultural world will affect you in every school you ever attend, every job you ever have, and every neighborhood you ever live in. How you deal with it will, to some degree, affect your success in every arena of your life.

You are one tile in the mosaic. But so is everyone else in your class, in your school, in your neighborhood, and in your town. Their efforts are just as important in making a successful future for this country as yours—even if the way they live is radically different from the way you live. If you are able

Food for Thought

A drawing that is traveling by e-mail can go from Quebec to Beijing on the Internet and be edited in a matter of minutes. The news network CNN tells us what is currently happening all over the world, twenty-four hours a day. Businesspersons in three different countries can all meet without ever leaving their offices, by using teleconferencing capabilities on their personal computers. We are all so accessible to each other that it makes the world seem quite small.

to accept and work with people and their differences, you will have a big advantage over those who cannot.

Ages, Stages, Abilities, and Values

Culture and ethnic backgrounds aren't the only contributing factors to our diverse world. You will also encounter people of different age groups, stages, and circumstances of life, as well as people who are differently abled and people with different value systems. Accepting this diversity and treating people of all ages and life stages equally carry as much weight as respecting different ethnicities, as Figure 2.1 illustrates.

AGE GROUPS

You live in a family of one type or another so you've probably already figured out that people come in different ages. Your parents are older than you are, your grandparents are older still, and any siblings you may have can be older or younger than you are. It can make for some interesting dynamics, as you well know. Take music, for example. The little ones may go for Barney while the older ones prefer Frank Sinatra. And you? Well, as long as it's loud and hot, you're listening.

Once you enter the workforce, you'll gain even more experience dealing with different age groups. There will be people who are about your age, some may be younger, some may be about your parents' ages, and some may be close to your grandparents' ages or older. In order to succeed on the job, you will have to learn how to work with people of all different ages.

Accepting and embracing diversity leads to . . .

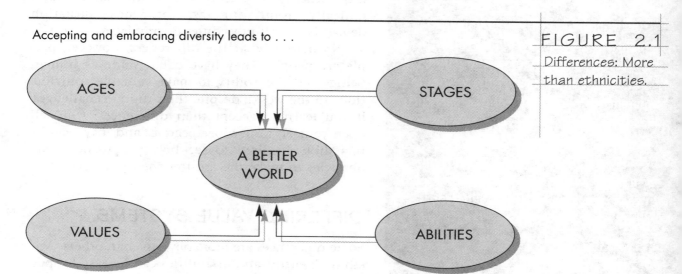

FIGURE 2.1

Differences: More than ethnicities.

STAGES AND CIRCUMSTANCES OF LIFE

Just like living with people of different ages, you probably already have experienced dealing with people in many different circumstances of life. For instance, some of your friends may live in homes with two parents while others live with only one parent. Some may live in huge houses with yards; others may call a small apartment home. You also encounter people in different stages of life. Just look at your high school. You have the freshmen who are just trying to learn the ropes, the sophomores and juniors who may be getting driver's licenses and starting part-time jobs, and the seniors who are busy applying to colleges and trying to figure out what to do with their lives after they graduate. Each grade level works in the same environment, but because they are at different stages, they experience it from different perspectives.

Whether at school or at work, people in different stages of life have different needs. Learning to adapt to those needs is an important part of living and working in a diverse society. Adapting often calls for some creative problem solving, trying to understand the other person's point of view, and enjoying the variety that this diversity brings to each situation.

Food for Thought

All of us know—or may be a member of—a family that has within its structure a deep-seated clash of values. One example is how a set of parents who believe in living together only after marriage may struggle against their young unmarried daughter who intends to move in with her boyfriend. Another is a son joining a band that he loves against the wishes of a parent who does not feel that particular lifestyle is healthy. Or even a sister who endures the disapproval of a brother because she decides to marry someone from a different background than her own. In each case, one side has a different value system than the other—each side has their own ideas about what is important, and those ideas collide against each other despite the close family ties.

THE DIFFERENTLY ABLED

People with physical, mental, or emotional differences are another kind of diversity you are sure to encounter at school and at work. The workplace, in particular, is changing to benefit from their unique abilities and to accommodate their special needs. Somewhere along the line you may find yourself sitting next to a person whose demeanor differs radically from your own or whose situation demands special procedures or privileges.

No matter what the differences, however, people are people. They have equal value as human beings and the ability to make valuable contributions to the world, despite their unique challenges. If you learn to accept their differences, you will open yourself to new perspectives and may even be incredibly inspired to see how people overcome obstacles to make the most of their potential.

DIFFERING VALUE SYSTEMS

Some differences are more obvious than others. Age, ethnic identity, and disabilities can be easy to spot. Other differences aren't so obvious. These differences have to do with our value systems—what we think is important and proper, and what we perceive to be standards of behavior and respectable living.

Value systems vary widely from person to person, even within groups (such as families and cultures) that tend to teach similar values to their members. We build our value systems partly with ideas passed on from families and friends and partly from our own inclinations. It's important to spend time thinking about your values; it will give you great insight into who you are and will help you set personal goals.

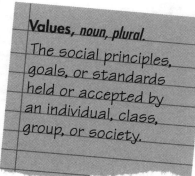

Values, noun, plural.
The social principles, goals, or standards held or accepted by an individual, class, group, or society.

Some specific ideas that comprise our value systems include our styles of living; the way we treat family and friends; how we prioritize family, peers, work, and other activities (how we rank them in order of importance); our religious beliefs; and our attitudes about childrearing. You will encounter a wide range of value systems as you make your way through life. Some you will understand, some will seem foreign to you, and some may upset or disturb you. It's important to remember: To each his own.

Make an effort to understand why different values work for different people. By doing so you, will stretch your tolerance and your knowledge considerably. Hold off on making judgments. Without the full story (which you seldom have), you can't really know what makes people think and act like they do. Although you may not agree with another person's choices in life, as long as they don't affect you or hurt anyone, those choices are, quite frankly, none of your business. Learn to create cooperative ideas to solve problems and keep your integrity in every situation.

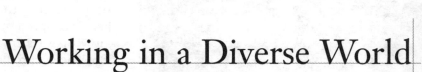

Working in a Diverse World

PREJUDICE AND DISCRIMINATION

Have you ever known anyone or heard about someone who was mistreated, denied work, or shown disrespect because he or she was somehow different? That is called prejudice in action or discrimination and, when left unchecked, can cause big problems.

Prejudice is the *feeling*, the unreasonable thought, and discrimination is the *action* taken by a prejudiced person. The good news is that this country has come a long way in overcoming prejudice and discrimination. The bad news is that there is still a long way to go before everyone really enjoys equal treatment and respect. There are federal laws regarding discrimination.

Prejudice, noun.
A judgment or opinion formed before the facts are known, usually unreasonable and/or unfavorable, often marked by suspicion or fear.

These laws are important and serve a valuable purpose. For instance, it is against the law for you to be denied work—or the chance to apply for work—based on your race, gender, ethnic origin, religion, or sexual preference.

So what can you do about prejudice and discrimination? Your absolute best tool is your own conscience. You can't change how someone else thinks, feels, or acts. But you can change your own actions, attitudes, and feelings. That's the way we will someday erase prejudice from the world—one person at a time.

Here are some ideas for keeping your own prejudices, and we all have some, at bay:

- Keep an open mind when meeting new people.
- Catch yourself when you jump to preconceived notions about someone because of differences, and turn them around.
- Make an effort to include those different from you in your life. You may be surprised how many things you have in common when you get to know them.

Do what you can to right this wrong in our world. But be aware that prejudice and discrimination will certainly continue to come up occasionally—these problems are still a reality in today's world. Just be ready to deal with them—with confidence, a good attitude, patience, integrity, and the other tools you acquire in your tool box.

Food for Thought

Assume you are a recent immigrant from Southeast Asia. You are having difficulty explaining what you need to a salesperson at a local hardware store, when you hear someone in the background mimicking your accent. Or, assume you are Hispanic. You are waiting at the counter of a busy fast-food restaurant. The server helps several Caucasian customers before he waits on you even though you were there first. How would you feel? Although seemingly small, unfortunately these incidents happen every day and they hurt. Let's appreciate and be sensitive to our differences, and do our part to diplomatically educate those who unconsciously are not.

PUT YOUR DIFFERENCES TO WORK

We are all different in one way or another. Those differences are what make us unique. They often reflect special talents that can help you throughout your life. If you present them proudly and show that you know of ways in which they can help others, your differences can become some of your most useful tools in this changing world.

Some of your differences may even become valuable marketing tools when you begin to enter the workforce. For instance, you may speak a language other than English. With an economy that is increasingly based on global relationships, your native language may open opportunities that would otherwise be closed to those who speak only English. Of course, you will still need a working knowledge of English, and you should always work to improve your English if it is not your first language. But your other language, or languages, may open doors for some interesting opportunities.

In addition, your differences may actually give you an edge in the marketplace. American business today is being forced to become more accepting of a

Reality Check

Here are some situations that may come up sometime at school. How could you handle them using the tools we've talked about so far?

- You go to a store and the clerks treat you rudely. You think it is because you are a teenager and they don't want you hanging around the store.

- A friend tells a joke putting down people of a different ethnic background.

- You overhear a classmate refer to another classmate with a racial slur.

Keep in mind that not every situation can be logically and calmly fixed. Sometimes people don't feel comfortable addressing the issue. Other times, trying to fix a problem like this only makes it worse. Each situation is unique. Just remember that sticking up for your principles may cost you some friendships—and not sticking up for them may cost you some inner peace. Look at each situation, and make the decision that best suits your needs without sacrificing your integrity. Just make sure you examine all your options and their consequences before you decide.

culturally diverse marketplace for two reasons. First, when a business seeks to hire someone, chances are increasing that the person will be of some non-European origin. Second, to sell a product or business, an employer wants to do business with all kinds of people. A good way to do that is to employ all kinds of people. In these ways, your differences can become valuable assets for future employers.

On the down side, if you are not of northern European ethnic origin, you or others close to you may have had experiences when they have been denied work because of their heritage or their appearance. Of course, both women and people who are differently abled also face this hardship. This has been a problem for a long time and is still a fact of life, now and again.

But what can you do about it? Certainly anger and violence won't change anyone's mind. You can fight it by working hard to prove yourself and your abilities. You can bring your battle into the legal system, although that is an expensive and time-con-

Real People, Real Stories

Ready to stretch your comfort zone a bit? Interview someone who is different from you to find out what life is like from his or her perspective. You may talk to an exchange student visiting your school from another country, someone from a different ethnic or cultural background, someone of the opposite sex, someone older or younger than you, or someone who is differently abled. Be sure that your interchange is respectful and sensitive. Your goal is to learn something about someone's life, not to try to change him or her!

Here are a few questions to get the conversation rolling (feel free to add your own):

- **What is it like to be you?**
- **Have you ever been discriminated against because of _____ (your race, age, sex—whatever fits)?**
- **What's the best part about being _____ (a woman, an African American, etc.)?**
- **What's the worst part about being _____ (same as above)?**
- **What do you wish people knew about people like you?**

After your interview, write a short, two-part essay about your findings. In the first part, describe what you learned about the person you interviewed. In the second part, describe what you learned about yourself by talking with that person about these issues.

suming solution. Or, as we said before, you can realize that your identity is a plus and find an employer who agrees with you.

Tolerance and Acceptance

Tolerance, noun.
1. The ability to recognize and respect others' beliefs, practices, etc., that differ from one's own.
2. The ability to allow, to permit.

Diversity is here to stay in a big way. That makes the likelihood pretty slim that you'll ever live, study, or work in a place where everyone shares the same ethnic background, the same abilities, and the same values—which makes putting two new tools in your tool kit a smart move. Tolerance and acceptance are essential tools that will help you function efficiently and happily in this new environment. Without them, you'll have a hard time fitting into our changing world.

You may have heard the saying, "If you are not part of the solution, you are art of the problem." It certainly applies to the diverse world we live in. If you are intolerant of differences, if you look down on others who live differently or have a different physical appearance, you are holding negative feelings that will come out in negative ways. Your attitude may hurt your performance at school or at work and make it difficult for others to enjoy working with you. You expect others to be tolerant of you—make sure you return the favor. Tolerance means live and let live, no matter what differences exist.

Tolerance comes first, and then comes acceptance. Tolerance is passive; acceptance is an action. Acceptance takes tolerance to an active, positive level. When you tolerate people, you recognize their existence; you understand that they desire to be valued and must be allowed to live in their unique style. When you show acceptance, you receive people positively, freely interact with them when the opportunity arises, and offer a deep respect.

Besides improving the interaction among ethnic groups, our tolerance and acceptance can bridge the gender gap in the workplace. Women still have trouble reaching certain job levels or categories in some occupations, and sometimes they receive lower salaries than men for identical work. As employers learn to tolerate the different needs of men and women and to accept the fact that proficiency on the job is based on skills and talent rather than on gender, the situation is gradually improving.

We need to accept the unique needs and welcome the gifts of those who are differently abled as well. Every person has something to give. If each of us is given the chance, we can do our best to contribute to society, and society will be richer for that contribution. If others are tolerant of our particular, and sometimes peculiar, ways, we will be free to be ourselves and to achieve to the best of our abilities.

Tolerance and acceptance are powerful tools. Make sure you have plenty of both tucked away in your tool kit.

Acceptance, noun. Approving reception; the act of receiving willingly and favorably.

Food for Thought

What if your family has a business that you plan to join? You might think that you can avoid the issues that diversity brings. But every family survives by bringing others into its structure. And, these days, intermarriage (marriage between people of different ethnic backgrounds or religions) is extremely common. Communities interact with each other so much that people interact and fall in love with others of different backgrounds whom they may not have ever met seventy years ago. If you prepare yourself to be tolerant, you will be able to adjust when changes occur. Asian-Americans, African-Americans, Native Americans, Hispanics, and Americans of European descent have learned that the bonds they forge can bridge ethnic differences.

Be Part of the Solution in Your Corner of the World

Figure 2.2 illustrates how we might use these tools. How can you put these new tools to use?

FIGURE 2.2

Embracing diversity.

Be part of the solution . . .

We are Brothers and Sisters

Let different people into your life

Be open minded

Accept different working styles

Celebrate your heritage with others

Look for commonality

. . . put your new tools to work.

Food for Thought

Think about conflict on the very smallest scale—within your household. You probably have opinions, on many varied issues, that differ from your closest family members. People who live together can disagree about all kinds of things, such as how to organize a closet, how to raise a child, how much television to watch, and what kinds of foods to eat. It's a miracle that anyone gets along at all! So you can see, knowing that you have conflict even with the people closest to you, that differences can easily arise in other places where you are often dealing with people from entirely separate backgrounds.

- Be open-minded about the kinds of people you encounter. Restrain yourself from making snap judgments based on externals such as skin color, body type, or gender.

- Allow yourself to learn about other cultures, ages, and stages by getting to know people who represent them. When you encounter those people, let them into your life as you would someone similar to you.

- Accept different ways of doing things as long as they don't break rules.

- Explore and be proud of your own heritage, whether your ancestors were from Africa or from Scotland or from any other country in the world.

- Share your heritage and/or situation with others. Give your family, friends, and peers the chance to learn about you and to understand your version of the world, as you work to understand their version.

- Look for what you do have in common. Do you like the same food for lunch? Are you both disorganized? Beyond the cultural and behavioral differences, you may find many things in common. You might just build a friendship on them, or at least a mutual respect.

■ Know that, underneath the skin, we really are all quite similar. We all love, hurt, think, like, dislike, hope, fear, and plan. Although we may express ourselves differently, we are all human.

The Diverse World and Your Future

How does all this relate to your future career? It all boils down to this: Your school, your workplace, and your neighborhood are all microcosms of the world, which means smaller versions of it. The more you understand about our diverse and changing world, the more you understand about your smaller sections of it. As the world at large changes, so does your world as well as the people in it. When you decide to be part of the solution in making your world a more tolerant and accepting place, you make it a more successful world for everyone.

Your Tool Kit at Work

Walk a Mile in Their Shoes

Can you imagine what it would be like to move to another country? You don't know the language very well, you are unfamiliar with the customs, and everything seems different than it did at home. Think about how you would adjust to your new life and find new friends. What would you do to try to fit in?

Pretend you are keeping a journal about your first impressions in the new country. On a separate sheet, record your first impressions as you do the following:

- Get off the plane.
- Meet your new neighbors.
- Go to school for the first time.
- Try to buy something at the store.
- Ride the bus across town to run some errands.

2.1 A Multicultural World

Countries stay strong when new, positive ideas are introduced. One reason the United States became a world leader was its ability to accept differing views and incorporate them into the culture. The multicultural workplace and world community of today demand more and more new ideas and understanding even as they continue to use traditional work customs.

Almost all U.S. families have come from other countries; the only non-immigrants are Native Americans. Chances are, your relatives or ancestors lived and worked in another country. One interesting way to find out the answers to the following questions is to talk with older relatives in your family. They often have a wealth of information, history, and stories that will enrich your sense of who you are as a member of a family and a culture.

My family arrived from _____

In their country of origin, they worked as _____

_____

In the United States, they worked as _____

_____

Reject the Rejection

2.2

If people in your environment reject you on the basis of differences, they are showing their own weaknesses, not yours. Work hard and maintain a good attitude—reject the rejection. You will come out ahead.

Our differences bring positives to the world, while at the same time they may bring challenges that require us to modify our attitudes or behavior. It is important to pay attention to your unique qualities in two ways. First, recognize their value. Second, explore any modifications you may need to make in your behavior to make the most of your qualities.

An example is Jenny, who is hearing impaired. She wants to be a graphic designer. Jenny brings good concentration and visual awareness (her qualities) to a graphic design program and career. However, she is having difficulty keeping up with her classes (the challenge). Learning to lip read or using an interpreter (some modifications) will enable her to be more successful.

To remember your importance in the diverse workplace, complete the following sentences.

1. A unique quality I bring to the diverse world is _____

   _____

2. This quality will help me in life because _____
   a. _____
   b. _____

3. To allow this quality to contribute positively to my future career, I may need to make the following modifications: _____
   a. _____
   b. _____

Your Diversity Quotient

2.3

Make a quick check of your global and diversity awareness by answering yes or no to the following questions.

1. Carnation Ice Cream is owned by a Swiss company.
2. You are uncomfortable working for a younger, female manager.
3. The Honda Civic is classified as a U.S.-made car.
4. Dim Sum is a Chinese food.
5. You want to learn a foreign language in anticipation of future opportunities.
6. Kwanzaa is an African celebration.
7. Squid is part of Italian and Japanese cuisines.
8. Bic Pens is owned by a French company.
9. Cinco de Mayo is considered the Independence Day of Mexico.

10. You enjoy trying different ethnic foods. _____

If you answered yes to:

7–10 questions, congratulations! You are sensitive to your global and diverse environment.

4–6 questions, you are aware. Consider deepening your use of global and cultural awareness.

0–3 questions, you might consider setting a goal of increasing your global and cultural awareness.

2.4 Getting in Touch with Our Prejudices

Discuss with a classmate or a friend how you would feel about the following situations:

1. You are ready to cross a busy street when you notice a blind person who is also crossing the street. This blind person doesn't have a seeing eye dog or any other assistance. What do you do? Do you ignore this situation? Do you help? Do you feel uncomfortable and don't know what to do?

2. You are on your way to school and find yourself driving behind a senior citizen. The senior citizen is driving the speed limit, which is slower than most other drivers on the highway. Do you view this driver differently from any other driver? Are you frustrated or patient?

3. You see an interracial couple walking down the street and you realize the woman of the couple is your sister. What is your reaction? How do you feel about this?

4. You are treated rudely and are receiving poor service at a coffee shop, where you notice others who are similar in appearance to the employees of the coffee shop are being treated with deference and good service. How do you feel? What might you do?

5. You think your male teacher is asking the females in class to meet more requirements than others in order to get a good grade. What do you do? How do you feel?

2.5 Your Positive Attitude List—Your PAL

The attitudes listed below are important in the workplace of today. Just as you did in Chapter 1, circle the attitudes on which you have a good grip and write the one you want to improve. Add this attitude to your card or note below your first attitude. For example,

I am Dependable

I am Unprejudiced

Now you have two positive attitudes (affirmations) to repeat daily.

Adaptable	Adjusts well to new situations.
Tolerant	Allows others to be themselves.
Trustworthy	Is dependable and loyal.
Insightful	Finds ways to understand unfamiliar work practices and people.
Thoughtful	Takes time to think things through before acting or passing judgment.
Unprejudiced	Accepts all for who they are.
Down-to-earth	Can go with the flow; realistic and practical.
Empathetic	Can put self in another's shoes and see a situation from that perspective.
Supportive	Helps others affirm their identity and encourages individuality.

I will develop my ability to be:_____

_____

Take New Tools on the Road

2.6

Look over the "New in Your Tool Kit" list at the beginning of this chapter. Choose and write here your three most important tools you gained from reading this chapter.

1. _____

2. _____

3. _____

For each tool you just listed, write one example of how you will apply that tool to achieve success in your future work life. Talk about changes you will make—things you will do differently—and how you will continue or reinforce tools that you already possess.

1. _____

_____

_____

2. _____

_____

_____

3. _____

_____

_____

3 Keys to the Tool Kit

UNLOCKING YOUR PERSONAL POWER

NEW IN YOUR TOOL KIT

Self-knowledge	Goals
Self-respect	Priorities
Talents	Career compass

Y ou were given a gift long ago—a gift like no other, a gift that no one else will ever have, a gift that will never exist in any other form. That gift is yourself—with all your ideas, thoughts, likes, dislikes, ups, downs, and dreams. Master the art of understanding yourself in those areas, and you will add one of the most important tools to your tool kit.

Know thyself—good advice from an ancient philosopher and a central theme of this chapter. Other tools we will consider are making goals and setting priorities.

Understanding Yourself

Self-knowledge and self-respect are the focus now—getting to know yourself and to respect yourself. Maybe you've heard the phrase, "You can't expect anyone else to love you unless you love yourself first." The word love can by replaced by any number of other words—respect, value, like, help—and the thought remains the same.

Put yourself first. You need to feel secure in knowing who you are. Your ultimate success depends on building a solid core of self-knowledge and self-respect. Why?

- Because you cannot believe in yourself without knowing what you are believing in.
- Because you cannot set smart and realistic goals for yourself without knowing where your talents and your difficulties lie.
- Because you need to learn how to care about yourself as you care for others.
- Because other people take their cue from what you project. If you act like you are unworthy of their attention, respect, and love, they are likely to believe you. But if you seem to care about and respect yourself and your abilities, they will follow your lead.
- Because it will stay with you through the tough times and help you stay strong.
- Because the more you know about yourself, the better you can determine your ideal job and lifestyle.

Food for Thought

You are what you eat. Eat a steady diet of fast foods, sweets, and sodas, and it will show—in more ways than one. Eating a balanced diet, including five daily servings of fruits and vegetables, may not be easy or as satisfying, but you will feel better and stay healthier. Exercising on a regular basis is also critical if you are to be at your best. Take care of yourself, mentally and physically. Eat right and exercise.

Let's face it, life can be tough. When it comes down to it, the one person you can always count on is you. Give yourself the best possible chance by knowing who that self is.

Know thyself. It sounds easy enough but, in reality, can be a pretty vague idea. There's a lot more to you than meets the eye. You have a personality, talents and abilities, likes and dislikes (see Figure 3.1). All these factors combine to make you, you. That's why we'll take the time to look at each one and help you get better acquainted with yourself.

PERSONALITY

It would probably be easier for the people who know you best to describe your personality than it is for you. They get the chance to watch you from the outside. When they spend time with you, they see how you relate to other people and how you react to situations. You, on the other hand, are so

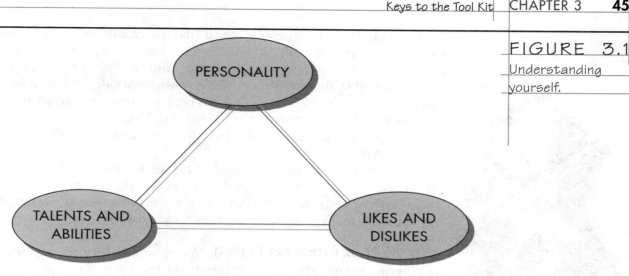

FIGURE 3.1
Understanding
yourself.

busy relating and reacting that you don't get the chance to take a good look at yourself.

In other words, personality is a way of describing who you are by looking at your actions and your views. It is the evidence of your unique qualities— the definition of you.

How can knowing about personality help you choose and succeed in a future vocation? Once you get a pretty good idea of your personality, you will have an easier time setting goals and making smart decisions for yourself. With a better understanding of your likes and dislikes, you will gain insight into what kinds of jobs will make the most sense for you. The best job for you will be the one that makes the most of your abilities and fits your likes.

Personality, noun.
Habitual patterns and qualities of behavior as expressed by physical and mental activities and attitudes; distinctive individual qualities.

What if you decide to become a police officer, not recognizing that you are extremely shy and prefer to work indoors? You might go through all the training only to learn that you really dislike your job. But if you are aware of your tendencies ahead of time, you can find a niche in the police or legal field that suits you better. What about legal assistant? Or an analyst in a crime lab? Or a court stenographer? There is a job out there that will fit you, whatever your personality may be.

A Personality Test

Now, let's see if we can put your personality into terms you can understand. One system that might help is called the Myers-Briggs Type Indicator®. Through asking simple questions about how you would handle situations and what you like or dislike, the indicator gives you a four-word definition of your personality type.

Talk to your guidance counselor if you'd like to actually take the Myers-Briggs test. He or she may be able to point you toward resources that make it available. Here, we will simply spend some time talking about the categories so that you can begin to find your niche. Even though we call it a test, it isn't possible to fail. Every score is a good score because the scores aren't numbers that measure ability; they are letters that stand for words that describe your personality. All of us are different and have different, but equally valuable, qualities and abilities.

The Myers-Briggs system uses four categories, each with two possibilities, to help you define your personality. Choosing one possibility within each category will give you a four-letter personality type. Let's take a quick look at each category.

EXTROVERT OR INTROVERT (E OR I). You've probably heard and used these terms before. They refer to the world that dominates your consciousness: your outer world (extrovert) or inner world (introvert). Basically, an extrovert is a person who receives energy from interaction with the outer world, a person who enjoys working with people and things, a person who is happy and comfortable interacting with the world outside the self. Other descriptive words you will hear to describe this type of person are outgoing or charismatic.

An introvert is someone who receives energy from time alone in the inner world, a person who enjoys ideas and concepts. People might call an introvert quiet or a listener.

SENSING OR INTUITIVE (S OR N). These categories might not be as familiar. They refer to how you perceive things, or how you look at and discover the world. A sensing person views the world primarily with the five senses. This person takes in the information that hearing, seeing, tasting, touching, and smelling provide, and sees the world in terms of facts that can be measured and proven through those senses.

An intuitive person goes with the gut feeling. This person discovers the world through the emotions, relationships, and deeper meanings felt inside, things that senses alone could not necessarily explain. Quite often that gut feeling will hold despite any facts that seem to contradict it. For instance, intuitive persons may have the feeling that they are going to have a good day and manage to have one even though it is pouring rain outside, they bombed out on a history exam, and they forgot their lunch at home.

Food for Thought

Think for a minute about people that you hear stories about in the news. Try deciding which category fits them—extrovert or introvert—by looking at what they do and where they seem to find their energy. How about Shaquille O'Neal, the basketball player? (An easy talker, probably an extrovert.) Barbara Walters, the reporter and interviewer? (Her whole job is talking to people, probably an extrovert as well.) Leonardo DiCaprio, the actor? (A thinker who usually avoids the press, perhaps an introvert.) Think about your family and friends too, and see if you can decide in which category to place each one.

THINKING OR FEELING (T OR F). The Myers-Briggs system uses these words to describe how you behave, how you decide to act on what you see happening in the world. Thinking people make decisions based on facts and figures. They like to follow logic and be able to concretely explain any decision they make. One might call these people logical, measured, or calculated.

Feeling people make decisions based on how they feel about the situation. They may even ignore facts in favor of what is important to them. People might call this kind of person sensitive or emotional.

PERCEPTIVE OR JUDGMENTAL (P OR J). The last category talks about how you relate to your outer world. If you are a perceptive person, you prefer to live day to day, happy to explore new things and ideas, focusing on how you view the world (through either senses or gut feelings) and not on making decisions about those feelings. This kind of person may be called spontaneous or flexible.

If you are a judgmental person, you focus on how you want to act on your worldview or feeling. The decision to act is more important than perception. You prefer to order and control your world, whether you do so based on fact or emotion. Words to describe this person include decisive, controlled, and structured.

Pay a lot of attention to your tendencies in this category. More than with any of the other three categories, your status as a perceptive or judgmental person will tell you about how you are likely to operate at school and on a job.

Your inner-world activity—what you ponder and think about in your mind—prepares you for school or work. The actual result happens when you act, which is the interaction of your energy with the outside that results in a change. What you do and the tasks that you accomplish happen as you interact with your outer world, whether that world is school, machines, people, numbers, clothes, forms, or ideas. Defining yourself as having primarily perceptive or primarily judgmental qualities will give you the biggest clue about how you handle the world outside. It's a clue that will help you define your school and work personality and style.

Put Your Type Together

Even without taking the test, you can put together a basic personality type for yourself just by thinking through those descriptions. Every answer is a correct answer for someone. Let's say you are a very outgoing person, and you decide that you are an extrovert. You are also emotional and act on your feelings rather than take the time to find out the facts. So you are probably an intuitive and feeling person. But you like your life organized. That means you would choose judgment for the last category. So your personality profile is ENFJ.

What would this mean for your career? It gives you valuable clues about what kind of job would make the most sense for you. Because you operate on feeling and enjoy dealing with people, you may want to consider a position that will involve service to people, for example, in health care or in a travel agency.

Real People, Real Stories

This is your chance to talk about one of your favorite people—you. Ask five people who know you pretty well (parent, sibling, friend, coach, teacher, etc.) to pick three words that describe you best. Write their responses on a separate sheet of paper. Compare the results. Are there any surprises?

For another example, consider the opposite. Are you more of a quiet person? Do you prefer to work alone? Do you like facts and figures and speculating on ideas for the future? You may be an ISTP. Your ideal job may involve details, mechanics, and independent work. Computer operation or repair, accounting, or auto mechanics may suit you well.

Do you see how knowing yourself will help you find your path to an ideal career? Thinking about who you are could save you time and mistakes down the road. It can take a lot of time, once you have begun a job that isn't right for you, to figure out that you are in the wrong place and to move ahead. The more you know about yourself and where you feel the most comfortable while you're still in school, the quicker you will find your niche in the working world.

Don't forget—these personality types are not exact. Nothing is set in stone! Each one is a unique combination of qualities, and you may have some of the characteristics of both sides of any one of the Myers-Briggs categories. Whatever you are is just right, whether or not you fit neatly into any definition. The important thing is to know who you are.

Don't worry that you are limiting yourself by defining your personality type. The point of the personality test is not to box you in but to broaden your self-knowledge. When you know your strengths, you can build on them and use them in school and in your career—and when you know your weaker areas, you can work to improve them.

TALENTS AND ABILITIES

As you think about your personality, your talents will come to mind because your traits tend to reveal those talents. If you are an extrovert, one talent might be getting along with people. If you are a thinker, your talent may be organizing facts and figures. Keep thinking about what you know about your personality as we talk about talents and abilities.

Some things you seem to be able to do naturally—these are talents. Other things you have worked hard to develop—these are abilities or skills.

Both are key tools in school and in your eventual search for the perfect career.

Give yourself time to consider what your talents and abilities are. What have you always been able to do well? What have you worked hard to learn to do? What do you do that earns praise from others? Use your knowledge about your personality to help you. Are you a thinking person? You may have a talent for working with words. You might look into writing advertisements. Are you a sensing person? You might look into medical technology, where sensing facts is very important. Are you an extrovert? Your talent may be working well with people so a job in sales might be a good option for you. Look carefully at your talents, and take them into account when making decisions about school or work.

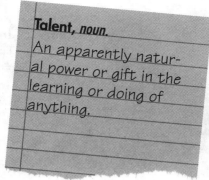

Talent, noun.
An apparently natural power or gift in the learning or doing of anything.

Remember, too, to consider your accomplishments. And not just the big "win a trophy" kind of accomplishments. Think about what you have done that has given you pride in yourself. Are you known as a good sport, someone who is a team player? Have you done volunteer work, serving meals at a homeless shelter or visiting at a senior citizens' home? Maybe you're the one your classmates come to when they have trouble with geometry or questions about the biology assignment. Accomplishments say a lot about your strengths as a person. Pay attention to what yours say about you.

We've already talked about how important it is to know yourself. Here's another old maxim that rings just as true: To thine own self be true. Modern translation: Be true to yourself. This is especially important when you are doing something as important as preparing for a future vocation. You sure don't want to get stuck in a career that won't be a good fit with who you really are and what you really want out of life. Beware of falling into some of these traps:

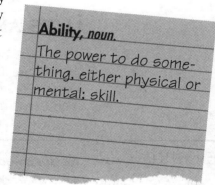

Ability, noun.
The power to do something, either physical or mental; skill.

- Choosing a career because your family or friends think you should do it
- Choosing a career because you think you will make a lot of money
- Choosing a career to prove something to someone or to one-up someone
- Choosing a career because everyone else is doing it
- Choosing a career just because it is convenient or easy

Sure, some of these factors may enter into your decision from time to time, but you don't want to base your entire decision on any of them. Trust us on this one! You don't want to end up wasting a lot of time, neglecting your true talents, and wearing yourself out trying to do a job you may not have the abilities to do. Challenge is one thing; completely ignoring your talents is another one altogether. If you find a career that will suit your talents and abilities, you'll find a career that you'll enjoy and one that you will do well.

There is, of course, another side to this picture. Just like we all have strengths, we all have weaknesses. Those are the things we aren't so good at doing. It's just part of being human. No one gets by without their fair share. The thing that separates the winners from the losers in this game is how you handle those weaknesses. The more you worry about your weak points, the weaker you'll become. Sometimes we can be our own worst critics-always putting ourselves down because of our short-comings. It's a self-defeating pattern that is sure to keep you stuck.

It's a whole lot better to just give yourself a break. That doesn't mean give up and not try to turn things around. It does mean that you encourage yourself and take credit for inching toward improvement. Each little success will lead to bigger ones. Talk yourself up in your head. It will help you keep a positive self-image, which, in turn, will allow you to take risks and grow.

A realistic assessment of both your strengths and weaknesses will help you as you make your way through life. Life is a series of decisions, a walk down a road that forks every few miles—sometimes every few yards. The more you know about yourself, the more quickly and easily you can choose the right path and be on your way.

LIKES AND DISLIKES

What's the big deal about finding a job that you will like? Look at Figure 3.2. This figure illustrates that people spend 40 percent of their time at work. That's more time than they spend doing anything else! Do you really want to spend that much time doing something you don't enjoy?

FIGURE 3.2

How we spend our time.

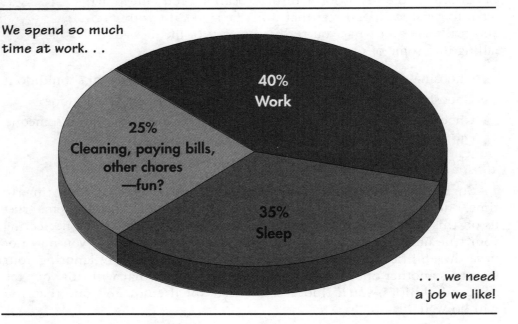

We spend so much time at work. . .

40% Work

25% Cleaning, paying bills, other chores —fun?

35% Sleep

. . . we need a job we like!

That's why this process of figuring out your talents and abilities is so important. It will probably come as no big surprise that you will be best at doing things that you like to do. So taking a good look now at what you like and dislike can help you get a better handle on what your talents and abilities really are.

How do you like to spend your time? What kinds of things can you do for hours without getting bored? What kinds of things make you crazy with frustration? Think about it, and you'll find some valuable clues about the best ways to invest that 40 percent block of time that will eventually be dedicated to work pursuits.

You'll be doing yourself—and everyone around you—a huge favor if you figure this out. You'll be satisfied at work, which will make your future employers and coworkers happy. You'll be easier to live with at home, and that will make your family happy. You'll feel as if you've had a choice in the matter, and that will make you happy, too. You'll be much better off in the long run than if you end up in a job that makes you miserable.

Of course, you can always (and probably will) change jobs from time to time. But the sooner you lock onto what you like, the sooner you will get your career focused and on track. You can then spend your time learning and growing and looking for ways to move up instead of always looking for a way out.

Identifying Meaningful Goals

Okay. You are in the process of getting to know yourself. You have a pretty good idea of your abilities, likes, and dislikes. So what's next? In order to move forward, you've got to use what you've learned to set some goals for yourself.

Whether you realize it or not, goals already drive much of your everyday life. You may not even think about the tiny goals you set for yourself each day, goals that help you accomplish what you need to do, such as study for a test, phone a friend, or take your little brother or sister to soccer practice. Every time you decide to do something, you've set a goal. What were your goals today?

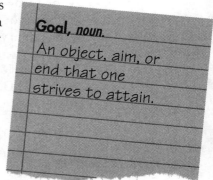

Goal, noun.
An object, aim, or end that one strives to attain.

Now all you need to do is apply the goal-setting skills that you already have to bigger purposes in life. If you do, you will be able to clear yourself a path into your future. Figure 3.3 illustrates how all this comes together. Setting goals lights up the path formed by linking your choices and helps to give you direction.

You've got some big questions looming ahead in your future. Setting goals can help you make good choices in these areas.

PERSONAL. What changes do you want to make in yourself with regard to your ideas, thoughts, tendencies, habits, and abilities? Do you want to change or improve your relationships? Do you want to improve your physical health

FIGURE 3.3
Unlocking your personal power.

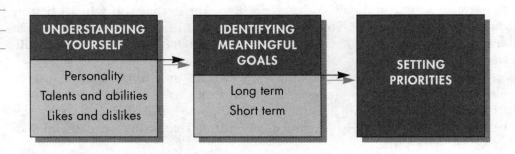

UNDERSTANDING YOURSELF	IDENTIFYING MEANINGFUL GOALS	SETTING PRIORITIES
Personality Talents and abilities Likes and dislikes	Long term Short term	

and/or appearance? Do you want to rekindle or alter your spiritual life and practice? Do you want to develop certain talents and skills or explore new interests?

EDUCATION. What's next after you graduate from high school? You do plan to graduate don't you? We urge you to do so. You'll really shortchange yourself if you don't. But, then what? Vocational school? Travel? Apprenticeship? Community college? Military service? Four-year college? There are a lot of choices. Make sure you explore all your options and find the one(s) that are best for you.

FAMILY. Do you want to marry? Do you want to have a family? How many children do you want? How much time do you want to be able to spend with them as they grow? Do you want to live near your parents, siblings, or other extended family? Do you want to strike out on your own?

CAREER. What specifically do you want to be doing on your job? To what level do you aspire in your field of choice? Do you want to manage? Do you want to own a business? Do you want to work as an independent contractor? Do you want to be your own boss? What kind of hours suits you best? What salary level? What benefits?

MONEY. How much do you want to earn? Do you want to invest some of your earnings? Do you want to pay off loans? Do you want to make major purchases such as a car, home, education, insurance, vacation, or appliances?

LIVING. Where do you want to live—city, country, or suburb? What style of housing do you want? Do you want to rent or own? What kind of community do you seek?

As mind-boggling as all this may seem, these questions are only the start of the issues you'll soon be dealing with as an adult. Pick a few to ask yourself, and they may inspire other dislikes, talents, and abilities. You know what you do well and what you like. Now, what do you want to do with it all? Here are three ways to help you find out.

TALK TO ROLE MODELS AND MENTORS

These are people you admire. Their experience and knowledge will help expand and enlighten your own. They might be able to tell you more about their career fields than you could find out on your own. They may also have some special insight or advice on where you might find success.

DARE TO DREAM

Dreams reveal to you your strongest desires. They may even surprise you sometimes! Look at what you daydream about when your thoughts wander. Think about those dreams seriously and look for clues in them.

Let's say, for example, that you daydream about being a disc jockey on a radio station. That might tell you:

- You like to talk.
- You like music.
- You enjoy working "off the cuff."
- You enjoy working with people.

These clues could translate into all sorts of goals; some may take you into a radio career, and some may not. But either way, you have learned about yourself, and what you have learned will help you focus more closely on your goals.

CONSULT YOUR CAREER COMPASS

Your career compass is a guide for determining direction just like a compass tells north from east, only its power to direct comes not from a magnet but from you. The three needles on your career compass represent:

1. **Your intelligence.** Your ability to take in and retain knowledge, your education, your training.
2. **Your experience.** The wisdom you have gained from all of life's experiences, at home, at school, and at work.
3. **Your intuition.** The honest wisdom of your gut feeling—that voice inside you that tells you when you're on the right track and when you're veering off the road.

If you trust these three forces, together they will guide your toward goals that make sense for your life. Just like a hiker, consult your career compass frequently to make sure you are heading in the right direction. Often what seems like the road leading toward where you want to go will take some twists and turns and will lead you somewhere else. Keep an eye on your

Compass, *noun.*

A device for determining directions by means of a magnetic needle, or group of needles, turning freely on a pivot (a fixed attachment point at the center of the needle).

career compass, and you will be able to change direction or turn back before you have gone too far.

There are two ways to read your career compass. Listen to your head and listen to your heart. Your mind will send you messages. Knowledge from experiences can provide you with valuable insight. Your heart will also send you messages—making you feel free and powerful when making the right moves and creating feelings of tension, fear, and unease when you are about to make a wrong move. Of course, some tension and fear are normal as we grow and change. But question yourself hard, and learn to tell the difference between normal fear and the tight inner feeling that comes from being in the wrong place.

REACH YOUR CAREER GOALS

Of course, setting goals and actually achieving them are two different things. Lots of people set goals, but not so many do what it takes to reach them. Well, what does it take to reach the goals you set? Here are eight ideas to help you reach your goals.

MAKE GOALS THAT YOU WANT TO KEEP. You'll have a lot less motivation if you try working toward a goal that someone else wants you to keep. When you set relevant goals, you'll get the inner drive and conviction you'll need to carry you through the tough times.

MAKE GOALS THAT ARE SPECIFIC AND MEASURABLE. Compare these two goals: "I will improve my grades in school" and "I will get a B on my biology test this week." See the difference? The first goal is vague and mushy; the second is so clear that you'll know exactly when you've attained it.

MAKE GOALS IN WRITING. It's been said that a goal is a dream with a date on it. Writing your goals not only helps you sort out your thinking but also makes it more real—something official that you can look at for inspiration.

MAKE GOALS THAT HAVE A BEGINNING, AN END, AND A DEFINED FIRST STEP. Otherwise, you're likely to fall into the trap of procrastination and never get around to doing what you need to do. The first step is often the most difficult, so make it easier to get yourself moving in the right direction.

MAKE GOALS THAT ARE ATTAINABLE. That means making goals that you have a realistic chance of reaching. If you shoot too high on the first try and miss, you may get frustrated and lose the courage to try again. Take things a step at a time, and you'll give yourself a better chance of getting there.

MAKE GOALS THAT CAN BE REVIEWED FROM TIME TO TIME. Revisit your commitment and refuel your enthusiasm to make a goal happen.

MAKE GOALS FOR YOUR SCHOOLING, YOUR FUTURE CAREER, AND YOUR PERSONAL LIFE. A well-balanced life requires TLC (tender loving care) in more than one area. Keep yourself on an even keel.

MAKE A PLAN AND IDENTIFY STEPS TO HELP YOU ACHIEVE YOUR GOALS. Without them, you won't know where you are going or how you are going to get there.

Goals help us make the most of our abilities and achieve personal, school, and career success. As you start making goals for yourself, because you know there are several different kinds of goals, you need to set priorities.

Setting Priorities

There's one more thing you need to do before you start setting goals, and that is to set your priorities. Setting priorities means ranking your goals in their order of importance. Setting priorities helps you decide what's most important to you so you know how to focus your energy and effort.

Like goals, priorities are unique to each individual. Your top priority may mean little to someone else, and vice versa. The differences can come from circumstances and preferences. If you are athletic, you may make working out a top priority; someone else may prefer reading or spending time with friends.

Your priority list may change from day to day, as well as from year to year. Some may show up every day during the week—school, sports practice, etc. Others may show up on weekends—attending church or synagogue, going out with friends, etc. Your priorities may change altogether as you get older and your needs are different. Some of common areas of priority are illustrated in Figure 3.4. What are your priorities right now?

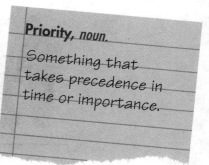

Priority, *noun.*
Something that takes precedence in time or importance.

PRIORITIES AND YOUR FUTURE CAREER

Making your future job search and career decisions a priority, for instance, by exploring your personality and interests and by researching education and training options, work environments, and so forth helps you zero in on the types of jobs that will fit in best with who you are and what you need most. Set priorities before you start looking, and you'll do yourself a big favor. That way you'll know what you are looking for and can rule out jobs, businesses, and areas that will not fit your personality, needs, and lifestyle. You'll save lots of time and energy that can be put to better use in finding a career that will make sense for you.

Even as a student, you can get in the habit of setting priorities right now. There will always be a variety of options competing for your time and atten-

Prioritize, *verb.*
To arrange items or tasks in order according to priority.

FIGURE 3.4

What are your
priorities?

tion, so deciding which ones are most important will enable you to put your resources into what really matters. Here is a sample priority list for a student, in no particular order. Think about which of these are priorities in your life, and rank them in order of importance to you:

—— School   —— Chores

—— Study time   —— Family relationships

—— Part-time job   —— Sleep

—— Friendships   —— Exercise

Learning to set goals and priorities now will not only help you make the most of your high school years; it will also prepare you for a lifetime of success. Use these tools—along with understanding your personality, identifying your talents and abilities, and determining your likes and dislikes—to get yourself ready for a productive and satisfying future.

Your Tool Kit at Work

Your Goals: Past, Present, and Future

3.1

Here is a chance to look at some helpful goals you've accomplished in the past, and to set some goals to work on in the present that you will accomplish in the future. Reaching for goals can be a long-term process. Writing what you plan to do will help you to structure your time and stay on track.

First, in the space provided, write things you've accomplished in the past month. You can include personal accomplishments, such as keeping your room clean, as well as school accomplishments. Write what you think each accomplishment means to your future career success.

MY ACCOMPLISHMENTS	HOW THEY WILL HELP MY CAREER
I made the volleyball team.	I am learning to be a team player and to be disciplined.
1.	
2.	
3.	
4.	
5.	

The following worksheets will help you define your goals and lay out plans for achieving them. Use one for a career goal, one for a school-related goal, and one for a personal goal. As you work, you will discover how you can achieve success in all three aspects of your life

LIFE AREA: CAREER

Goal—Be specific and positive (e.g., instead of writing "I will find a good job," write "I will talk to a career adviser next week.")

_____

_____

_____

Obstacles—Why haven't I reached my goal by now?

_____

_____

_____

Solutions to obstacles

_____

_____

_____

Action steps—Things I will do and dates to be completed

_____

_____

_____

Benefits I will receive—What will it mean to me when I accomplish this goal?

_____

_____

_____

What I have accomplished and by what dates these accomplishments con-firm for me that I am serious

_____

_____

_____

LIFE AREA: SCHOOL

Goal—Be specific and positive

_____

_____

_____

Obstacles

_____

_____

_____

Solutions to obstacles

_____

_____

_____

Action steps—Things I will do and dates to be completed

_____

_____

_____

Benefits I will receive

_____
_____
_____

What I have accomplished and by what dates

_____
_____

_____

LIFE AREA: PERSONAL

Goal—Be specific and positive

_____
_____
_____

Obstacles

_____
_____
_____

Solutions to obstacles

_____
_____
_____

Action steps—Things I will do and dates to be completed

_____
_____
_____

Benefits I will receive

_____
_____
_____

What I have accomplished and by what dates

_____
_____
_____

3.2 Priorities: One Size Doesn't Fit All

Priorities are different for different people and may change at various stages of your life. First, make a list of your own top three priorities. Now, ask a friend to share his or her top three priorities with you. Next, ask a parent, teacher, or another adult who is still raising children and working. Finally, ask a grandparent or another older person who has grown children and is retired from a job. Compare the different responses:

PERSONAL PRIORITIES

1. _____
2. _____
3. _____

FRIEND'S PRIORITIES

1. _____
2. _____
3. _____

PARENT'S OR WORKING ADULT'S PRIORITIES

1. _____
2. _____
3. _____

GRANDPARENT'S OR RETIRED ADULT'S PRIORITIES

1. _____
2. _____
3. _____

3.3 Your Positive Attitude List

Your PAL for Chapter 3 takes another look at your personality. The traits on the list are considered necessary personal qualities for today's successful employee.

As in the past chapters, circle the personality traits about which you are confident, and write in the space indicating the one that you will work to develop first.

These skills are essential for your success, so don't stop improving on the ones that you already do well. Make a note of the traits that need extra work, and set goals for yourself to work on them.

Adaptable	Adjusts well to new situations.
Truthful	Is honest and sincere and straightforward.

Thoughtful	Takes time to think things through before acting or passing judgment.
Industrious	Works hard and steadily and completes tasks efficiently.
Tenacious	Holds firmly to ideals and strong values; never gives up.
Understanding	Has perspective on the needs and situations that affect self and others.
Dependable	Is reliable and trustworthy.
Empathetic	Can put self in another's shoes and see a situation from that perspective.
Self-controlled	Knows how and when to act, and can defuse anger when necessary.

I will develop my ability to be: _____

_____

Take what you just said you want to develop and write it on one of your cards or Post-It® notes. Put it with your other cards from earlier chapters.

Take New Tools on the Road

3.4

Look over the New In Your Tool Kit list at the beginning of this chapter. Choose and write here the three most important tools you gained from reading this chapter.

1. _____
2. _____
3. _____

For each of the tools you listed, write one example of how you will apply that tool to achieve success in your career. Include changes you plan to make as well as how you will continue or reinforce existing behavior.

1. _____
_____
_____

2. _____
_____
_____

3. _____
_____
_____

4

Managing Your Time and Money

MAKING THE MOST OF KEY RESOURCES

NEW IN YOUR TOOL KIT

Time management

Scheduling

To-do lists

Financial management

As you get older, how you manage your time and money will directly affect the opportunities available to you as well as your ability to pursue and achieve your personal and career goals. In fact, to a large degree, the overall quality of your life will depend on how well you manage these resources.

You've already learned about the importance of identifying meaningful goals and setting priorities. In this chapter, you will develop skills in resource management and the ability to focus on your time and money, as noted in Figure 4.1, which are skills and resources crucial for achieving your goals.

There is nothing so degrading as the constant anxiety about one's means of livelihood. Money is like a sixth sense without which you cannot make a complete use of the other five.

—WILLIAM SOMERSET MAUGHAM

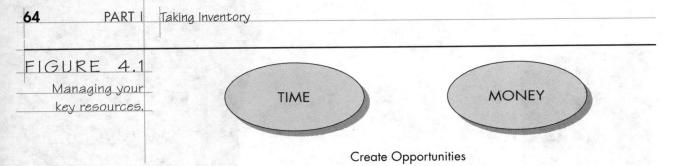

FIGURE 4.1
Managing your
key resources.

Managing Your Time

No matter who you are, you only get twenty-four hours in a day. To effectively achieve the goals you have prioritized, you need to know how to manage that time. Time management is a tool that, if used every day, will help you to achieve your goals in the quickest and most efficient way possible. Without it, you may find your days slipping by without accomplishing much of anything. With it, you will make the most of your time and energy to reach your goals and enrich your life.

How can you put your twenty-four-hour days to best use? First, take away your sleeping time, and you have around sixteen hours left. How can you manage that time without making yourself crazy, overestimating, or scheduling so tightly that you can't deal with surprises?

Take some time to consider what you know about who you are. Remember your personality profile—it will tell you much about how you handle time and help you decide what to do to make the most of it. Are you an ISTJ? You may be a natural-born list maker. The T for thinking and the J for judgmental combine to create a thoughtful, deliberate person who likes to write a schedule on paper. If you make reasonable lists and stick to carrying out the tasks you have listed, your tendencies will serve you well.

What if you are an ENFP? You probably are on the go a lot, but you may not spend much time organizing your schedule, and your inefficiency may cause you to lose time. Take a lesson from the list makers, just as they can learn from your drive and enthusiasm. Keep a calendar with you all the time, and write down a few essentials every day to keep you on track.

Different hints work for different personality types. Look at your own tendencies, and decide what works and what you would like to change. Don't rule anything out—you won't know until you try it! Use the Rule of 21 that we introduced in Chapter 1 to give new habits a chance.

Here are several suggestions for managing your time, as illustrated in Figure 4.2.

FIGURE 4.2
Seven ideas for
managing your
time.

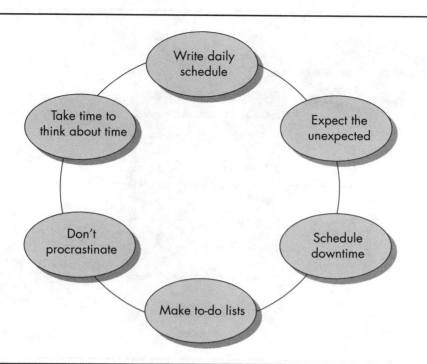

WRITE YOUR DAILY SCHEDULE

First things first—get yourself a date book. You will find two major types: one that lets you see a day at a time and one that shows a week at a time. The books that display one day give you more room to write in each day's activities but don't give you a good look at what is to come, so you may forget important events coming up later in the week. With a "week at a glance" book, you have less room to write about each day, but you have a perspective on the whole week. The choice is yours—decide whether you need more space to write or a larger perspective.

Then start to write your schedule. At the end of the chapter, you'll get the chance to schedule one week just to see how it works. Divide your activities—on paper or just in your head— into three categories: essential, regular, and if there's time. Essentials are things that have to get done, no matter what, like doctor's appointments, tests, etc.

Next are the regular tasks, the things that you do each day or each week at approximately the same time. You can adjust or miss these activities if you have to, but it's generally best not to. Typical regular tasks include school, work, after-school practices, a favorite TV show, etc. Write these in, and think about how to balance them with the essentials of that day.

Last is the "if there's time" category. You'd like to do these things if it doesn't throw your whole schedule out of whack, but you can sacrifice them or

FIGURE 4.3
How much time do
you have for a life?

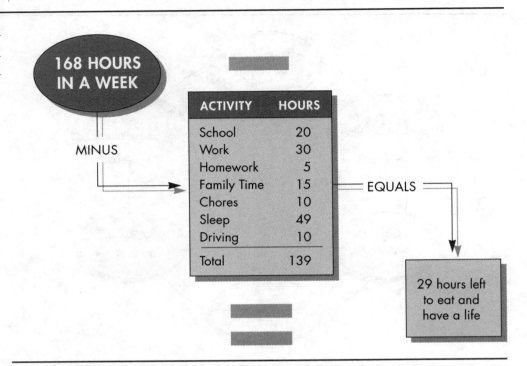

ACTIVITY	HOURS
School	20
Work	30
Homework	5
Family Time	15
Chores	10
Sleep	49
Driving	10
Total	139

168 HOURS IN A WEEK

MINUS

EQUALS

29 hours left to eat and have a life

bump them to another day if you just can't squeeze them into your schedule (see Figure 4.3). "If there's time" activities could include a shopping trip to the mall, visiting a friend, or doing your nails. (Some of these could become essentials, depending on the situation! You be the judge.) Take a look at your schedule, and see what you can fit in after you write your essential and regular activities.

This kind of schedule will work for you now while you are a student and later when you become an employee. It's all part of making the most of your time.

EXPECT THE UNEXPECTED

Life throws all kinds of curveballs! Just when you think you have your act together, something comes up to mess things up: Sometimes it's weather, sometimes it's other people, sometimes it's an emergency of one kind or another. Whatever it is, you'll handle it better if you keep an open mind and keep your plans flexible. Circumstances change plans. It's as simple as that. Go with the flow, and do what you have to do—just get back on track as soon as you can.

SCHEDULE DOWNTIME

Leave time for yourself every day, time to just goof around and relax. Even the littlest bit of downtime will refresh you and give you a chance to reenergize.

Just fifteen minutes a day can give your brain a break from running in the constant "on" mode. Get in the habit of setting aside time for just you; otherwise, the days will fly by without giving you a chance to stop.

MAKE TO-DO LISTS

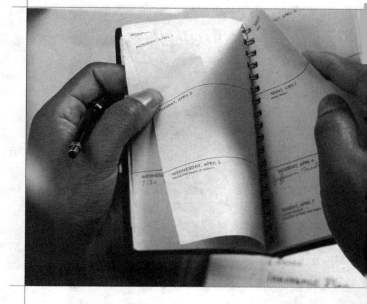

To-do lists are just what they sound like—lists of the things that you have to do or would like to do. They complement your daily schedule because they show detail that would otherwise crowd your date book. If your schedule for the day is something like school 8:00–3:00, practice 3:30–5:30, and mall 7:30, a to-do list for all the day's activities might include the following:

- Go to appointment with academic advisor
- Take test in English
- Eat lunch with Sarah
- Prepare project report for history class
- Exchange sneakers for different size
- Get birthday card for John

A to-do list helps you achieve little goals by reminding you of duties that can easily slip out of your mind. It can keep you on track so that you do things when it is easier for you to do them.

We have just been talking about a daily to-do list. You may also want to keep a long-term to-do list, on which you write activities you want to accomplish when your schedule lightens up. You don't assign these activities to a certain day, but by writing them down and keeping the list handy, you remind yourself of what you want to do. That way, you can take advantage of unexpected free time. A long-term to-do list might include:

- Start holiday shopping
- Sort through clothes and give unused clothing to the needy
- Put photos in album

DON'T PROCRASTINATE

Procrastination is the number one enemy of time management. When we procrastinate, we put things off without a sensible reason. The excuses for procrastination can get pretty creative—so creative at times that it would take less energy to just do the job we are avoiding in the first place! Maybe you've

Food for Thought

Depending on individual factors and our health, we have up to roughly sixty to eighty quality hours per week available for work, study, and other important commitments. After using our quality hours, we lose our efficiency; that means we take longer to accomplish tasks, and we find ourselves making too many careless mistakes. Unfortunately, with our busy lives, many people find themselves with commitments that exceed the sixty to eighty hours per week. How many hours of commitments do you have? Do you find it difficult to maintain your concentration? Do you find yourself having to reread the same paragraph several times? Setting goals and defining your priorities will help you best use your quality hours and avoid "burning the candle on both ends."

been guilty of procrastination regarding completing a homework assignment or studying for a test.

Whether you procrastinate due to dread, fear, lack of self-confidence, unrealistic goals, or just plain old habit, here are some ideas to help you conquer this enemy of successful time management:

- Ask for help with projects or schoolwork. Teachers, tutors, or supervisors are great sources of information and assistance.
- Try your hardest and do your best, but don't worry about doing everything perfectly.
- Give yourself a pep talk, and use positive self-talk to get yourself motivated.
- Make yourself commit to spending just fifteen minutes on the task. Getting started is the hardest part! Once you get started, you will find it easier to keep going.
- Think about the rewards of completing the project. Better grades? Parents off your case? Or, how about promising yourself a special treat when you get done?

TAKE TIME TO THINK ABOUT TIME

Sometimes it feels like days are so jam-packed that there just isn't time to sit down and plan anything. But, interestingly enough, taking time to plan will actually save you time in the long run. Try getting up a few minutes earlier in the morning to quickly sketch out your day. It might save you hours! No matter how pressed for time you feel, make yourself a plan. You know what they say—a stitch in time saves nine.

Managing Your Money

Sure, money isn't everything. It will never equal love, family, education, or a satisfying career. But money sure does come in handy at times. It pays for food, clothes, and housing. It finances the education and training that lead to a career. You don't necessarily need huge amounts of it—you just need to know how to manage what you've got. A small amount of money handled well will go much further than a lot of money handled carelessly. Bottom line, money is a basic resource. Manage it well and it will serve you well. Figure 4.4 illustrates key factors in money management.

Sometimes people go overboard trying to make money at all costs. They put all their energy into earning money at the expense of the more impor-

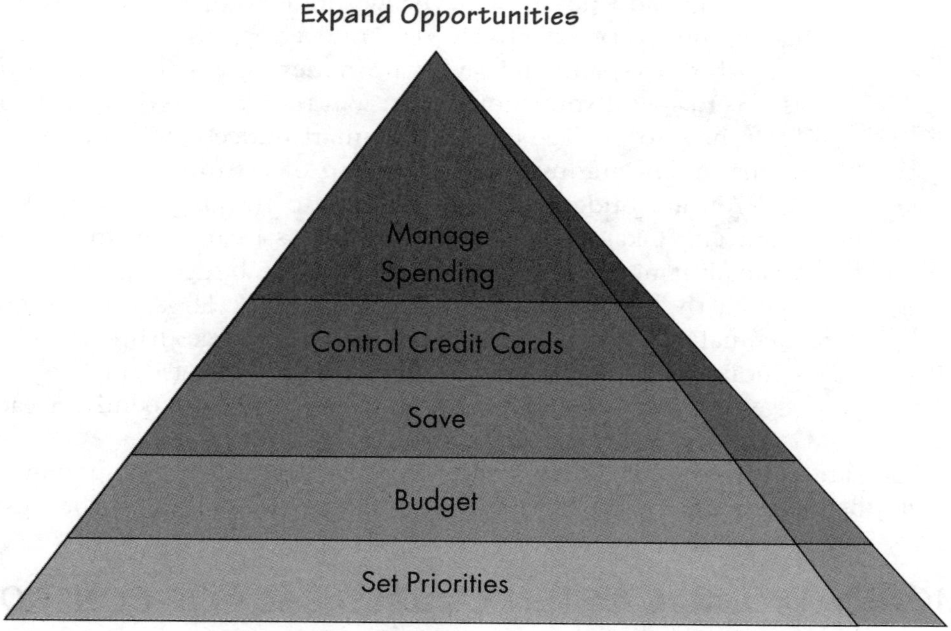

Expand Opportunities

FIGURE 2.3

Building your financial foundation.

Manage Spending

Control Credit Cards

Save

Budget

Set Priorities

tant things in life. This approach only goes so far. It's best to strike a balance between expecting money to magically appear on its own and becoming obsessed with earning as much of it as you can. It's all about control—you controlling your money without it controlling you. If you already have a paying job or earn an allowance, start now to learn how to manage that ebb and flow of cash.

Good money management is the right tool for every high school student and every worker. It means more than simply watching the money come in and go right back out again (even though that's how it often feels). Money management tools are strategies you can use to maximize and save your money. In this chapter, you will learn how to budget and how to spend and save wisely. You will read about the pros and cons of using credit. After taking in all this information, you will be able to evaluate it and make choices that best fit your needs.

Balancing Your Budget

Budgeting is setting goals with your money. If goal setting helps you organize and control your future plans and activities, then budgeting likewise permits you to control the flow of your money. The further ahead you can envision your plans, the more in control you will be.

Budget, verb.

To plan activities and expenditures according to the amount of income available.

noun.

A list of needs and the money spent on each.

You already do this, maybe without even realizing it—and maybe not very effectively. It's budgeting, making decisions about how to spend and save your money. As easy (and even fun) as it is to spend your money, you will thank yourself later if you learn how to manage it wisely. A smart budget and solid money management are investments in your own future.

You are budgeting when you go to the mall and think to yourself, "Okay, I have $50. That means I can buy this pair of jeans but not that pair of shoes." You are budgeting when you are at the movies deciding whether to get a large popcorn and a small drink or a small popcorn and a large drink with the money you have left after paying for the tickets. You are budgeting when you decide how much you can spend on each member of your family during the holidays.

You can see that you've already had a little practice! But it is important to look at the bigger picture—to budget over a period of a week, a month, or a year.

MONEY TROUBLE OFTEN EQUALS LACK OF CONTROL

Losing control of spending happens to people all the time. But such a loss of control does not mean that you don't have the power to control it. It usually means that you haven't tried! Control comes from long-term vision. If you look ahead, you will be able to control your funds.

Here's an example. You get paid $25 a week for doing extra chores around the house and $50 a week for your part-time job. You want to go with your class on the senior trip that costs $500. Your parents have said that is fine as long as you pay for it yourself. You have 3 months to save up, which means you need to save about $167 each month or $41.75 each week. That leaves you $33.25 a week to spend and save as you like. As long as you stick to that budget, you are on your way. What happens if you blow it? No senior trip!

BUDGETING

It isn't hard to budget. It simply takes a bit of time to keep track of everything. Right now, your budget will probably be fairly simple. Learn the ropes, and get yourself in the habit of good money management so you'll be ready when the big bucks (and the big bills!) start rolling in. Here is the basic process, in four easy steps.

STEP 1. Determine how much you will make in the coming month. Add up how much you expect to earn from allowance, part-time jobs, baby-sitting jobs, etc.

STEP 2. Determine what your expenses will be (clothes, entertainment, college fund, etc.). Figure out how much you spend on a regular basis. Add up the cost of a typical week's expenses—

lunch money, movie tickets, gas, car insurance, etc. If you have no idea what your regular expenses are, buy a small notebook or tack a piece of paper to a bulletin board, and keep track of what you buy and how much you pay each time you spend money.

You don't have to list everything to the penny. Just get a fairly close estimate of what your regular expenses are likely to be in a given week, and multiply it by four weeks.

STEP 3. Subtract expenditures from income, and look at how much you have left over—if there is any left over, that is. If you have more coming in than going out, your best bet is to save it (more on that strategy later). Some months, you may not have anything left over. Trim costs where you can, and be careful about overspending.

STEP 4. Make adjustments wherever necessary so that all essentials are covered. Be smart. Learn the difference between needs and wants; make sure what you really need is covered before spending on wants. You will be glad in the long run.

As you add budgeting skills to your tool kit, remember to go with your strengths. If you think you'd find keeping a weekly or monthly budget too much of a hassle, make a yearly budget. You won't be able to be quite as specific in estimating expenses, but you can get close enough to make some decisions about what your financial goals should be for the year.

Spending and Saving Wisely

Steady now, stay in control. The first step is to know where your money goes. You handle that when you budget. Then you need to know how to distribute that money. That's where wise spending and saving come into play.

LIVE BENEATH YOUR MEANS

It's the golden rule of smart spending and saving: Live beneath your means. That means to spend less than you make. The other side of the coin is to live beyond your means, which means to spend more money than you make and to create debt for yourself—not a good idea.

For example, if you were living beneath your means, you might bring in $200 a month, spend $160, give $20 to a favorite charity, and save $20. The savings, however small, will give you a buffer zone that will come in handy if something comes up that requires some extra cash (a new car or college, for instance).

Living beneath your means doesn't mean you have to become a penny-pinching scrooge; it just means being careful with what you've got and saving for a rainy day.

PAY YOURSELF FIRST

If living beneath your means is the golden rule of personal finance, then pay yourself first is the silver rule. Paying yourself means putting money away in savings, where it can grow until you need to use it. You owe it to yourself to teach yourself how to save money. It is a habit that will serve you well throughout your lifetime.

We all like to spend extra money on things that we don't really need—things we want to buy, entertainment, or dinners out. It's better to save the money, keeping an eye on it as it gains interest and grows so you'll have a nest egg of savings to keep you afloat when unexpected expenses come up.

An important tip: Don't think of your leftover money as extra. If you include it in your budget as a payment to yourself that carries equal weight with your other bills, you will honor your commitment to yourself. Giving yourself a strong financial base is an important part of the commitment to your success in life.

Remember this before we get into our suggestions for saving: When we talk about ways to budget and save your money, we don't mean that you should sacrifice all the little extras that make life enjoyable! Life is too short to restrict all your fun activities so that you can save money. At that rate, by the time you retire, you will have worked so hard that you will be too tired to enjoy the money you have put away! But we've had to economize too, so we want to share our tips with you. Even if you don't have to worry about money right now, stay conscious of where it goes—you never know what the future holds.

The purpose of this chapter is to encourage you to deal with money matters intelligently—to help you reason through your financial needs, apply budgeting strategies, make wise decisions, and work to attain financial goals. So you want to go to the amusement park with friends? Attend a movie or a basketball game? Buy a new outfit or the latest CD? Don't deny yourself. Just do yourself a favor by thinking before you spend.

What can you do to save in other areas so that you can indulge in what you want? What about making your lunch instead of buying it for a week or two? How about saving all the money you usually spend on sodas for a while? There are usually lots of ways to have fun in your life without hurting yourself financially. Give it a bit of thought—it will be worth it.

There are all kinds of ways to save a few dollars here and there. If you make a habit of taking advantage of them, you will build some savings. Then you will be able to use your hard-earned money when something important comes up, whether it's an emergency or a long-awaited purchase. Saving strategies help you to be financially prepared for the unexpected.

Using Credit Cards

Show me the plastic! This seems to be the rallying cry of people everywhere. Credit cards can be an incredible lifesaver or a black hole of debt. It's up to you because, as Eric Clapton says in one of his songs, "It's in the way that you use it!"

Real People, Real Stories

Want the inside story about what life is like after high school? Talk to someone who recently graduated, and find out how life changed after obtaining that awe-inspiring diploma. Depending on your own next-step goals, you may want to talk to someone who is in college or someone who decided to take a job soon after graduation. If you don't know anyone in these categories yourself, ask around. Surely some of your friends or classmates will have recent graduates in the family. Ask them to tell you what their new situation is like. Find out what changes they've noticed in their time schedules and their budgets. Record your discoveries on a separate sheet of paper.

You can benefit from using credit cards wisely. You can get yourself into a lot of trouble if you don't. Let's take a look at the benefits and problems associated with having credit cards.

CREDIT, noun.
A sum of money made available by a bank or credit card company, on which a specified person or firm may draw.

BENEFITS OF CREDIT CARD USE

First, we list the good points of credit card use.

ESTABLISHMENT OF A GOOD CREDIT HISTORY. Having a credit card that you use moderately and pay off regularly on time can give you a good credit rating. Companies such as TRW track credit histories of everyone who has any sort of credit. The history is your record of your credit use itself; the rating is the score that a company like TRW will give you based on how good or bad your credit track record is. Your credit rating becomes important for both job hunting and major purchases (cars and homes, primarily). Many prospective employers look into the credit histories of applicants to see if they are reliable bill payers. If the credit rating is good, it will help the applicant qualify for the job. Also, when you want to make a major purchase, you will often need a loan from a bank. Banks will more readily loan money to someone who has a good credit rating because it shows responsibility and reliability.

HELP IN EMERGENCIES. Credit cards can come in handy if you are caught somewhere without cash and need to pay for something. These kinds of situations can happen anytime—you run out of gas, you get stuck somewhere and need to stay in a hotel, you need to find transportation in a hurry—and your credit card can get you out of a jam.

Sound Bite

I think knowing that you need to put some money away is the most important idea. Opportunities will come up later, and you will need money to get into them. You don't need to buy that extra this or that you need to put some money away in savings or investments and watch it draw interest. I know that a lot of people coming out of school are younger, and they're not thinking to invest their money. But if you're making enough and you can do it, then by all means, do it. When I was younger, I was so busy, and at that time life was very simple and I didn't have a lot of bills. Things get more complicated—you're not buying new shoes, you're buying new furniture, and there's a big difference in price.

—K. Mitchell,
independent consultant

A RECORD OF PURCHASES. Some people like to use credit cards because they get a record each month of the purchases that they made, where they made them, and exactly how much they paid. This can be useful especially if you make purchases for work on your credit card and need to keep records of them for tax purposes.

BONUSES OFFERED BY CREDIT CARD COMPANIES. In recent years, many credit card companies have begun to offer bonuses to attract more people to their particular credit card. For example, the Shell Oil Master Card offers points that you earn for using the credit card, and you can exchange the points for free gasoline. Many airlines have cards that give you frequent-flier miles in exchange for dollars spent, and General Motors offers credit toward the purchase of a General Motors car. If you know that a bonus will be useful to you, and you use the credit card consistently and pay it off just as consistently, you can benefit from the situation.

PROBLEMS OF CREDIT CARD USE

In spite of their many benefits, credit cards have a few features that can get you into trouble if you aren't careful. We list some of these problems.

YOU ARE SPENDING SOMEONE ELSE'S MONEY. It's a fact! Until you pay it back, the money you spend is not yours. It belongs to the credit card company, and it pays the money to the retailer. The credit card company counts on you to pay it back later. The problem is, it can be very tempting to overspend when the money isn't really yours. Because you don't have to face up to paying your own money right away, you may feel free to spend more than you should. And that can lead to trouble later if you are unable to meet your credit card payments.

YOU ARE TAKING OUT A HIGH-INTEREST LOAN. When you spend credit card money, it is the same as taking out a loan. You are using money with the promise to pay it back. In exchange for the privilege of using that money, you pay interest and fees. The problem is, credit card interest rates range from 11 to 23 percent, and they are more often on the high end of that range. Taking out a loan at such high percentages is extremely costly! Let's say you have $2,000 in a savings account at 5 percent interest, and you owe $2,000 on a credit card, on which you pay 15 percent interest. Chances are that you don't want to pay off your credit card because you don't want to erase your entire savings. But you should notice that you are paying 10 percent more interest on the money owed than you are receiving in interest from the money saved! You are losing some money, in this case, $200 a year or $16.50 a month. Not much, but every little bit counts. We wouldn't advise you to wipe out your savings, but perhaps you could pay off half of your credit card balance and then get rid of the rest in installments. Generally, try to keep your credit card debt lower than the amount of money you have saved. If you need funds for a large purchase, try a bank loan. The interest rates will beat credit card rates any day.

CREDIT IS ADDICTIVE. Spending money can be like a drug. It's fun, and it seems painless because you don't see the damage (the bills) for a while. But if you get too hooked on it, if your material desires get the best of you, you can wind up thousands of dollars in debt to credit card companies. You will see your debt grow by leaps and bounds because of the high interest. Having such debt will hurt you in many ways: Your credit rating will fall, you will be unable to take out loans for mortgages, you will lose the ability to use your credit cards, and money that you could spend on things that you need will have to go toward repaying your debt. You can avoid making this kind of trouble for yourself.

A BAD CREDIT RATING CAN HURT YOU. Anytime you miss a payment, default on a payment, or in any way misuse your credit card, that black mark will show up on your credit history and lower your credit rating. If a prospective employer investigates you and finds that out, that person may be less likely to trust you. And if you apply for a bank loan, the bank may refuse the loan if you have a history of missing payments or other credit card problems.

Do yourself a favor. Don't create unnecessary stress for yourself by getting into credit card trouble. It can be tough enough to get by in the world without getting financially strapped! Don't get into a hole with credit cards.

If you do have credit cards, restrict yourself to one because the fewer the cards, the less temptation to spend. Pay your bills regularly, even though it is not always possible to pay off credit cards in full each month. If you cannot pay off the bill completely, commit yourself to making a good dent in it, and pay the minimum at the very least. Remember that the credit interest you pay is almost always higher than the savings interest you earn. You will be

Food for Thought

You have credit card bills and car payments. You are making just enough to get by. Despite not liking your job, you don't feel you can make a change. You feel locked in by the monthly payments you have to make. Many adults find themselves in this situation. It's no fun. What can you do to avoid making the same mistakes? Open up your options. Create a financial foundation so that you can pursue your dreams. Start saving, control your credit card spending, and use a budget to help manage your money.

Sound Bite

These are challenging times financially because of the instability of the work world. You have to prioritize—pay the most important things first because it's not always realistic to be able to pay off all your bills all of the time. Don't forget about the things that you numbered 2, 3, and 4 just handle those things on smaller levels—do a little bit this month, a little bit that month. It's like building a house. Build your finances brick by brick, and you will eventually come to a point where everything is being paid consistently and you are on some kind of schedule. When I had my first job in New York, I was starving! I got a second job selling real estate part-time at night, and then I just knocked off one bill at a time. I would focus on my Visa, pay as much as I could, and only pay minimum on the others until Visa was paid off. I'm not a financial expert, but that's how I did it.

—L. Durden, career counselor

smart to put some of your savings toward your credit card bill. And if that hurts, just grit your teeth and do it—and then curb your credit card spending next time!

IF YOU BLOW IT

It happens. Many people get into trouble with credit cards. Sometimes difficult and sudden events occur; sometimes they just weren't paying attention to their money. But the result can be a bad credit history. What do you do?

Here's the solution: Admit it, fix it, prevent it. You cannot undo what has been done, so don't let it keep you up nights.

Admit It

Acknowledge that you made a mistake. It sounds like a breeze, but most people get tripped up on this first step! It's hard to admit responsibility for what's happened. So people often go right ahead like nothing ever went wrong. And that's when things really go wrong because the hole that has been dug only gets deeper.

Admit your mistake to yourself and to your creditor (the bank or company to which you owe money). Then you will be ready to do something about it.

Fix It

This step usually involves payment. If you are in credit trouble, you need to find a way to pay off as many of your credit card bills as you can. You cannot erase the damage, but correcting the situation quickly, pleasantly, and completely can help to minimize it.

Don't hesitate to call the bank or credit card company to talk to someone about the problem. Often the bank or credit card company will agree to a payment plan that allows you to pay the debt gradually, in amounts that your budget can manage. Creditors would rather have an honest payment plan than no money and no idea when it will arrive.

Prevent It

Learn from your mistakes. If you have to, tear up the cards and live on a cash-only basis. Otherwise, consider what changes you want to make in your credit card use and credit history, and what steps you need to take.

Drawing Your Financial Future

Getting your financial facts together will give you a solid base from which to make decisions. When you are job hunting, you will know what knowledge to use and what actions to take, no matter what the situation. Perfecting the use of your personal finance tools will make you an old hand by the time you have your first job. Ensuring the smooth transition from study to work is worth the discipline that this chapter suggests.

Your Tool Kit at Work

4.1

Your Time—Spend It Like Money

We are all on equal footing where weekly time is concerned. We each have 168 hours per week to spend as we choose. And just as with money, you get less for your time if you don't spend it wisely.

Start planning your time by discovering how you use it. Estimate how you manage your time in hours per week.

WEEKLY TIME PLANNER

Activity	Time in Hours
School	
Work	
Sports, other after-school activities	
Study	
Sleep	
Meals	
Commuting to school and work	
Personal business (shopping, doctors)	
Household chores	
Communication with family and friends (include telephone time)	
Leisure activities (include social events, television, exercise)	
Religious activities	
Dealing with the unexpected	

GRAND TOTAL: _____

With only 168 hours to spend, do you

Feel too tightly scheduled? _____

Have too little scheduled? _____

Have the right balance? _____

To check your estimates, keep track of exactly how you spend your time for a week. Write in the number of hours that you spend each day on each activity.

Activity	Mon	Tue	Wed	Thu	Fri	Sat	Sun
School							
Work							
Sports/Activities							
Study							
Sleep							
Meals							
Commuting							
Personal business							
Household chores							
Communication							
Leisure activities							
Religious activities							
Dealing with the unexpected							
TOTALS:							

GRAND TOTAL (add totals): _____

Compare both grand totals. Do they match? If they don't, look at where the differences are so that you know how you are currently spending your time.

Now that you know how you spend your time, how can you change your schedule to accommodate your responsibilities? Look over your current time allocations and make cuts and increases where needed. The television and telephone are often the major time wasters. Cut back on those culprits, but don't shortchange leisure time or time that can help you handle unexpected events.

If you plan to get a job, have you left enough hours open? If not, go back and make more cuts. If there are no more cuts to make, realize that you may have to live the way you are now while you're in school.

You're ready to spend your time like money—carefully and realistically. Fill in your revised weekly time planner.

WEEKLY TIME PLANNER

Activity	Time in Hours
School	
Work	
Sports/Activities	
Study	
Sleep	
Meals	

(continued)

WEEKLY TIME PLANNER (continued)

Activity	Time in Hours
Commuting	
Personal business (shopping, doctors)	
Household chores	
Communication with family and friends (include telephone time)	
Leisure activities (include social events, television, exercise)	
Religious activities	
Dealing with the unexpected	

GRAND TOTAL: _____

Transfer those hours to a weekly master time chart. Fill in your activities under the best times for you to accomplish them. Of course, you need to put the actual times you work, go to school, and complete your other time-specific tasks and activities.

	Mon	Tue	Wed	Thu	Fri	Sat	Sun
7:00 A.M.							
8:00 A.M.							
9:00 A.M.							
10:00 A.M.							
11:00 A.M.							
12:00 P.M.							
1:00 P.M.							
2:00 P.M.							
3:00 P.M.							
4:00 P.M.							
5:00 P.M.							
6:00 P.M.							
7:00 P.M.							
8:00 P.M.							
9:00 P.M.							
10:00 P.M.							
11:00 P.M.							

Technology at Work

4.2

Use a personal computer to help you budget your time. Software programs such as Quicken, Daytimer Organizer, or Microsoft Schedule+ are designed to help you manage your time. Or you can use a spreadsheet program such as Excel to develop a daily schedule, a weekly plan, and a place to write your goals, priorities, and to-do lists.

To Do or Not To Do

4.3

We all know about to-do lists. But not everyone consistently uses this tool. Writing major tasks is a must if we plan to get things done! Try this to start a habit of making to-do lists.

Jot down everything you need to do tomorrow.

1. _____
2. _____
3. _____
4. _____
5. _____
6. _____
7. _____

Look at your list. Which three items are the most important things to do? Put an A, B, and C by those items according to their order of importance.

Now you have your to-do list for tomorrow complete with priorities. Make a quick list every morning or evening, and you've added a valuable tool to your tool kit.

The best place to write your to-do list is on a monthly calendar. That way you can see at a glance what you need to (1) do each day, (2) plan for the week, and (3) accomplish in a month. Following is a calendar for you to fill out for the current month. Fill in those items now that you know that you need to do, attend, complete, and so forth. Include school assignments, projects at work, personal business and social events.

Sun	Mon	Tue	Wed	Thu	Fri	Sat

Compare your goals with your monthly to-do calendar. Are steps toward each of your goals part of your to-do list? If not, determine why. Maybe your goals need revising if they aren't important enough to include. Or, maybe when you make your to-do list you're not thinking in terms of your success and what you want to do to reach your goals. Either way, before you proceed, make sure steps toward your goals are included every week on your calendar.

Color code the to-do's that deal directly with your goals. For example, use red for your career goals, yellow for school goals, and green for personal goals. When you finish, you'll have an eye-catching chart as well as an easy way to know you're taking the necessary steps to success.

Make a calendar for every month as it approaches, and color code it. In that way you can change and revise steps as required.

4.4 Virtual Budget

Pretend that you've finally made it. You've graduated from high school, completed college or another advanced training program, and landed the perfect job. The pay is decent—$33,000 per year. Use that base salary to work out a budget using the following common expenses as a guide. Ask your parents and teacher for ideas on the realistic cost of these expenses as well as checking ads in the newspaper for things such as the going rates for apartment rents and car payments.

As with your time, you need to know how you're spending your money to make changes and improvements in your budgeting. A good plan requires a solid starting point. Here's yours.

Estimate your current expenses in dollars per month:

Income	Amount
Regular work salary (full-time or part-time work)	$ 33,000

Expense	Amount
Rent or mortgage	$
Utilities (electric, gas, water)	$
Food	$
Telephone	$
Loan payments (student or bank loans)	$
Car expenses (repairs, insurance, payments)	$
Gasoline	$
Clothing/personal items	$
Entertainment	$
Child care (caregivers, clothing and supplies, other fees)	$
Medical care	$
Miscellaneous/unexpected	$ _____
GRAND TOTAL:	$

To find out your cash flow each month, subtract the grand total of your expenses from the grand total of your income.

My income is $_____   per month $_____
My expenses are $_____   per month − $_____
                           CASH FLOW $_____

Choose one:

I have $_____ positive cash flow.

I have $_____ negative cash flow.

I break even.

The Real Thing

4.5

Back to reality. Chances are that you aren't making anywhere near $33,000 yet. How much do you bring in each month? What kinds of expenses do you have now? Use the space below to put together a budget using your current income and expenses.

INCOME (LIST ALL SOURCES SUCH AS ALLOWANCE, ODD JOBS, PART-TIME JOB, ETC.):

- _____
- _____
- _____

EXPENSES (LIST ALL REGULAR EXPENSES SUCH AS LUNCHES, CLOTHES, ENTERTAINMENT, COLLEGE FUND, ETC.):

- _____
- _____
- _____

Your Financial Future

4.6

Think ahead to some of the big things you'll need money for in the near future—things like cars, college or training programs, your own apartment, etc. Use the space below to write some financial goals for the next few years. What kind of major expenses to you expect to have? How can you meet these obligations?

- _____
- _____
- _____

4.7

Take New Tools on the Road

Look over the New In Your Tool Kit list at the beginning of this chapter. Choose and write here the three most important tools you gained from reading this chapter.

1. _____

2. _____

3. _____

For each of the tools you listed, write one example of how you will apply that tool to achieve success in your career. Include changes you plan to make, as well as how you will continue or reinforce existing behavior.

1. _____
_____
_____

2. _____
_____
_____

3 _____
_____
_____

GETTING STARTED

II

No one is better than you.

We are all human.

Regular people can do anything.

And you're never too good to

learn more.

LISA DURDEN, CAREER CONSULTANT/MOTIVATIONAL SPEAKER

5

Sharpening Your Tools

YOUR BASIC SKILLS

NEW

IN YOUR TOOL KIT

Effective communi-
cation skills

Reading

Writing

Thinking

Proofreading

Test taking

Lifelong learning

One critical SCANS category that you learned about in Chapter 1 is basic skills. Underneath all your abilities, ideas, styles, and talents, you need these basics to function successfully in the working world. To put it bluntly, if you can't read, write, and think, you won't make it very far in the real world. Hopefully, you've realized, by this point in the educational process, that there really is a reason for learning all the things you've been learning in school. The time will come when you'll need to put all that learning to work. These basic skills give you access to what John Adams calls the "sluice of knowledge"— the flow of all other information and learning.

When Adams talks about the "means of knowledge," he refers to how these skills enable us to find and receive knowledge. Here, "means" indicates the skills that expose us to the knowledge that we need in the working world. We define these skills as listening, concentration, memory, note taking, reading, writing, proofreading, and test taking. Everyone, regardless of profession, needs these skills.

Success in the workplace requires that workers have solid reading and writing skills. In some areas of employ-

Let us . . . cherish, therefore, the means of knowledge. Let us dare to read, think, speak, and write . . . Let every sluice of knowledge be opened and set a-flowing.

—JOHN ADAMS, 1765

ment, the necessity of good basic skills is more obvious. But you will need those basic skills for any job that you take, at any time in your life. Words are everywhere. Being able to hear them accurately, read them easily, and communicate them clearly on paper will serve you in any and all professions you will encounter.

There's no escaping reading and writing—or any of the other basic skills. These tools will be well worn because you take them out of your tool kit often. Before we launch into basic skills, there is one thinking skill you need to consider as you read, a skill that involves many aspects of the basics. That skill is called knowing how to learn. The techniques involved in knowing how to learn can free your mind to take in the knowledge you encounter. They enable you to evaluate, retain, and use what you have studied.

At the end of this chapter, you will look at a list of how-to-learn skills in detail, and you will evaluate your own aptitude level for each. Some of them involve the reading, writing, listening, concentration, memory, and test-taking guidelines that you will cover. Some talk about the kind of study environment that you set up for yourself. Some address your attitude toward your studies and your habits. Used together, they are a simple guide to opening your mind to the knowledge presented to you at school and on the job.

Listening

Everyone has this skill to some degree. Even most people who cannot hear can "listen" to what hands, lips, or facial expressions say. We are not really taught how to listen in school, other than to hear our teachers say, "Listen up!" We know we should do it, and we know we can. But often we don't listen as well as we could.

The fact is, an ability to listen well is one of the most sought-after qualities in employees of all professions (and friends, too). It comes down to two basic facts. First, we all love to be understood. When we talk, we want to know that someone hears us, takes in what we have to say, and understands our message. Do you feel good when you pour your heart out to a friend who takes it all in quietly and attentively? On the other hand, do you feel annoyed when you are trying to communicate to people who use your words only as springboards on which to bounce stories about themselves back to you? It is frustrating to feel like no one hears what you say.

Second, the success of any organization, be it a classroom or a company or whatever, depends on communication among its members—from the top down and from the bottom up. If everyone listens when someone communicates ideas and instructions to them, things will roll along as they should. If people don't listen well, communication breaks down, and the classroom's or company's operations can be placed in jeopardy.

Have you ever played the game gossip? It's the one where one person whispers something in another person's ear, he or she repeats it to the next person, who repeats it to the next person, and so on down the line. The last person says the message out loud, and the group compares the original message with the final one. As you might imagine, there is often quite a big difference between the first message and the last, which goes to prove that what you think you heard isn't necessarily what was said.

Miscommunication happens often wherever there are at least two people trying to get a message across. Many avoidable mistakes are made and misunderstandings occur because people don't always listen well. It only takes a tiny bit of effort to make a big difference. If you are a good listener, you will find that people will listen to you in return. It's simply another application of the golden rule: Do unto others as you would have them do unto you. It will pay off. Figure 5.1 identifies key steps for listening success.

Food for Thought

You have worked hard to complete an important project. You scheduled a half-hour appointment with your teacher and are now meeting with him to review it. Yet, he doesn't seem to be paying attention. As you talk, he reads some other material on his desk. How do you feel? Your teacher may think there is a one-way mirror, and you don't see what he is doing or that his poor listening habits are not rude. As a student or an employee, don't make the same mistake as the teacher in this example. As you sit in class or at a meeting at work, practice active listening. Not only will this help your performance, but active listening will let others know you care about their work and respect what they are doing.

Enhance listening skills. FIGURE 5.1

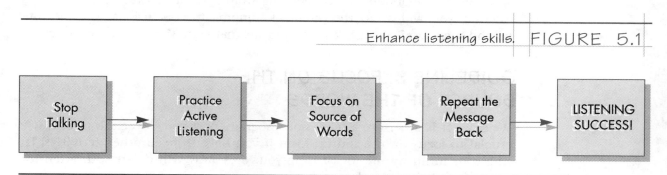

GUIDELINE 1: STOP TALKING

It seems pretty obvious, but one of the most effective ways to begin listening attentively is to stop talking. It is very hard to hear what others have to say when you are saying things yourself, so don't interrupt. Close your mouth and concentrate. Let someone else have a chance to speak, and you will find yourself able to hear what he or she has to say better because you aren't throwing your own words into the mix. By the way, if you get restless, don't worry. The more you let someone else have a turn, the more likely you are to have yours—and to have people listen to you silently, too.

GUIDELINE 2: PRACTICE ACTIVE LISTENING

Active listening involves a few different concepts.

ONLY LISTEN. It is easy, in our hurried world, to get into the habit of doing many things at once. But your listening skills can suffer. If you are studying and taking a phone call at the same time that your friend is telling you something important, what do you think the chances are that you will hear it correctly? Not too good. We are all guilty of this kind of attempt to do it all. So when you must listen to someone, make a conscious effort to stop everything else you are doing, if only for one moment. The computer, phone, or television can wait. Start your listening with the first word out of the other person's mouth.

QUIET YOUR BRAIN. We also stifle our listening ability by thinking of how we will answer someone while he or she is still in the process of talking to us. If we read our own meanings into what we hear right as we hear it, we might not hear correctly. Listen before thinking. Try not to react until you have it all purely, without mixing it with your own thoughts. Hear each word as if it were the most important thing in that moment, more important than your thoughts about it.

STAY OPEN AND RECEPTIVE. Sometimes even our reaction to the person speaking, especially a negative reaction, can distract us from what the person tries to communicate. Hold off on any judgments of the speaker; be open to hearing what is being said. Your reaction will come into your head naturally without any premature or additional effort—let it happen after the person finishes speaking. You may hear emotional or challenging words, but if you take it all in before reacting, you will avoid the pitfall of jumping to conclusions. The meaning behind such words may sink in if you wait that extra time before you react.

GUIDELINE 3: FOCUS ON THE SOURCE OF THE WORDS

Whether it is a person, a television program, or a voice over the phone, it is crucial to focus on the source. Even if you have stopped other activities, letting your mind wander or turning your eyes away will divert your attention as much as would another activity.

It's amazing what a simple visual focus can do for your quality of listening. Letting your eyes concentrate on the person speaking to you guides your energy toward that source and allows you to take in the information freely. Plus, it will help you ignore distractions. If you take listening one step further by using open facial expressions and body positioning to show your interest, you will encourage the other person to open up even more.

What if you are talking on the phone? If you can't see the person who is speaking to you, how can you focus on that person's image? This situation is a bit different. Some people find it helpful to use an inner focus, a technique in which they focus on an image of the person they conjure up in their mind. It works well, but only if you have an idea of what the other person looks like. A more consistently useful idea is to simply make sure that your eyes are not focusing too hard on anything else such as a book, TV program, or another person within your field of vision. Eliminating any other distractions will help you concentrate, even though you cannot see the other person.

GUIDELINE 4: REPEAT THE MESSAGE BACK

This technique adds a few more moments to the listening process, but it is worthwhile. After you have listened to someone speak to you, take a minute to repeat the message back to the person to see if you heard it right. Repeating gives you a chance to check your understanding of the message.

For example, suppose you miss math class one day because you were sick. The next day, you ask the teacher what you need to do to make up the missed assignments. She says, "Read pages 49–56 in your math book, work through all the problems in the first section, but only the odd-numbered problems in the second section."

You might say back, "Read the next chapter, work all of section one, odds only in section two." Wait to hear a verbal response that you are right, and politely request one if you don't receive it: "Is that correct?" If you are wrong, the person will tell you, and it's up to you to make the correction right away.

Repeating serves three purposes:

1. You assure the speaker that you are listening.

2. You reinforce what you heard by saying it out loud.

3. You get a chance to correct a misunderstood direction before you act on it.

Concentration

The dictionary lists two definitions of concentration (see below), and what you need to know involves both.

When we talk about concentration, we are referring to the first definition, to the act of focusing your thoughts on one thing or concept. But the very act of focusing in that way brings in the second definition because it increases the intensity of your thought power.

Think about it. You have a certain amount of available brainpower at any given time. What if you are in class and the teacher is talking, but you have three or four other things on your mind? Your father is sick, you forgot to finish your biology assignment, and your best friend is mad at you. All those things compete in your head with the need to listen to the teacher, and the listening ends up with only one-quarter of your brainpower. You won't get nearly as much out of the class as you would if your thoughts were focused 100 percent.

Concentration, *noun.*

1. The act of collecting one's thoughts and focusing them toward one center.
2. The act of increasing in density or intensity.

GUIDELINE 1: KEEP A SINGLE FOCUS

You will always get more out of whatever you do if you let your brain focus on one thing at a time. We all have times when our brains are rushing around worrying about ten things at once. Have you noticed that you rarely solve any of your problems at those times? You cannot concentrate. Your thoughts flit around and come to no conclusions, except for the conclusion that you have a lot of worries—and you knew that already. Sometimes people realize that they've wasted a whole hour worrying when they could have solved the problem in that time!

So instead of flitting for an hour, divide and conquer. Concentrate your energy on one issue at a time. So you have six concerns? Devote ten minutes to each, and don't let your mind wander while you focus on one at a time. You can bet you will take a few steps in the right direction on every one. Have respect for your brain! If you don't overload it, if you let it work on one issue at a time, it will reward you with good progress.

Food for Thought

Think of yourself as a participant in a bicycle race. A successful racer has only one thing in mind: to keep going and move ahead. If the racer worried about how fast the other racers were going, or who was ahead, or how many miles were left to go, her concentration would scatter, and ultimately the racer would be unable to find holes in the pack through which to plow ahead with increased speed and thus improve her position. The racer would lose a bit of her brainpower, and it would hinder her success.

GUIDELINE 2: BE HERE NOW

Concentration thrives best in the here and now. Thinking about something that happened in the past, or something that concerns you in the future, will take you away from what you should concentrate on in the present. Don't shortchange the present. It is all that you have at any given moment; it is the solid opportunity you hold in your hand. The past has slipped away, and the future is only a dream. Staying "present" in the present also saves you time. If you concentrate on what is happening at the moment, you will not need to spend as much time remembering it later or going over it to fortify your knowledge. The more energy you devote to the information in front of you at the moment you take it in, the less you will have to expend trying to recapture it later.

GUIDELINE 3: USE PROVEN CONCENTRATION TECHNIQUES

You may find it hard sometimes to concentrate. We all do. Sometimes your brain can relax and focus, and sometimes it is too busy to land on any one concern. When you find you are in the busy stage and you want to get out, there are three things you can do. Try them all, and see what works best for you. You may like some better than others, and some may be better choices than others for certain situations. For example, if you are in the middle of class, you don't want to breathe so loudly that you appear bored, and you cannot change your environment. In that case, try the focus technique.

BREATHE. It's amazing what a few minutes of deep breathing can do. Breathe slowly and deeply, and think of exhaling your busy brain activity along with the air you blow out. Close your eyes so that what you see doesn't get in the way of your brain's clearing. Don't do this for too long—you may end up taking a nap! Only a few minutes should calm you down and clear your head so that you can choose your focus.

FOCUS. Focus your eyes on something. Sometimes gazing at something intensely and focusing your vision will bring your thoughts into a similar focus. Looking at something may naturally lead you to think about what you are seeing, and other thoughts may fall away. When you feel focused, you may have more power to turn your thoughts in your chosen direction.

FIND A RELAXING ENVIRONMENT. Certain places make it harder to concentrate—perhaps for you it's a busy lunchroom, a family room where children are playing, or somewhere with a loud television or stereo. You know yourself, and you know what kinds of distractions bother you. If you sense that your environment is making it hard for you to concentrate, try to move yourself or change it. Build yourself a bubble of peace! Find a quieter room or remote corner in the cafeteria. Ask someone to turn down the television or music. Give yourself the best chance to concentrate by minimizing your distractions.

GUIDELINE 4: GIVE YOURSELF A BREAK

All work and no play will make anyone pretty antsy. It's tough to concentrate when you are tired and would rather be doing something else. That can eas-

Food for Thought

Jana was so looking forward to her weekend trip that she daydreamed through the day and forgot to complete two important tasks. Ben was so caught up in how angry he felt at himself over a mistake he made yesterday that he couldn't bring himself to make the phone calls today that might partially correct it. Did you know that most people spend up to 90 percent of their time thinking about the past (how the date went last night) or the future (what to have for dinner tomorrow)? Forgetting that we exist 100 percent in the present, we often spend only 10 percent of our brainpower on it. Think what we can accomplish with a mind and time fit—matching 100 percent brainpower to the present!

Real People, Real Stories

This time out, we'll stretch your boundaries a bit. Identify someone who has an interesting job, maybe even one that you are considering for yourself. Ask if you can talk to him or her about the profession. State that the focus of this assignment is communication. Let the person tell you how good communication skills come into play in the work. Record your discoveries on a separate sheet of paper.

ily happen if you study, work, or concentrate for lengthy periods of time. Listen to your mind's hints. If you cannot concentrate because you keep dreaming about playing ball outside, going shopping, or taking a long lunch, go ahead and take the break you want. Enjoy yourself; when you return to work later, you will be able to concentrate once again.

Be sure to put leisure time in your schedule. Plan ahead so that you know when you will work and when you can play. That way, you won't take up your working energy wishing you could escape to some more pleasant activity. You free your mind to concentrate when you know you have fun time scheduled later.

When you are studying or working at home and become too tired to concentrate, give your brain a rest and try one of the following:

- Read or watch television.
- Do a mindless task such as cleaning up, raking, or organizing your room.
- Take a nap or turn in for the night.

The next time you return to your task, you will feel refreshed and ready.

Memory

Memory is a tool that people use throughout each day. We all have some ability to recall facts and experiences, but as with listening, we rarely work deliberately to improve this skill. Many people have trouble remembering names, phone numbers, or directions. We take in so much information every day that it is tough to keep track of it all.

Good memory skills help save time—and time is one of your most valuable commodities. The more you can accomplish in the time you have, the more you will progress. If you can retain information and recall it quickly without always having to refer back to something or ask someone, you will save a great deal of time.

GUIDELINE 1: USE YOUR OTHER TOOLS

A couple of additional basic skills give memory power a jolt. One is listening. If you don't listen well, you won't know what you need to remember! The second is concentration. It's tough to remember things that you read or hear unless you focus on them at the time. The more you concentrate on something, the more you will burn it into your brain.

Have you ever read a whole page of a book and then realized that you don't remember a word of it? You had no concentration, so to retain any of the information on the page, you had to go back and read it again! Neglecting to listen also interferes with memory. Often in conversation, you will hear phrases such as "Come again?" or "I'm sorry, could you repeat that?" or a even a simple "What?" that may indicate someone hasn't been listening. When that happens, the person needs to listen to the information twice before being able to remember it accurately. This is a waste of both the speaker's and the listener's time.

GUIDELINE 2: REPEAT

When you repeat verbally—to yourself or others—or you repeat by writing important concepts on paper, you increase your chances of remembering information. Verbal repetition works especially well with remembering names of people you have met. Have you ever been introduced to someone and then found that you had forgotten the name not two minutes later? Try using the name right away when you meet someone: "It's a pleasure to meet you, Jerry." Just saying the name, letting your mouth and tongue form the words, helps to inscribe them in your memory. Saying your notes aloud to yourself also helps.

GUIDELINE 3: ASSOCIATE

If you can associate new information with something that you already know, it will help you to remember the concept. Putting something new in the context of something familiar helps you relate to it much more easily.

A more specific association trick is especially helpful with recalling names. Suppose you meet Stacey Long and she's tall. You have a natural association that will help you remember her—her height and her last name! Or perhaps she reminds you of your best friend, Tracey. In that case, the association of rhyming names will help. You can even make up an association to help you, such as "Stacey lives a long way from me." Any of these associations can work.

GUIDELINE 4: WRITE

Writing helps whether you write something you heard or rewrite something you already wrote. If you take notes in a class, for example, and want to remember certain key points, take a clean sheet of paper and rewrite a simple list of those points. Write important numbers or names. The more you write, the more you will remember.

GUIDELINE 5: USE MNEMONIC DEVICES

Mnemonic (pronounced "neMAHNick") devices are word tricks that can help you retain information in your memory. Whether or not you have trouble remembering things, you may already use some of these devices occasionally. Mnemonic devices are for those with strong memory skills as well as those who could use some help. Far from being sneaky, they are essential.

These word games help you remember specific sets of information. One kind uses the first letters of words to make a funny sentence. Another, called an acronym, makes a memorable word from the first letters of words you want to recall. A common example is the word WAJEMMA, made up of the first letter of the last names of the first six U.S. presidents (with the "E" added for pronunciation). You can even take words out of context and make funny sentences. Mnemonics are easy to remember because they are designed to be catchy—and they are especially efficient when you make them up yourself.

Taking Notes

Although you may think you can leave it behind when you finish your time in school, note taking is one of those skills that you'll need beyond the classroom. When might you need this skill in the workplace?

- At an orientation meeting when you start a job
- At staff meetings
- When learning rules of your workplace
- When learning how to operate equipment
- When taking phone messages
- When learning essential information such as lock or alarm combinations, emergency phone numbers, or intercom numbers

Specific jobs will offer other opportunities to take notes. Use this list as a springboard for your own ideas about when you will need to write things down. Figure 5.2 identifies actions you can take to improve your note taking.

Taking good notes is also important right now as you pursue your studies. You are investing valuable time to educate and train yourself for your future. Listening helps you make the most of your time, but taking good notes enables you to take what you have heard away with you and reconsider it later. It gives you a second chance to learn what the teacher covered in class.

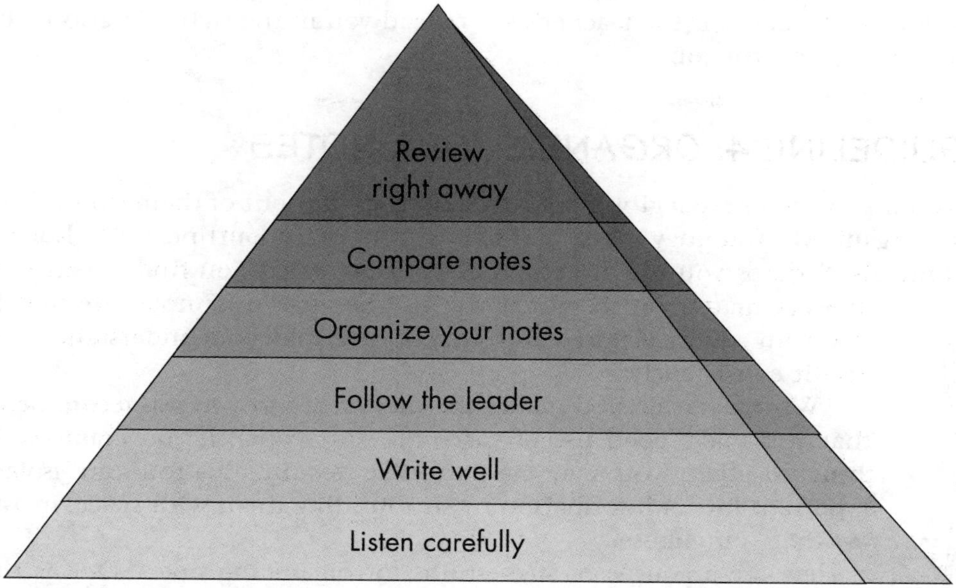

FIGURE 5.2
Guidelines for good notes.

Review
right away

Compare notes

Organize your notes

Follow the leader

Write well

Listen carefully

GUIDELINE 1: LISTEN CAREFULLY

Refer back to the listening section! So many of these skills are interrelated. You cannot take good notes when you have not been listening to what you need to write. You have to hear the message before your brain can translate it to your writing hand. Have you ever been tired in class, realized that your notes had suffered, and compared them with those of a classmate? You may have hardly recognized the information your friend wrote! Your fatigue reduced your listening power and closed you off from much of the information.

GUIDELINE 2: WRITE WELL

So you have listened well and written all the important things you have heard, but you cannot read what you wrote. What good will it do you? Not much! When you take notes, follow Guideline 1 in this chapter's later section on writing. If you use good penmanship, you will benefit from what you write.

GUIDELINE 3: FOLLOW THE LEADER

Whether your teacher, boss, coach, or coworker is the leader, follow that person's lead when taking notes. If this person writes something on a board or pad, copy it. If this person emphasizes something, write it—perhaps with a star next to it. If this person repeats something or says that something will be on a test, write it. In class, whatever receives emphasis—even when the teacher simply speaks louder, slows down, or shows excitement—is important. Follow the leader. It is the teacher's job to lead you in the right direction. The same is true on the job.

GUIDELINE 4: ORGANIZE YOUR NOTES

Even if your notes are legible, you won't get the most out of them unless they are organized. You may have learned in school to outline with Roman numerals. Perhaps you use a method of your own that you find effective. It doesn't matter much which you use because your notes are mostly for your own purposes. But choose one that you understand, and use it consistently.

Whichever method makes the most sense to you, we recommend that you make good use of space on your paper. If you cram everything together, you may have trouble reading it. You can isolate important bits of information by surrounding them with space, in any way that you choose.

Here are a couple of suggestions for organizing notes. One is the standard outline form that you have probably seen before. The other is called a think link, developed in Lexington, Massachusetts, in 1965 by Dr. Frank Lyman, a learning theorist. It is a creative way of tying related ideas and examples together using geometric shapes and lines drawn to connect them. Experiment with both methods in class sometime (see Figure 5.3). Do you see how the space helps you to see the parts of the notes better? It draws your eyes to important points. Don't be afraid to use lots of it.

FIGURE 5.3

Ways to organize notes.

The Classic Outline

I. Potatoes
   A. French Fries
      1. Frozen
         a. Ore Ida
         b Gorton's
      2. Fast Food
         a. McDonald's
         b. Wendy's
         c. Burger King
   B. Mashed Potatoes
      1. Fresh
      2. Powdered

A Think Link

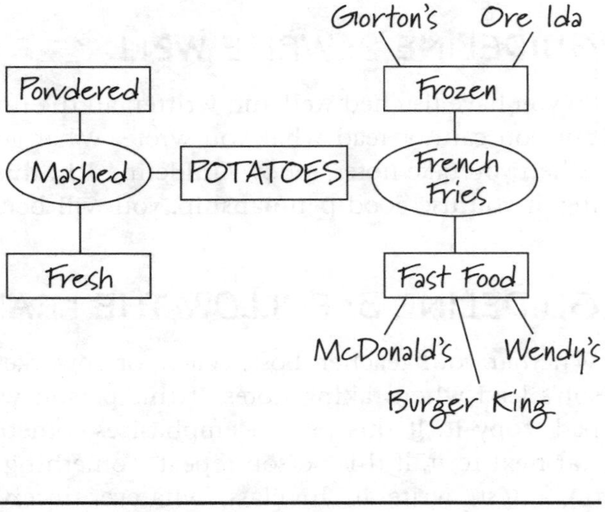

GUIDELINE 5: COMPARE NOTES

After class, after work, or during a break, take a moment to compare notes with your peers. Do they have something you are missing? Did you emphasize something that they missed? An episode of daydreaming, a brief loss of focus, or even a trip to the rest room can result in your missing an important point. Together, you and your classmates or coworkers can help each other fill in the gaps. Two (or more) heads are better than one!

GUIDELINE 6: REVIEW RIGHT AWAY

If you take notes on something that you will have to know later, review your notes soon after you take them. If you look at them within twenty-four hours, filling in any blanks that you have, you will stand a much better chance of retaining the information. We lose 50 percent of what we hear in the first day and at least 20 percent more in the next week. Keep everything fresh in your mind by reviewing soon and often.

Reading

Whether you consider yourself a strong or weak reader, you started learning to read a long time ago. You may still be working on it, or you may have stopped trying to better your reading ability if you think you are already a good reader or if you believe you won't often need reading for your future career. No matter what, keep working on your reading! Learning to read is a lifelong task for people of all ages. Building your skill and your vocabulary continues over a lifetime; the more you read, the more words you know and the more you know about how to put words together.

Take a look at the world around you, inside and outside your school. Words are everywhere, helping you find out which way to go, how to use things, what facts to know, and what to do. Information comes to you constantly in the form of the written word, and you can receive it only if you can read.

What if you eventually work as an electronics technician, a hairdresser, or a cook? Why would you need to be a good reader? For one thing, those jobs will require you to use equipment with great care. You would need to be able to read directions for computer installation, a hair-perming kit, or the meat slicer. If an inability to read caused you to assemble the computer incorrectly, mix the wrong amounts of perm chemicals, or insert the slicer blade incorrectly, the results could be disastrous. You might hurt someone, or (in the case of the botched perm) someone might hurt you! You could even lose your job.

Good reading skills are not only for people who work in libraries or for managers. Continually working to improve these skills is not only for those

Food for Thought

Take a day in your life, and try to count the number of times you use written information to get through the day. You will be amazed! You may count ten or fifteen before you even get started at school—directions for hair-care products or prepared foods, road signs, memos, take-out menus, brochures, etc. By consciously focusing on how much you read, you will realize what an enormous role reading plays in your daily life.

who have trouble reading. Even people who spend most of their evenings poring over a book are improving their skills, just by using them. This skill will serve you well through your life only if you keep it in good condition through regular use. Reading is truly a skill for life.

A note for readers who didn't grow up reading and speaking English: English is the business language of the United States, as well as for much of the world. To succeed in your future career, you need to know how to read and speak English well; the more you read, the more you learn. Of course, your native language can also be a marketable skill in today's growing global economy, but you've got to master the English skills, too.

What follows are guidelines for all levels of readers and all levels of interest. Some of you may not like to read. You may find it boring, slow, or too quiet. Some of you may not believe you need to improve your English for your particular future career choice. Others of you may think you are simply no good at reading and that your reading skills aren't worth trying to improve. Don't sell yourself short. You are capable, and you can only benefit from improving your reading skills.

As for those of you who enjoy reading and feel like you have a knack for it, these hints also apply to you. You have many years ahead of you in which to build both your reading abilities and the base of knowledge that you gain from reading. Don't stop now!

GUIDELINE 1: SIMPLY READ A LOT

Want to be a better reader? Then read! It's as simple as that. Read as much as you can. The more words and combinations of words that sift through your brain, the more you find out about them. With any skill, one primary way you learn is by doing.

GUIDELINE 2: MAKE A DECISION TO READ

How can you include more reading in your day? It takes a conscious effort. You have to make a decision, just like you decide to practice a musical instrument or drop by a store to pick up an item. Especially if reading is not currently an important part of your life, you need to be very deliberate about saving some time, energy, and attention for it.

Reading what your teachers assign you for school is a good place to start. Knowing that you need to complete the reading, use the next guideline to find a time when your mind is alert.

GUIDELINE 3: LOOK FOR TIME TO READ

Once you make the decision to read, search actively for the time you need. It can be hard to find! Life moves quickly, and most of your time is taken up by classes, family, and everyday tasks. So when can you find a time to read? Hunt through your schedule for multipurpose time. The following are examples of times when you can do two things at once:

- Read during breakfast or lunch.
- Read during your ride to school—if you're not driving!
- Read before dinner.
- Read when you ride the bike at the exercise club or before a sports practice.

You may also be able to discover hidden pockets of unused time when you can squeeze in some reading. Here are a few:

- Read before you go to bed.
- Read during a break between classes.
- Read for an hour instead of watching television.

Reading may not seem appealing at first, but it will boost your mind power and creativity. When you sit in front of the television, you take in someone else's images. When you read, your imagination creates its own pictures and expands to take in the information that you are reading.

Look at these proposed lists, think about what times might be convenient for you, and then make the commitment. Keep in mind what you read in the sections on procrastination, habits, and time management—the key is to simply get started. Then it won't be so hard to continue. Try devoting fifteen minutes a day to reading, and progress from there.

Some people feel too distracted when they try to read in short periods of time; they need more time to feel they can read efficiently. In that case, don't worry about fitting it into tight spaces, and try to schedule a longer block of time for your reading. Many people also prefer, and even require, a quiet place to read that won't distract them too much. What kind of conditions do you prefer when you read?

GUIDELINE 4: READ WHAT YOU LIKE TO READ

Outside of your school assignments, you can choose the other materials you read. You don't have to pick up an imposing novel immediately. Read what you enjoy reading because if you don't enjoy it, you won't benefit from it as much as you might otherwise.

You can benefit from almost anything that you read: newspapers, magazines, fiction or nonfiction books, cereal boxes, pamphlets, or instruction books. Do you like astrology? Find a book on it. Do you like to work on your car? Pick up a book on car repair. Mysteries, fitness magazines, self-help books, and sports statistics books all have information from which you can learn.

GUIDELINE 5: USE SPECIFIC TECHNIQUES

This guideline contains different hints to be used primarily for school and work reading instead of leisure reading. The more you concentrate on specific techniques as you read, the more quickly you will improve in speed, efficiency, and information retention. Remember what you just read about mnemonic devices? We have one for you as the first hint:

- Be a CHARTER member of the reading comprehension club:

    Concentrate (follow those guidelines from the Concentration section).

    Highlight important passages and/or use a pen to write in margins and take notes (make sure that you own the book first).

    Associate (relate what you read to ideas and events in your own life).

    Reread one page before beginning new material.

    Take as much time as you need.

    Enjoy something in everything that you read.

    Review right after reading, if you need to recall the information for a test (statistics show that reviewing within twenty-four hours of reading will greatly increase your information retention).

- Don't vocalize (read out loud). It will slow you down.
- Don't regress (go back over words). Allow yourself to read at whatever speed you need to get all the information the first time.
- Read in groups of words. Let your eyes take in groups of words together (it will speed up your reading without sacrificing your understanding).

The more you structure your reading with these hints, the more your reading will improve.

Writing

Knowing how to write flows from knowing how to read. If you are a good reader, then you gain a sense of how to combine words in a way that makes sense to others. As stated, certain professions will require strong writing skills, usually the same ones that will require a lot of reading: marketing, word processing, and legal work. But you will have to use your writing skills in any future job—not to mention all your present classes.

You will encounter many situations in which you will need to write something to communicate with someone else, for example, an office memo, a message taken over the phone, or an order given by a customer. As we will discuss further in Chapter 6, success in school, work situations, and relationships is built on good communication. Good writing is one key to being able to communicate.

Whether your classes or part-time job require you to write letters, orders, or reports, you will find that the ability to write well makes everything easier. If your written word communicates clearly and directly, the people who read it will be able to understand what you are saying. You will save the extra step of having to rewrite an assignment or explain yourself again in person. You will be an efficient and understandable writer. Think about a typical day for you. What do you have to write and when? What important task does each of your written communications perform? Inform your parents of your whereabouts in a note? Gain essential course credit with a written report?

Following are some guidelines essential to good (and successful) writing. Again, these apply equally to those who like to write and to those who don't.

GUIDELINE 1: WRITE LEGIBLY

If no one can read it, why bother to write it at all? It is pretty basic but something that an awful lot of people overlook. It's no fun to try to decipher someone's messy scrawl. And no matter how intelligent your writing may be, it loses big-time credibility with a sloppy visual image. Some people have such messy penmanship that they can't even read their own writing minutes after they've written something! It doesn't matter what style you write in as long as it's legible. If your cursive is neater than printing, write in cursive, or vice versa. Use all uppercase letters or even all lowercase letters if you must. Make the choice that is most comfortable for you and most legible for your readers.

GUIDELINE 2: FIND OPPORTUNITIES TO WRITE

Writing is a lost art these days. The world moves fast and furiously, and the speed of telephones and e-mail has established them as the leading modes of communication. No wonder good writers (and readers) are hard to find.

You can change the situation in tiny ways. Look at your daily life for opportunities to write something. Here are some ideas for chances to write (others may come to mind as you read):

- Lists (of things to do, school assignments, etc.)
- Letters to relatives and friends
- Thank-you notes
- Notes to tape onto gifts you give

- Summary of meetings
- Letters to companies praising good products or telling about problem ones
- Letters to accompany job applications
- Thank-you letters after job interviews
- Advice via e-mail for friends or relatives going into high school or trying to get a part-time job

You may even find others as you go through your daily routine! Take advantage of them.

GUIDELINE 3: KEEP A PERSONAL JOURNAL

One excellent way to improve your writing is to keep a journal. Write in your journal as often as you can—every day would be ideal but not always realistic. When you run out of space, get yourself a blank notebook and keep going. It doesn't matter what you write. You can write about people, events, things that happen to you, your thoughts about the world, poems, angry feelings, song lyrics, meaningful phrases, jokes you want to remember—anything.

You don't have to pressure yourself to write every day. At times, you will be too busy or will not feel like it. But you may discover that writing can help you organize your thoughts, let off steam after something upsetting has happened, spur creative ideas, or provide a ritual for you (for example, before you go to bed). If you don't force the art of writing, you may end up actually enjoying it. Writing is a means of relaxation and an emotional release for many people.

GUIDELINE 4: REMEMBER THE THREE CS

Here is a mnemonic that will remind you of three practical hints for efficient writing:

Cis for   CLEAR.Write what you need to say and nothing else.

Cis for   CONCISE.State your case in as few words as possible.

Cis for   CONCRETE.Keep it simple and understandable.

For example, here is a memo written without considering the three Cs:

There will be a meeting this evening, October 5, at 6 P.M. for all those who might have an interest in participating in the volunteer group this fall. If you want to participate but can't make the meeting tonight, please let Mel McMadden know, and he will talk to you at another time. Leave your evening conflicts on his voice mail so that he can see if you will be available for the scheduled activities. We will be in the conference room, and we need to finish by 7 P.M. so that the office can close. Thanks—see you soon.

And here is a three Cs–approved version:

MEETING TONIGHT—All Welcome

5 October, 6:00–7:00 P.M. in the Conference Room

Topic: Fall Community Activities for Volunteers

** Interested persons not able to attend: Contact Mel McMadden at x 213**

The reader gets the picture much more easily and quickly when the writer remembers the three Cs.

Proofreading

After writing something, you need to proofread it. Read it again, and check for any changes that you want to make. Be sure that what you give to someone else to read is as clear and free of mistakes as possible. Figure 5.4 highlights three actions you can take as you write and proofread.

Who needs to proofread? Everyone does, if only to check the phone number on a phone message. Have someone proofread your work if you have written something longer than a phone message! It always helps to get another perspective. Somehow another pair of eyes can often see things that the writer cannot.

Our discussion of proofreading will be of value to all. We won't go into the specifics of proper syntax and grammar or letter forms and detailed punctuation. Here we will address the basics of proofreading that will help you in any class or at any kind of job that you will take—whether you proofread your own work or someone else's.

GUIDELINE 1: ALWAYS PROOFREAD

No matter what you write, take a moment to review it if possible before you pass it in. Even if it is a short-answer test or a telephone message for someone that doesn't require much writing, you will want to make sure that you

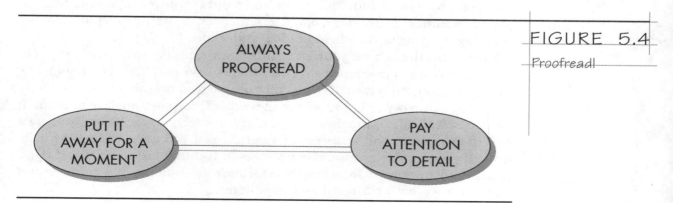

FIGURE 5.4

Proofread!

have made it readable. Can you remember a situation in your life when a problem occurred because someone didn't proofread? It happens. Someone shows up at the wrong place or time, you get docked points on an English assignment, or you wind up looking kind of silly by misunderstanding a message full of mistakes.

Food for Thought

Given our personal and work commitments, most of us don't get enough sleep, and it shows! You have a hard time focusing. You are irritable and short-tempered. You're just plain tired. When you have slept well, you work hard and can keep a cool head throughout the day. You can't always get a good night's sleep (an emergency, the flu, outside noises, etc.), but you can determine the frequency of your late nights out, the noises inside your home, or whether you eat and drink before bed. Sleep is important for your mind and your body. Getting enough sleep will help you achieve your goals at school and work.

GUIDELINE 2: PUT IT AWAY FOR A MOMENT

This rule applies to anything longer than a brief message. We recognize that sometimes you won't have an extra moment before you have to pass it in, but when you do, take the time. It will make a huge difference.

Somehow, when you give yourself a bit of time before you look again at something you've written—a day, an hour, even a few minutes—you are able to look at it with fresh eyes. Taking time gives you the ability to look at your writing from the perspective of someone who has never seen it. Pretend you are the person who will be reading it. Do you understand everything you are reading? Does it make sense? Would you know what the correct information was if you were the person reading the essay or report? Be honest and objective, and then make any necessary changes.

GUIDELINE 3: PAY ATTENTION TO DETAIL

Proofreading is all about detail. You are looking for ways to correct and/or improve what you have written. Correcting refers to checking over information that is either right or wrong, for example, historical facts, formulas, phone numbers and addresses, name and word spellings. Improving refers to paying attention to writing complete sentences, using proper punctuation, breaking for paragraphs where needed, and so on.

For correcting, check yourself against your sources—your notes, the telephone book, the encyclopedia, or the friend who told you. For improving, sometimes you can rely on having other people read over what you have written. They can tell you if and where the writing becomes unclear to them. If no one is available to proofread for you, try this technique: Pretend you are a television reporter, and read the information as if you were reading the daily news. If you stumble over words or phrases or if things just don't sound right, you'll need to tighten things up a bit. Here's an example of a message and how it can be both corrected and improved:

THE MESSAGE

The barbecue will be held at Tresh's place on Satrday, 21 June, on Harper's Farm Road, and everyone should bring what they can make to eat or drink.

CORRECTIONS

Tresh becomes Trish.

Satrday becomes Saturday.

Complete the address.

IMPROVEMENTS

Put the address next to "Trish's place."

End the first sentence after the address.

Clarify what, and how much, everyone should bring.

THE NEW MESSAGE

The barbecue will be held on Saturday, 21 June, at Trish's place—3942 Harper's Farm Road, #6. Please bring either one bottle of something to drink (soda, water, juice) or one food item to share (chips, salad, casserole).

Now it is easier to read because it is correct in spelling and grammar, it gives more complete information, and it communicates its message more clearly.

Test Taking

Taking tests is probably a regular part of your life in school. We hate to be the ones to break it to you, but you can count on this sometimes fearsome process following you into the workplace as well. The good news is that tests won't be a regular part of most jobs. The bad news is that doing well on a specific kind of test may be your "ticket" into a certain position or the means for progressing into even higher positions. There's no need to worry, however, if you master the following test-taking techniques.

GUIDELINE 1: STAY HEALTHY AND ALERT

Get enough sleep and eat healthy regular meals on the day of the test. Don't risk being drowsy, hungry, or low on energy. Give yourself a chance to do your best.

GUIDELINE 2: DON'T OVERSTUDY

You probably know the material better than you think—you've covered it for a long time! Trust yourself. Study enough so that you feel confident, but don't cram to the point of feeling overloaded.

GUIDELINE 3: PLAN AHEAD

Make sure you know the date, time, and scope of the test. Plan to arrive at class on time so that you can feel prepared and calm.

GUIDELINE 4: RELAX WHEN YOU TAKE THE TEST

This is sometimes easier said than done, but you can do it. Focus your mind. Take your time. Remember that you know the material and feel confident that you will complete the test in the time allowed. You are in control.

GUIDELINE 5: KEEP IN MIND YOUR BASIC TEST-TAKING SKILLS

You've been taking tests for a few years now! Here is a summary of the basics to remember as you take any test:

- Look over the entire test before you start. Notice the number of questions so you can determine how much time to allow for each question and how many points each question is worth. You will also get a general idea of the scope of the test.
- Read the directions carefully. Listen carefully, too, if the teacher comments on them or reads them aloud. There are important clues in the directions about how to complete the test.
- Answer the easiest questions first. Unless your test is on a computer, you usually don't have to do the questions in order. This warm-up will give you confidence and extra time to spend on the tougher questions.
- When in doubt, go with your first guess. It is often fairly accurate.
- Don't waste time pondering. If you get stuck, go on to another question, and come back when you are ready (if you have time).
- Check over your answers before you hand in your test. It's easy to make careless errors. Don't change answers unless you are positive you have made a mistake.

GUIDELINE 6: BE KIND TO YOURSELF

Don't be hard on yourself if you feel like you failed the test. You did the best you could at that time. And you don't yet know the results for sure! If you do receive disappointing results, take it easy. You are not a failure simply because you fail one test. You are still you, with as much value and worth as you had before. You simply didn't do well on the test. Look at what went wrong—whether you got nervous or didn't know the material well enough—and think about how to improve for the next time.

Lifelong Learning

Times have changed. Today doing a job—in fact, doing a job well—does not necessarily mean that someone will keep a job. There was a time when doing a job well meant an annual pay raise and long-term employment. There was an unwritten employment agreement: I'll take care of the company, and the company will take care of me.

That is no longer true in today's workplace. Layoffs, downsizing, takeovers—these have become commonplace occurrences in even the most respected companies. So how can you prepare to earn a living in this climate?

Lifelong learning is the key. Lifelong learning means keeping abreast of how technology and changes in the job market will affect your chances for employment and then seeking experiences to prepare yourself accordingly. Lifelong learning means developing new, relevant skills in school or on the job. Lifelong learning means embracing the learning process as fun and essential rather than as work. Lifelong learning also means recognizing these learning myths.

MYTH 1: After I get my diploma, certificate, or license, my education is complete. *Truth:* No, it is actually just the beginning. Today, the average person will have at least five to seven jobs, if not entirely different careers, during his or her working life. Is it realistic to believe these jobs or career changes can be made successfully without learning new skills? No way!

MYTH 2: Learning is not necessary. *Truth:* Sorry. If you hope to keep pace with rapidly shifting demand, fierce global competition, and rapid technological innovation, you'd better keep that thinking cap firmly in place after you graduate. Keeping good jobs and moving ahead require lifelong learning.

MYTH 3: Learning can wait. *Truth:* Wait for what? Until you've been laid off and discover that, even with a diploma, your skills are obsolete? Don't think so. Make learning a lifelong habit. You'll never regret it. We promise.

Hang On to Your Basics

You have a large set of valuable basic tools. All of them, separately and together, will serve to make the other tools you have already collected more useful to you. Take time to discover how each tool works and to test it out. The exercises at the end of the chapter will help you do just that. You will find that you will use them now, as a student, and later, as an employee. They will always be there to make what you do easier and more successful.

Your Tool Kit at Work

5.1

Knowing How to Learn

Honest appraisal of your learning skills is critical for your success. Knowing how to learn is a lifelong skill that you will use again and again both during school and in your career. Unless you know how to learn, you will have trouble building the know-how that helps you adapt to different situations. The knowledge you find in courses and books is only useful if you can efficiently learn and retain it.

Review your how-to-learn skills in the following exercise by checking the answer box that most fits your present skill level. In this chapter we have focused on how-to-learn skills as they apply to your school experience; later, in Chapter 9, you will complete a similar exercise that shows how these skills function in the workplace.

Skill	Rarely	Sometimes	Often	Almost Always
1. I have a regular place to study.				
2. I have a regularly scheduled study time that corresponds to when I'm most alert.				
3. I plan my study time and set priorities.				
4. I read the table of contents before beginning a textbook.				
5. I scan reading assignments first and then reread them carefully.				
6. When I read, I underline, highlight, or make notes in the margins.				
7. I ask myself questions on what I just read.				
8. I look up words that I don't know in the dictionary.				
9. I attend class.				
10. I come to class early.				
11. I listen intently in class.				
12. I keep a notebook for class notes.				
13. I take notes in class.				

(continued)

Skill	Rarely	Sometimes	Often	Almost Always
14. I know how to determine the key points my teachers make.				
15. I include these points in my notes.				
16. I write assignments in the teacher's exact words.				
17. I review my notes within twenty-four hours of class.				
18 I study my most difficult subjects first.				
19. For a writing assignment, I write a first draft.				
20. I proofread.				
21. My concentration is good; I am able to focus on what I read and study.				
22. I know and use memory aids.				
23. I review my notes and assignments weekly rather than cram for a test.				
24. I ask a teacher, a counselor, or a tutor for help when the need arises.				
25. I reward myself when I complete studying.				
26. I arrive early for tests.				
27. On a test I answer the questions I know first.				
28. I check all my answers before I hand in my test.				
29. I spend more time studying than I do worrying about school.				
30. I know that ultimately only I am responsible for how much I learn.				

Give yourself 4 points for every Almost Always, 3 points for an Often, 2 points for a Sometimes, and 1 point for every Rarely. Total your score here:

110–120: Congratulations! You have excellent learning skills. Keep working on making your skills even better.

100–109: You have good learning skills. Try new hints to achieve excellence.

90–99: You have average learning skills. If you change some habits, you'll do better in school and feel more confident in your career

Below 90: Your skills have weaknesses that most likely cause you difficulty. Increase your potential by putting these learning skills to work.

5.2

Are You an Active Listener?

Assess your listening skills by checking the appropriate boxes. You will notice other skills mixed in with the listening skills, primarily communication skills that you will study in the next chapter. This shows how closely good listening skills and successful communication are linked.

Listening Skill	Rarely/ Sometimes	Often	Almost Always
1. I avoid interrupting others.			
2. I start listening with the first word.			
3. I put away what I'm doing when someone is talking.			
4. I encourage others to talk and say what they think.			
5. I ask questions.			
6. I listen even if I don't particularly like the speaker.			
7. If I don't understand, I tell the person and ask to have the material clarified.			
8. I respect other people's right to their opinions.			
9. I think of a disagreement as an opportunity to share opposing views.			
10. I think of a disagreement as an opportunity to understand a person better.			
11. I enjoy listening.			
12. I use good eye contact.			
13. I listen to the tone of a person's voice and watch gestures to understand the real meaning of the words.			
14. I look for points on which we agree and not for points on which we disagree.			
15. I realize the speaker's meaning is not necessarily what I would mean with the same words.			
16. I listen equally well to a person of a different age, gender, race, or culture as I do to a person similar to me.			
17. When appropriate, I take notes.			
18. When I respond, I avoid lecturing, prying, or topping the story with my own experiences.			
19. If I don't hear the speaker, I ask politely for the information to be repeated.			
20. I know listening is an important success skill, and I continually work to improve it.			

Give yourself 2 points for an Almost Always and 1 point for an Often.

30–40: You're all ears. You'll hear clearly what others need to communicate to you in any environment.

20–29: You're a fair listener, but you may be missing some important points.

0–19: If you activate your listening skills, you'll do much better at school and at work.

Whether you scored high, low, or in between, pick five skills that you know you could improve. Write them here:

1. _____
2. _____
3. _____
4. _____
5. _____

In the next two weeks, concentrate on improving those skills. Reread the Listening section in the chapter for help. Discuss briefly here two incidents in which your hard work paid off. They can be classroom situations in which you understood something that you may not have before, conflicts that were resolved more easily, important directions that you heard clearly and carried out, or any other situation in which your skills saved you some trouble.

1. _____
   _____
   _____
   _____

2. _____
   _____
   _____
   _____

Do You Know What You're Reading?

5.3

To determine your skill in concentrating and understanding while you read, scan the paragraph quickly and then read it through carefully once. After you finish, cover the paragraph and answer the questions.

Ergonomics

With most Americans spending 70 percent of their waking hours at work, the office environment should be as safe, healthy, comfortable, and productive as possible. Then why don't we feel more at home in the workplace? Because traditionally, workplaces have expected us to conform to them. However, workers have not conformed as expected by management. One reason has been that as computer technology advanced and more office workers began using computers, problems of user comfort arose. Since the introduction of personal computers in the 1980s, an entire market of products has evolved that supports computer workstations. With much emphasis being given to the development of computer products and the work environment, the field of ergonomics evolved. Ergonomics is the science of fitting the workplace to the worker to meet the physical and psychological needs of the worker. Everything that affects the worker must be considered—layout, decor, furniture, lighting, amount of workspace, quality of air, heating and cooling, acoustics, and placement of equipment.*

1. What percent of their waking hours do most Americans spend at work?

   _____

2. Your office environment should be _____, _____, and _____.

3. What have workplaces expected us to do in the past? _____

4. As we began to use computers, problems related to worker comfort rose.

   T_____   F _____

5. The field of ergonomics is:

   a. The science of advanced computer technology.

   b. The process by which the worker becomes accustomed to the workplace.

   c. The science of fitting the workplace to the worker.

6. The workplace needs to meet only the physical needs of the worker.

   T_____   F _____

7. Name four office factors that affect workers.

   a. _____

   b. _____

   c. _____

   d. _____

*Procedures for the Automated Office. Lucy Mae Jennings, Sharon Burton, Nelda Shelton. Prentice Hall, Inc., 1994, p. 8.

Go back to the paragraph and check your answers. How did you do? Don't feel down if you didn't answer all the questions correctly. To remember what you read, scan the material first, read it carefully a second time, and then ask yourself questions about what you just read. Also, review often. Use this process every time you pick up a textbook.

Calibrate Your Basic Skills

5.4

Answer yes or no to the following questions:

_____ 1. Remembering names is easy for me, even when meeting a lot of new people.

_____ 2. I rarely if ever daydream in a class at school or at a meeting at work.

_____ 3. I read a newspaper on a regular basis.

_____ 4. I write notes, underline, or highlight as I read this book.

_____ 5. I use the spell-check feature when writing with a word processing program.

_____ 6. I have taken tests when applying for jobs.

_____ 7. I find the need to use computers and adapt to new technology increasingly a basic skill for a good job.

_____ 8. I tend to take notes at during classes and meetings at work.

_____ 9. I usually set aside what I have written, then reread it, and then make any necessary changes.

_____ 10. I take a short break when I find myself losing my concentration.

If you answered yes to:

7–10 questions, you have a grasp of basic skills. Keep it up!

4–6 questions, you have a foundation for your basic skills. Use your tools to build upon it.

0–3 questions, you will gain significant benefits from working on your basic skills.

Your Positive Attitude List—Your PAL

5.5

Your Basic Skills PAL is set up differently from the positive attitude lists that you have seen thus far. Circle the attributes that characterize your behavior and write in the trait that you need to develop now.

Produce good notes

Attend all classes

Listen in class

Study class notes and materials

I will develop my ability to _____.

Write on a reinforcement card or Post-It® note the quality that you just indicated you will develop. Put it where you keep your other cards, in a place where you can see it every day.

Now you can reinforce those skills with another pledge. You made a habit pledge in Chapter 1 and a money pledge in Chapter 4. Make a study pledge that will help you prepare for your future career efficiently (using waste-cutting, productive ideas) and effectively (using methods and skills that bring excellent results).

Sign the study pledge only if you have every intention of living up to the guidelines.

I WILL ATTEND ALL MY CLASSES WHERE I WILL LISTEN ATTENTIVELY AND TAKE NOTES. I WILL REVIEW THE NOTES WITHIN TWENTY-FOUR HOURS OF THE CLASS.

Name _____

Date _____

How can you stick to your pledge? Avoiding distractions will help a great deal. Unless you concentrate in class, when you study, and on the job, you may waste time. No one, and certainly not you (the student, employee, or future employee), can afford to lose time. You discovered with your time planner how important every hour is.

When your mind is distracted, you can't concentrate. What's on your mind right now that will interfere with your concentration? You may be letting the date you had last night, the phone call you hope to receive tonight, or the errands you have to run after school interfere with the present.

For one minute, jot down everything you're thinking about right now.

I AM DISTRACTED BY:

1. _____

2. _____

3. _____

4. _____

5. _____

Now, leave all those distractions on the page. Turn to the next page. Close your eyes. Bring yourself into the present with a clear mind ready to concentrate. After class, the interfering thoughts will still be waiting on the paper for you, but you'll have retained the new ideas you learned while concentrating. Well-used class time can save you study time too.

Use the exercise whenever the past or the future seems to block out the present. Daydreaming and to-do lists have their place, but not during class, study, or work.

Take New Tools on the Road

5.6

Look over the New In Your Tool Kit list at the beginning of this chapter. Choose and write here the three most important tools you gained from reading this chapter.

1. _____

2. _____

3. _____

For each tool listed, write one example of how you will apply that tool to achieve success in your career. Include changes you plan to make as well as how you will continue or reinforce existing behavior.

1. _____
   _____
   _____

2. _____
   _____
   _____

3. _____
   _____
   _____

6 Becoming Marketable

GETTING THE JOB DONE THROUGH COMMUNICATION

NEW
IN YOUR TOOL KIT

More effective
  communication
  skills

Teamwork

Anger management

By now, you have quite a variety of tools in your tool kit that you know how to use to your best advantage. You know how to take good care of yourself, your time, and your finances, and you have a strong sense of your talents. Next up is adding tools that will help you function efficiently and effectively with other people. We are talking about communication skills. It's the tool that helps you build and maintain relationships both now and throughout your life.

Communication skills fit under more than one of the SCANS umbrellas. They are crucial in the interpersonal category so that you can work comfortably with others. They involve thinking skills because good communication requires that you reason well and know how to solve problems. The basic skill of listening is necessary to communicate. And personal qualities such as integrity, self-control, and sociability will go a long way toward improving communication.

Different types of communication skills and styles will be covered in this chapter. You will read about verbal and nonverbal communication as well as building relationships with people at school and on the job. We

Good, the more communicated, More abundant grows.

—JOHN MILTON

will deal with important topics such as handling criticism, conflict resolution, and effective speaking.

The ability to communicate well makes a student more successful at school and a worker extremely valuable to an employer. The smartest person in the world cannot function in school or a working environment if that person cannot ask questions or talk with others about what is expected, what needs to be done, or how things should be done. The most talented people will create problems at school or at work if they keep to themselves and don't collaborate with others. Collaboration through communication—working together toward a common goal—fuels the fire of the classroom and the workplace.

Communication Skills

Communication is the giving and receiving of ideas and information. It takes thought and effort to communicate efficiently. Figure 6.1 illustrates this. Three conditions have to exist for clear communication to occur.

First, people take turns playing the roles of sender and receiver in a communication situation. You cannot play either the sender or the receiver role well if you try to do both at the same time. What kinds of situations illustrate this problem?

- Two people talking to each other at the same time
- One person talking to another person who is talking to a third person on the telephone
- One person addressing a group in which a second person is chatting with a friend (this probably happens at school a lot)

In each situation, the first person is playing sender only. But the second person is trying to receive information from the first person while sending information elsewhere—back to the first person, to a third party, or even to a task (information in the form of energy and concentration). The second person will be unable to receive information clearly or send it efficiently if both happen at once.

FIGURE 6.1
*Communication
is giving and
receiving.*

IDEAS   INFORMATION

When you communicate, choose your role and play it to the hilt. If someone talks to you, stop what you are doing and focus to clearly receive what the person is saying. If you want to communicate with another person, make sure that person isn't muddling your communication by trying to send information to you or to a third person.

Second, reasoning must support your ideas. Ideas can be difficult to explain to people because they are often general and hard to pinpoint. You may need to clarify your idea through explanation. Link your idea to solid and simple examples—examples of how it works and/or examples of what could result from what it does. Think of an idea as a large ship, with reasons and examples as anchors to which the ship is tied. Reasons and examples keep the idea anchored and reachable.

We just used this technique in condition 1. We communicated the idea that sending and receiving at the same time causes problems, and then we provided three examples to illustrate the concept.

Third, people must speak in terms of their own needs rather than focus on what they think someone else needs. Communication can involve tension, especially when it concerns conflict or a touchy subject. Anger, fear, or other emotions can hamper your ability to speak clearly about what you need.

To communicate effectively, the sender must say "I" instead of "you." "You" statements point the finger at the other person. They put the other person on the block and attack them, sometimes making it seem as though that person is being accused (often unfairly and prematurely) of wrongdoing and blamed for the problem at hand. The other person will most likely feel wronged and launch a corresponding set of "you" statements back at you. The result is much anger and resentment, two people feeling unjustly blamed, and no reasonable and fair solution.

"I" statements soften the conflict. They promote conversation and resolution because they keep people focusing on their own needs and problems

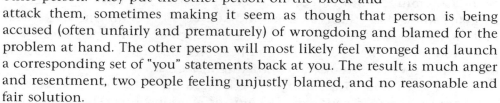

instead of on how another person may have made a mistake. When you turn your statements toward yourself, the other person will feel more welcome in the conversation, will more likely offer to help, and may even acknowledge where mistakes were made. Consider the following rephrasing of accusatory statements:

- "You didn't lock the door!" may become "I felt uneasy when I came home tonight and found the door unlocked."
- "You never called when you said you would!" may become "I was worried about you when you didn't call."
- "You always leave me out of the decision!" may become "I felt disappointed and left out when I realized the decision had been made without my input."

Expressed calmly and honestly, these statements leave room for the other person to offer an explanation. They express feelings rather than harsh judgments. What if the other person wasn't the one who left the door unlocked? The "you" statement would have created anger in addition to being unjust. The "I" statement leaves the judgment unmade. You might be glad you stayed neutral if you hear a response such as, "I agree, and I talked to Dad about it this morning. He's really sorry; he was the last one to leave home yesterday morning, and he was in a rush to get to work. He had an important meeting."

Give yourself some time to adjust to this kind of communication. Most of us aren't used to it! It takes some thought and planning. Jumping into "you" statements can be easier and feel more natural; however, your efforts to stay calm and use a different kind of statement will pay off. When you feel angry about something at school or at home, before you lash out at someone, think first about why you are angry. Translate your anger into an "I" statement about your feelings. Try it out to see if you can make progress. After you express how you feel, invite conversation by saying, "Can we talk about how to fix this problem together?" Ask the other person, "How do you feel about what happened?" Slowly but surely, the "I" statement will seem more natural—and it will bring results.

VERBAL AND NONVERBAL COMMUNICATION

People communicate in two different ways: verbally (expressing yourself by speaking words that others can hear) and nonverbally (sending messages with body language—the way you walk, sit, gesture, twist your facial features, or move your eyes). Often people communicate verbally and nonverbally at the same time—they can even send conflicting messages!

If you learn how to use and receive both kinds of communication, you will increase your efficiency in all kinds of relationships. Believe us, you'll save yourself a lot of time and trouble caused by miscommunication if you get this straight now.

- Choose to communicate!
- Think before you speak.
- Do it ASAP.
- Try for optimum listening conditions.
- Choose your moment carefully.

- Speak clearly.
- Be precise.
- Be brief.
- Be honest.
- Watch your tone.

FIGURE 6.2

Effective verbal communication.

Verbal Communication

This is often where the trouble starts—with the spoken word! We frequently speak unclearly, use words that convey a meaning we don't intend, or leave out important words or thoughts. But when we say what we want to say and the person hears it as we mean it, it makes all the difference. Figure 6.2 identifies ideas to consider as you try to improve verbal communication skills.

CHOOSE TO COMMUNICATE! First and foremost, you need to make the choice to speak. No one can change or improve anything if they don't know it needs fixing. No one can help you if you haven't said that you need help. If you have something to say, choose to say it. You have the right to speak your mind, stand up for your needs, and express your suggestions and opinions.

THINK BEFORE YOU SPEAK. It's an old saying, but it works. Give yourself a chance to figure out what you mean to say before you say it. If the message is important, take time to rehearse it. It's easy to say something without thought. But once you say it, you can't take it back. Sure you can admit, "I didn't mean it that way!" But the damage is already done.

DO IT ASAP. This acronym stands for "as soon as possible." When you have something to say, say it as soon as you possibly can. Especially if it's to compliment someone or express a positive feeling. There's never too much of that going around. On the other hand, if it's a problem that needs discussing, get it out in the open before it has a chance to grow.

TRY FOR OPTIMUM LISTENING CONDITIONS. What would happen if you went to your teacher with a question when she was pulling on her coat and rushing out to a meeting? How about if you met a friend in a crowded, noisy lunch area to talk about something serious? One thing is sure—you won't get your message across! The conditions just don't lend themselves to clear communication. Make sure that the person you intend to talk to is ready to listen—that you have the right time, the right place, and the full attention of your listener.

CHOOSE YOUR MOMENT CAREFULLY. How? Ask the person what time might be good—whether you are speaking face-to-face or on the phone. Avoid noisy or distracting places. Don't initiate an important conversation when someone is busy or distracted. Try to avoid talking when someone is under pressure to be somewhere else—that person's brain might be traveling to the next place, leaving you talking to the air. Give yourself the best possible chance to be heard.

SPEAK CLEARLY. Tell it like it is, so the person can understand! Avoid mumbling or speaking too fast. Use words that can be understood.

BE PRECISE. As for the actual words that you use, don't include too many extras. The quicker you get to the point and the fewer words you use, the more efficient a communicator you will be. Overdo it, and you may irritate the listener or lose the hearer in the onslaught of verbiage.

BE BRIEF. This hint goes with the previous one. If you work to speak precisely, you will probably have no problem being brief. These two work hand in hand and are always a crowd pleaser. Waiting for a long-winded person to state a case can be like watching the grass grow. Speak your mind quickly and precisely—your listener will appreciate you for it.

BE HONEST. This hint will help you stay brief. It takes more time to run verbal circles around what you really want to say than it does to be honest and direct. Sometimes honesty can be tough when you have to say something that will make the other person unhappy. But it is usually better to just get it over with. People cannot begin to solve problems until they know the truth about what is happening. When you supply the truth, you will get results.

If you are consistently firm and gentle but honest in your communications, you will develop a reputation as a person of integrity. People will learn to count on you for an honest answer. They will also be more willing to talk with you when they know you to be a person of integrity.

Food for Thought

Consider times in your life when a mistake in communication has cost you time, money, or happiness. Did you ever wait for a long time at a specified pick-up location only to find out that your friend was waiting somewhere else? Someone heard incorrectly or spoke unclearly, and it cost time, caused anger, and may have made someone late for an important appointment. Have you ever fought with someone only to discover later that you had misunderstood something that the person said? It may have made you so upset that you couldn't stop to hear the person clear up the misunderstanding. It saves a lot of trouble if you try to get it right the first time.

WATCH YOUR TONE. The people to whom you speak pick up 35 percent of your message from your tone of voice. Stay aware of your tone, and make sure that it communicates what you intend to say. Sometimes you need to adjust your tone to your words—perhaps when you are angry but cannot let that show in the words you choose. Sometimes you change your words to fit your tone; for example, you decide that you need to stop denying the anger that wants to come through in your tone. Keep your tone and your words in harmony; otherwise, you will sabotage your communication efforts.

Nonverbal Communication

All of us say things with our bodies, often without thinking about it. People pick up on our nonverbal signals even when we don't want them to. In truth, we read the body language of others. Our thoughts and feelings can color the words that we speak—they can reinforce them or change them. For example, when you first meet someone, you base your impression on a combination of elements: nonverbal signals, tone of voice, and actual words spoken. The nonverbal element makes up 55 percent of a first impression, while tone makes up 35 percent and words only 10 percent. It makes sense that when you meet someone, your eyes take the first reading before anyone speaks a word. You make assumptions based on posture, degree of eye contact, and speed of movement. Even when introductory words such as "Hello, nice to meet you" are spoken, they won't tell you too much about the person inside. You find out more from the tone—bright or apprehensive, bored or interested, upbeat or sullen—that the person uses when greeting you.

Deciding what someone is saying without words is a tricky and subjective business. It's tough to find a clear answer, but it is important to take a look at how it comes into play. Understanding nonverbal communication can give you important insights into your own feelings as well as those of others. Figure 6.3 highlights three suggestions to improve your nonverbal communication.

BE AWARE. Start by simply taking a look at what people say to you with their bodies. It will help you understand more about their true thoughts. If a friend compliments you while making eye contact, standing up straight, and smiling, you can be fairly sure that the person means what he or she says. If that same person says the same words but doesn't look you in the eye, barely stops walking to talk, and doesn't have a happy expression, that person has left something unsaid. Of course, it is up to you whether you need to deal with that "something." If that person feels jealousy, you may not need to address that. On the other hand, if the problem will interfere with your relationship, you might want to bring it up. The choice is yours; paying attention to body language will give you that choice.

USE IT TO SUPPORT YOUR WORDS. As you learn to look at the nonverbal language of others, start noticing your own as well. You can use it to help clarify your thoughts with others. For example, if you are meeting with

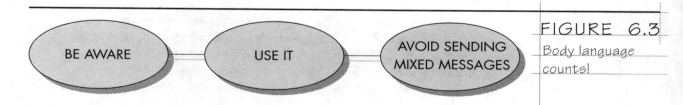

FIGURE 6.3

Body language counts!

your teacher to make a case for a higher grade, express confidence with your body—sit up straight, look the teacher in the eye, relax your shoulders, and calm your hands.

AVOID SENDING MIXED SIGNALS WITH YOUR BODY LANGUAGE. If your non-verbal message goes against your verbal one, you may confuse the receiver. Nonverbal messages come across before verbal ones. What if your teacher didn't give you the higher grade and you said that was fine and it really wasn't? Your body language—sagging posture or a defiant expression—may show your true feelings and belie the words you speak. Both of you would suffer: Your teacher would be confused, and you would have to carry the hurt inside that comes from not expressing your true feelings.

Don't say anything with your body that you aren't willing to say with your mouth. Body language comes through more clearly than you might think. If you want to hide something and you choose not to talk about it, it might come through loud and clear in how you hold yourself and what facial expressions and gestures you make. If you think you might convey something nonverbally that you don't feel comfortable about, make a choice. Either face up to talking about what you really feel, or make a major effort to turn off your body language.

COMMUNICATION STYLES

There are as many different styles of communication as there are people in the world! We as individuals have particular ways of expressing ourselves. Some people come right out and talk about feelings; some hide them. Some people speak quietly and carefully; some let it all hang out without censoring their words. Some get right to the point, and some talk circles around the central idea of a conversation.

When these different communication styles interact, clashes can result. But if you become aware of your own style and the styles of those with whom you have regular contact, you can begin to avoid the problems that come up when one person says something and the other person takes it the wrong way.

To give you an idea of how those communication styles work in real life, the following paragraphs contain a few types of responses you may have heard of or will encounter. Put yourself in this situation, and think about how you might respond. Examine your style and make any necessary changes.

THE SCENARIO

You participated in a project at school that involved two major tasks—we'll call them X and Y. Y was new to you, although you have a lot of experience with X. You want to know what your teacher thinks of your performance, and you leave him a note asking about it. What follows are responses you might receive from teachers with different communication styles.

Direct. This person is honest about both compliments and criticism and rarely dwells on unimportant chatter. The note reads, "Your idea about X was great, and I'm glad you followed through on it because it worked. You need to improve your technique with Y; I see it cost you some extra time. Stop by after class, and I'll tell you about some other ideas you might want to consider."

Indirect. Someone like this has a hard time getting to the point. This teacher will meander around the question and may never really answer it. "Everything seemed fine, I guess. I don't know whether Y could have happened faster or not, but, oh well, it seemed okay. By the way, did you think about Z?"

Noncommunicative. This kind of teacher will almost always choose to say nothing at all. You probably wouldn't get a response to your note, leaving you to assume that nothing is wrong, even if something is. If you asked again, maybe in person, you might receive a brief evaluation.

Confrontational. This kind of person has no fear of an argument and will usually express opinions in no uncertain terms—in other words, confront you, focusing too much on the negative. You'll hear directly from this teacher without even asking: "Problem Y is a disaster. Find a way to take care of it."

Nonconfrontational. This person will avoid confrontation at all costs and dislikes conflict. You may have to dig to get any kind of helpful criticism. But you will probably get an answer if you ask directly. "Oh, yeah, sure, I approved of everything you did. It was fine."

Unexamined. This type of person rarely thinks before speaking! You might have to weed through jumbled, off-the-cuff words to pick out the important information. "Wow, I'm late—what? Oh yeah, X was terrific. Did you do that by yourself? Have you thought about Z? I'm looking for that. I thought Y was a nightmare. You need to get your thoughts organized."

Building Relationships

As important as your specific skills may be in school and in the workplace, the ability to get along with people can carry even more weight. You may have wonderful skills and great talent, but if you are difficult to be around, it will hamper your success. This is especially true in the classroom and workplace. A teacher may not give a difficult student the extra attention needed. A boss will often take the easier route and hire someone with less developed skills but an easygoing personality. Teaching skills beats trying to teach human relations and kindness any day.

There's something you need to know before you begin a career. People are hired, promoted, and fired based on 80 percent attitude and 20 percent job skills. 80 percent! Attitude can make all the difference—at home, at school, and at work.

Our attitudes show mostly in our relationships with other people. Why is building good relationships so important? Because that's pretty much how real work gets done. When people get along in class, on a team, or on the job, everything progresses more quickly and efficiently. When people clash, everything suffers. People cannot work well together when personal issues and egos cloud the picture.

The fact is, you can rarely choose your fellow students or coworkers. But you can choose how you deal with them. Think about what you learned about yourself and others in Chapter 3. You'll always have an easier time getting along with certain personality styles, but the better you understand what makes other people tick, the better you will be able to get along with all kinds of people and have effective communications (see Figure 6.4).

Here's a way of looking at your personality in terms of your working style. It's a four-sided grid that divides people into four general workstyles (see Figure 6.5). Each corner of the grid represents a combination of two of the four named qualities: task-oriented or people-oriented and passive or aggressive. Even though your probably haven't had much experience in the workplace yet, think about how you approach your school assignments and see if you can figure out where you fit in.

Use this grid as a way to evaluate yourself and others. Through your evaluation, you will begin to understand how different people work and why you either get along or clash. Understanding is the bridge to improvement. This process can help you work on some areas that may need some fine-tuning and others that may need cultivating to give you the best chance for success now and in your future career.

FIGURE 6.4

Getting the job done through communication.

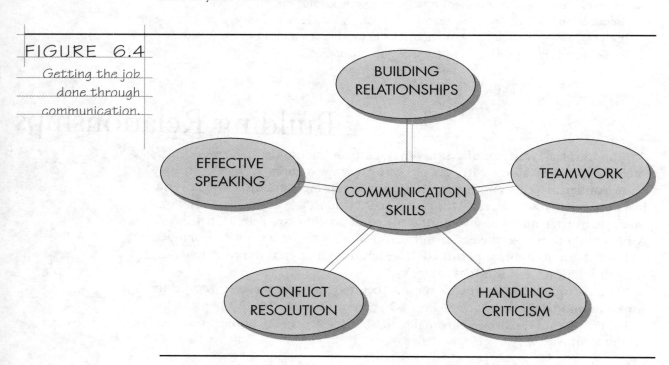

FOCUS: *TASKS* IN THE WORKPLACE

The ANALYST

Acquires & Evaluates Information
Gathers & Examines Facts/Weighs
   Evidence
Makes Decisions Slowly
Works Carefully
Loves Stability/Low Risk Taker
Dislikes Conflict
Speaks Quietly/Firmly
Priority: To Be the Expert

The DIRECTOR

Interprets & Processes Information
Acts/Produces Results
Makes Decisions Easily
Works Hard
Takes Risks/Challenges Stability
Thrives on Conflict
Speaks Forcefully
Priority: To Be in Control

TIMID/PASSIVE	BALANCED/ASSERTIVE	BOLD/AGGRESSIVE

The MEDIATOR

Organizes & Maintains
   Information
Harmonizes Workplace
Makes Decisions Reluctantly
Works Thoroughly
Likes Stability/Rarely Bored
Can't Stand Conflict
Speaks Supportively
Priority: To Be Needed

The ENTERTAINER

Communicates Information
Energizes Workplace
Makes Spur-of-the-Moment
   Decisions
Works Fast
Loves Risks/Easily Bored
Accepts Conflict
Speaks Spontaneously & Well
Priority: To Be Recognized

FOCUS: *PEOPLE* IN THE WORKPLACE

FIGURE 6.5

Personality and working style are interrelated.

GETTING ALONG WITH PEOPLE AT HOME, AT SCHOOL, AND AT WORK

Unless you plan to live as a hermit in a cave, something we don't recommend, there will always be people in your life. People with whom you'll live, go to school, work, and play. These people will have many different kinds of roles in your life. Some may be in charge of you; others may be peers. You'll need to use different kinds of techniques and different kinds of behaviors with different kinds of people. We've named three groups of people to consider.

People in Charge

The authority figures are those that who some control over what you do—parents, teachers, and bosses. These relationships are best when built on a foundation of mutual respect. People relate to their superiors in many different ways: buddy-buddy, strictly business, strained, or almost no contact. Regardless of the flavor of the relationship, both people must show respect for one another. It's a lot easier to take orders from someone if you respect them—even if you don't spend your free time with them.

What personal qualities, basic skills, and interpersonal skills can help you relate to a higher-up?

- Listen (review the section on listening in Chapter 5).
- Behave in a respectful manner.
- Follow directives pleasantly. Trust that the person has good reasons when deciding what you should—or shouldn't—do.
- If you have a problem or complaint, make an appointment and address the person directly and calmly in private, instead of blowing up or talking behind the person's back.
- When the person compliments you or does something nice for you, show your appreciation.

Colleagues

Colleagues are peers—people who study or work together on the same level. It may be fellow students or coworkers on a job. In either case, good relationships will keep things running smoothly.

Some of the skills that will help you get along with colleagues are the same skills needed to get along with superiors, and some are different:

- Listen.
- Show respect for one another.
- Be familiar with the way things are done in a given situation or organization, and behave accordingly.
- Keep out of anyone else's territory—actual physical space or assigned task—without asking that person first.
- If it is important to you, make an effort to get to know the other person, either at lunch or school or work.
- Address any problems, bad feelings, or complaints in private with the person involved. Avoid gossiping about it to everyone but the person with whom you have a problem.

Family and Friends

What does your relationship with your family and friends have to do with being able to get along with others in school and at work? Quite a lot, actually! The state of your personal relationships has a strong effect on your mood, attitude, self-image, and energy. You need a good and positive personal support system to function well with people you encounter in your life outside your family. This will be important as you go to school or search for a part-time job as well as after you begin working full-time later on. If your personal life drags you down, your school or working life will suffer as well.

Your two best strategies for making sure your personal life supports your stability elsewhere are:

1. Make your personal relationships a priority. We will talk in the next chapter about ways to keep your personal relationships in balance. That balance forms the core of your strength. Put it above all else. Go out of your way to maintain or repair relationships with family or close friends.

2. Leave personal problems and moods at home. When you do have problems that occupy your mind, when your home life makes you feel unsettled or a particular event has put you in a bad mood, try to leave it all at home. Why?

- **School is a necessity and deserves your full attention.** You need to study to earn the diploma that will help you achieve your goals. Letting emotional issues keep you from working efficiently at school can be the same as missing classes altogether.

- **Focus on school issues at school, and home issues at home.** Remember what happens when you attempt to pay attention to more than one thing at a time? When everything receives only a fraction of your attention, only fractions of each problem improve. When one issue at a time receives 100 percent of your attention, you can solve problems completely, one at a time.

- **Give yourself a mental and emotional break.** Sometimes when you have a problem that upsets you, your thoughts run in circles and go nowhere for a while. Taking a mental break and focusing on something else, such as your extracurricular activities, can free your mind from its regular paths. You may find that new, fresh ideas pop up at the end of the school day as you ride home.

Remember, many facets of your life—family, friends, school, work, teachers, coworkers—are intertwined; what happens with one can easily affect your situation with another. The more you can separate them and be at peace with each of them, the easier it will be for you to stay balanced, efficient, and happy.

Teamwork

Imagine a basketball or volleyball team if every player tried to score as many points as possible. Or, imagine a football or soccer team if each player only thought about his or her own performance. You would not expect these teams to achieve their potential or perhaps even be successful. Teamwork will be as much a part of your future success on the job as it is on the playing field.

Teamwork—as simple as the sharing of resources, information, or customers—is critical to achieve the potential of any business. But how often do you see people protecting their turf or using selfish, prima donna behavior that gets in the way of team success? Unfortunately, whether this behavior is based on selfishness or on not being sensitive to how their actions affect others, the results are the same: missed opportunities. Individual success does not necessarily translate into business success.

Eventually, when you accept a position with a company, your personal success will be linked to your employer's success. If your employer fails, in part or in whole, jobs and opportunities are lost. Team success, personal success, and business potential are a package deal. Team success sustains the company, and it will enable you to be rewarded, to continue to grow, and to deepen skills. Clearly, becoming a team player is in your best interests now and in the future.

Handling Criticism

Ouch! Criticism—sometimes negative and harsh, sometimes useful for improvement—can hurt. No matter what kind of criticism we give or get, it can create tension and bad feelings, especially on the receiving end. Learning to accept criticism and making corresponding changes in behavior are tough for most people. But if you can do it, it will enhance your happiness and productivity.

Criticism often follows a vicious cycle. If one person criticizes another in a harsh way that says, "I'm right and you're wrong," then the other may resist the criticism and respond with more criticism or even personal slights. Consider these two medical assistant students, talking in an empty hospital room.

Jamal: I can't believe you forgot to pick me up again! I was late for school and now I have detention.

Damon: How was I supposed to know you needed a ride? Do I look like a taxi driver to you?

Jamal: I told you my mom's car was still in the shop.

Damon: So what? That's supposed to mean come pick me up again?

Jamal: What am I supposed to do—beg on bended knee?

How might you start this conversation over and make it a more productive one? You can make changes on both the giving and receiving ends.

GIVING CONSTRUCTIVE CRITICISM

- **Think about the behavior you intend to criticize.** Make sure it is something that can be changed. If not, don't even bother to address it. Think of ways you can work around it.

- **Decide on the exact behavior you want to criticize.** Don't drag any other dirty laundry (unrelated issues) into the conversation. Stay as specific as you can.
- **Carefully choose the time and place where you intend to talk.** Arrange it as soon as possible, but make sure it is private and at a convenient time for the person with whom you need to speak.
- **Stay calm and clear and be as brief as you can.** Avoid threats, ultimatums ("If you don't do X, then I will have to do Y"), and accusations.
- **Choose your words carefully.** You don't want to sound hostile or sarcastic. Stay cool.
- **Explain the reasons behind your criticism.** Try to make sure the person you are criticizing understands why the change should happen.
- **Offer help in improving or changing the behavior you are criticizing.**

RECEIVING CRITICISM

- **Consider the criticism carefully when you hear it.** If you accept its truth, say so. If you are unsure, hear the person out. Regularly repeated criticism is probably valid.
- **Resist the desire to defend yourself blindly against criticism before you've heard the details.** Use all your good listening tools, listen attentively, and ask for more information.
- **Ask for solutions to the criticism.** You might want to say, "How would you handle this if you were in my place?"
- **Before you finish the conversation, summarize the criticism and your response to it, and repeat it back to the person who offered the criticism.** That will make the situation clear to both of you.
- **If you feel the criticism is warranted, plan a definite, specific strategy for correcting the behavior.** Think about what you learned from the criticism and how you will change. Explain your behavior change to the person who has criticized you.

A MORE REASONABLE VERSION OF THE CRITICISM EPISODE:

Jamal: Did you forget that I needed a ride to school again this morning?

Damon: You did? Why didn't you ask me to pick you up?

Jamal: I thought I did. I told you my mom's car was still in the shop. I guess I figured you'd know what I meant.

Damon: Oh man! I'm sorry. I didn't realize what you were getting at. Next time just give me a call in the morning. I'll be glad to come get you.

Not all such conversations will be that easy, but you can see how taking a nonaccusatory approach can soften the situation. Take each situation as it comes. If you handle criticism calmly and effectively, you will bring about positive change while maintaining good relationships.

Conflict Resolution

We've talked a bit about conflict as we discussed your relationships with the three categories of people in your life; however, it deserves more attention. All relationships experience conflict! As much as we may dislike it, conflict is a normal part of everyday life; it is unavoidable. In fact, trying to ignore or deny problems can eventually make them worse. One important skill to develop is learning how to effectively handle conflict. If you learn to resolve conflict with relative speed and ease, you will benefit from the experience by retaining knowledge of the solutions that you can use to make your relationships stronger and better in the future. One key to resolving conflicts is knowing how to handle anger. Anger is a natural emotion that everyone feels from time to time. It's how you handle your anger that makes a difference. Here are three suggestions for controlling your anger as you resolve conflicts.

AVOID AGGRESSIVE BEHAVIOR

Aggression will only escalate the conflict and any violent tendencies that the people involved may have. When people behave aggressively, they focus on fulfilling their own needs rather than considering the needs of others. This self-centered focus often leads to anger and impatience when the need is not immediately satisfied. These are examples of aggressive behavior:

- Name-calling and verbal insults
- Physically violent encounters
- Blaming
- Walking out of arguments in a huff without resolving the problem
- Loud, heated fighting

If you find yourself wanting to behave in any of these ways, the best thing to do is to take time out! Stop before you say anything to anyone. Cool down. Count to 10—or even to 100 if you need to. Wait until you feel like you can discuss your problem calmly and reasonably.

AVOID PASSIVE BEHAVIOR

Just as aggressive behavior will hurt you, so will pretending that you don't feel angry. People behaving in a passive manner deny themselves power by focusing on the needs of others and reacting to actions, instead of taking action to fulfill their own needs. Some kinds of passive behavior are:

- Concealing feelings
- Denying anger
- Doubting the right to be angry

Rather than hiding your feelings, acknowledge them. Then, decide what to do with them. Sometimes you may choose to talk to the person about them. Sometimes you may decide that the problem is so small that bringing it up may cause more harm than good. In such a situation, you may find it appropriate to say to yourself, "I'm angry, but I will let it go this time because I value my relationship or my part-time job."

Food for Thought

Here's a quick look at three different approaches to phrasing a request. How would you respond to each of these requests?

Passive
Do you think maybe you could work on that letter this afternoon for me?

Assertive
I need to have the letter by 2:00 P.M. because the messenger will be by to pick it up. Can you have it ready by then?

Aggressive
Have that letter on my desk by 2:00 P.M.

BE ASSERTIVE

Assertive behavior strikes a balance between aggression and passivity.

When you are assertive, you defend yourself without being negative, nasty, or overbearing. You can say what you want and ask others what they want, while taking both into account. You state your case calmly and express hope that the situation can be resolved to benefit all parties involved. You involve the other people who share the conflict by making sure that they have a chance to talk and by listening carefully to what they have to say. You use statements such as the following:

- I am angry that . . .
- I would like . . .
- How do you feel about . . .
- I need . . .
- Does it make sense to you if . . .

Assertive, adjective. Able to insist on one's rights and express one's thoughts in a positive, confident, and persistent way.

When you act assertively, you will be able to resolve conflicts to the best of your ability. You use smart strategies and see the conflict through.

Remember, not every conflict will end in your favor. You win some, you lose some, and some will end in a compromise. Be willing to accept the outcome, knowing that you have negotiated and discussed as <u>fairly and as calmly as</u> you could. Your best effort is all you can ask of yourself.

Effective Speaking

The term *speaking* refers to the most presentational and public form of communication. The ideas about good communication that we already discussed apply to speaking. But speaking at length in front of others—whether one person or a group of twenty—involves some special techniques, in addition to those for communicating well in an informal conversational setting.

Some of you may have jobs that never require you to speak formally in front of others; however, the principles of effective speaking apply to situations such as interviews, meetings with your manager or boss, or group planning sessions. In school, you may need to present a project or demonstrate something you built or repaired. Some people can feel just as nervous about a discussion or an evaluation meeting with a supervisor as they feel about standing before many people and talking. A meeting or interview requires you to prepare some statements beforehand, as does a speech.

Don't worry if you have a fear of meetings or of speaking in front of others! You are not alone. You may think that others don't seem afraid, but often they conceal their fears. No one wants other people to think that they are afraid. If speaking makes you nervous, you are in good company with most of the world.

One of the best ways to conquer your fear is to remember that what you say in a speech or at a meeting is no different from what you would say in a conversation with one friend—only you say it to more people. Think of it as a conversation, with a group. That way you have more of a chance of hanging on to that comfortable feeling that allows you to carry on a one-on-one conversation easily.

We have identified three stages in making an effective speech:

- Mental preparation
- Preparation of your speech
- Presentation of the speech

Within each of these stages we will list advice that will help you prepare and present your ideas clearly and thoughtfully.

MENTAL PREPARATION

The first question to ask yourself is, "Why do I need to speak and what do I gain by speaking? Will I inform, persuade, or motivate?" You might need to present some facts and figures to your department. You might want to present a case to your boss for a raise in pay. You might need to motivate a group of new employees. Whatever you need to accomplish, establish that goal for yourself before you do anything. Your audience won't get the point unless you have a strongly established purpose.

Once you decide on a goal, ask yourself if you're capable of achieving it. Build and maintain a strong sense of self-confidence. Until you believe that you can achieve what you want with your talk, no one else will believe it either. We all have our moments of doubt, of course. But if you don't push them aside and move ahead confidently, you may never prepare yourself adequately, and you become your own worst enemy.

Beyond believing in yourself and in your own abilities, you must speak with sincerity and believe what you say. The person or people listening to you will quickly notice if you don't seem to believe in your own words, and consequently, they won't believe in them either. Only say aloud what you feel you can truthfully say silently, in your heart.

PREPARING YOUR SPEECH

A very important step, after you make sure that you believe in yourself and what you will say, is to know what you are talking about. After your audience sees that you believe in what you say, they will listen to the words. Make sure those words make sense! Gather facts, evidence, true stories, and other fuel for your fire. For example, if you want a raise, demonstrate how you have helped the company since you were hired. Did you raise production? Do other supervisors have good words to say about you? Did you boost sales? If you want to persuade, research your topic.

As you plan, keep your communication skills in mind. Speaking is a form of communication and all guidelines apply. Illustrate your points with examples, stories, facts, and explanations. These will anchor your ideas and help your audience understand what you say.

Organize your talk ahead of time. If you are preparing for an interview or small group discussion, you may only need to prepare answers to questions you know you will hear. If you are planning to present a speech to a group, you will want to outline your whole speech. You can write ideas, comments, or key words on index cards. Or you can use the cards to create a chain think link, with each link on a successive card instead of all on one piece of paper.

Begin with a catchy fact or idea. Then introduce the central concept(s) of your speech. Plan how you will make your points in the middle. Then summarize at the end. Work on the outline until it flows comfortably and feels like "you."

Consider your audience. Is it your boss? Is it an informal group of co-workers? Customers of your company? The type of audience will determine how formal or informal you will need to be, which in turn will help you decide what style of speech to use, what to wear, how long to talk, and what points to make.

Don't go in cold. Practice alone and with others listening to you. Practice makes perfect! The more you rehearse your speech aloud, the more freely and comfortably you will speak when it really counts. Try out your talk in front of people who will give you a good honest critique of your speech. Ask for feedback on your ideas and your delivery.

Try to eliminate overworked words and expressions. Many of us pepper our casual conversation with words that serve very little purpose. Phrases such as "you know," "right," "like," "okay," "um," "well," and "I think" take up time without adding substance to your speech. Using them is a habit that is tough to break (see Chapter 1 for suggestions on breaking habits). Ask your practice audience to let you know when they hear them. You can even have them use tactics such as ringing a bell when they hear one or making you pay a nickel for every one you use!

Although you want to know your talk well, do not memorize it. Memorizing will lock you in to an exact speech, not allowing for the give-and-take that occurs with any conversation (and your talk is a conversation with others, even in cases when they don't have a chance to reply). The ability to speak in a spontaneous way, adjusting to audience response and ideas simultaneously, is one mark of a talented speaker.

PRESENTING YOUR SPEECH

Speak clearly, audibly, and slowly, but not so slowly that you put your audience to sleep. If you have messy handwriting, no one can read your brilliant thoughts; likewise, it won't matter how wonderful your talk is if no one can hear or understand it. When you practice in front of others, ask them if they understood everything you said.

Maintain eye contact with your audience. You can't look at them constantly, of course, because you will probably need to glance at your notes. If your audience consists of more than one person, you will have to shift your gaze from one audience member to another. It can be difficult, but make the effort, because people are more likely to pay attention if someone catches their eyes. They feel as if the person speaking is addressing them directly, and they may take more of an interest.

Do not read your speech off the page. Like memorization, reading may make your talk seem too preset and dull. The audience may feel like they would have received the same benefit from silently reading a photocopy of your speech! Use the advantage of a live presentation to deliver your ideas with emphasis and individuality.

Let a little humor into your talk! Whether you plan it or you insert it in reaction to something that happens at the moment, humor relaxes people and draws their attention. Begin with something upbeat or funny, and then get to the more serious points; however, be careful about jokes—they can backfire. Use them only if you are comfortable telling jokes and, most importantly, if they are appropriate for the topic and the audience.

Stay aware of your audience, but don't let audience reaction throw you off. For example, if your audience seems bored, increase your energy and enthusiasm. But if a few faces seem unmoved, don't automatically assume that they take no interest in what you say. They may be thinking hard, or they might be the kinds of people who don't reveal their feelings immediately. If you assume they dislike your talk, your self-confidence will shrink and you will cancel yourself out before you even get rolling. If your audience reacts well to certain points, expand on them. The more you focus on your audience rather than on yourself, the more relaxed and in tune you will be.

Make sure that when you close, you summarize by reiterating one or two major points and stating your own conclusions. If it suits the topic, take a moment to offer your projection of what may develop in the future. The summary gives you the opportunity to emphasize your most important ideas. It is at this point you will present the thought you want everyone to remember. Even if you have lost a few people along the way, you have a chance at the end to rein them back in.

After you have spoken, review your presentation alone or with someone who heard it. Think about what went well and what could be improved. What you learn from each speaking engagement will enable you to speak more effectively in the future. Reviewing is a chance to improve your skills and even your material.

Remember, a speech is an opportunity to communicate. Think of it as a chance to convince others of something that is important to you, rather than a frightening ordeal. The more you speak, the better speaker you will become. Even if you decide that making speeches doesn't suit you and doesn't make you happy, the experience will have taught you something about yourself.

Keep the Lines of Communication Open

Communication is the lifeline of the family, the school, the workplace—and the world. Everything that happens does so because people communicate to others what must be done. When you know how to communicate well with all kinds of different people and in all kinds of different situations, you will be a key link in that lifeline, one that your family, friends, and employers value. With good communication skills, you will build lasting relationships at school, at home, and at work. The more you give and receive communication, the more marketable you will become.

Your Tool Kit at Work

6.1

Words, Words, Words

Listen to yourself and others, and you'll hear them: "You know, it's like this, I mean, ummm, yeah, well, like I said, I think you gotta do like what you gotta do . . . if you know what I mean, OK, right?" You may not even know how often you're filling sentences with words that say nothing.

Are you tired of these same old words? Employers are, and they will hear overworked slang and tired phrases if you use them during an interview. Under stress people tend to revert to old patterns, and you might find yourself using words that you thought you had eliminated from your vocabulary. The time to apply the Rule of 21 is now—well before you're ready to interview. When it's time to go in for the real thing, your same old words won't be hanging around to hurt you.

Put a check by your particular culprits. You know yourself—be honest. If you really aren't sure which ones you use, ask a close friend or family member what they hear you say.

_____ 1. You know

_____ 2. Right?!

_____ 3. OK?

_____ 4. Ummm

_____ 5. Yeah

_____ 6. Say what?

_____ 7. Like . . .

_____ 8. I mean

_____ 9. Well

_____ 10. Any other slang you overuse _____

_____ 11. Profanity you use _____

Write your problem words in a notebook, and carry it with you. For two days, each time you catch yourself using a particular offender, put a check by it. Then take a look at your top three and bring the Rule of 21 into action against them. For the next twenty-one days, stop when you use an overworked word. If you don't know what to say in its place, try silence. Pauses make good, thoughtful impressions, but they're difficult to adjust to at first. Pay a nickel into a jar each time you goof, and buy yourself something with your change at the end of twenty-one days (you should have made the major contribution to your jar in the early part of those days).

You may need to repeat this exercise several times. The phrase took years to get into your speech patterns; give yourself time to get it out! By the time you walk into your first real interview, you'll be ready to express yourself clearly and without slang.

Working Styles

6.2

As we discussed in the chapter, work styles fall into four general categories. We usually, but not always, exhibit the same characteristics at home.

FOCUS: *TASKS* IN THE WORKPLACE

The ANALYST	The DIRECTOR
Acquires & Evaluates Information	Interprets & Processes Information
Gathers & Examines Facts/Weighs Evidence	Acts/Produces Results
Makes Decisions Slowly	Makes Decisions Easily
Works Carefully	Works Hard
Loves Stability/Low Risk Taker	Takes Risks/Challenges Stability
Dislikes Conflict	Thrives on Conflict
Speaks Quietly/Firmly	Speaks Forcefully
Priority: To Be the Expert	Priority: To Be in Control

TIMID/PASSIVE   **BALANCED/ASSERTIVE**   **BOLD/AGGRESSIVE**

The MEDIATOR	The ENTERTAINER
Organizes & Maintains Information	Communicates Information
Harmonizes Workplace	Energizes Workplace
Makes Decisions Reluctantly	Makes Spur-of-the-Moment Decisions
Works Thoroughly	Works Fast
Likes Stability/Rarely Bored	Loves Risks/Easily Bored
Can't Stand Conflict	Accepts Conflict
Speaks Supportively	Speaks Spontaneously & Well
Priority: To Be Needed	Priority: To Be Recognized

FOCUS: *PEOPLE* IN THE WORKPLACE

To determine where your personality style fits on the chart, read each line below, and circle the words in each line that most closely resemble you. Then count the words you circled in each column. Write the total at the bottom of each column.

Self-controlled	Quick tempered	Patient	Nervy
Tenacious	Leader	Responsible	Quick
Loyal	Persuasive	Supportive	Sociable
Considerate	Competitive	Empathetic	Convincing
Faithful	Forceful	Friendly	Animated
Scheduled	Efficient	Obliging	Playful
Determined	Strong willed	Sensitive	Spirited
Detailed	Effective	Adaptable	Spontaneous
Shy	Positive	Peaceful	Charming
Perfectionist	Doer	Team player	Promoter
Analytical	Resourceful	Considerate	Energetic
Realistic	Opportunistic	Idealistic	Optimistic
Planner	Decision maker	Listener	Storyteller
Consistent	Daring	Reliable	Creative
Organized	Bold	Tolerant	Delightful
Persistent	Productive	Reasonable	Upbeat
Respectful	Frank	Thoughtful	Flexible
Expert	Problem solver	Helper	Inspiring
Careful	Headstrong	Responsive	Verbal
Deep thinker	Pragmatic	Compromiser	Demonstrative
Structured	Confident	Diplomatic	Imaginative
Introspective	Independent	Reserved	Mixes easily
Quiet	Strong opinions	Eager to please	Talkative
Hardworking	Mover and shaker	Negotiator	Popular
Dedicated	Sure of self	Sensitive	Fun
Polite	Adventurous	Join in fun	Lively
Skeptical	No-nonsense	Permissive	Restless
Critical	Argumentative	Hesitant	Forgetful
Worrier	Impatient	Submissive	Unorganized
Fact seeker	Solution seeker	Harmony seeker	Attention seeker

TOTAL	TOTAL	TOTAL	TOTAL

Remember to answer honestly about who you think you *are*, not who you think you would *like* to be. None of the answers are negative—all are positive in different ways. The more honest you are, the more accurate a picture you will have of your personality, and the more you will be able to use what you know to your benefit in school and in the workplace.

If you scored the highest in the first column, your personality style is primarily the analyst; second column, the director; third column, the mediator; fourth column, the entertainer. You may have a tie or other close numbers. No one personality is typical of only one style.

You now have an idea of your personality. Like most of us, you probably have characteristics from a combination of styles, although one will dominate. Did you already know you were most comfortable with this working style? You may have, but you may not have ever defined it for yourself. Now you can figure out the parts that hold you back. For instance, to be successful, people of all personality styles need to assert themselves, communicate their needs clearly, and ask other people what they want. By nature, the analyst and the mediator are often passive. If your personality falls on this side, you need to practice stating your own opinions and desires. If you're primarily the director or the entertainer, you achieve balance by toning down your opinionated nature.

Ask yourself what qualities you need to develop to balance your style. Be aware of where you want to stretch your style and start practicing. How about beginning with twenty-one days?

Who Gets the Raise?

6.3

No matter how satisfying careers may be, everyone wants raises along with the recognition. Rosina, Ivan, and Lucy are no exception. They have worked for Dumore Digital for over a year and have received excellent evaluations. However, their supervisor, Mr. Dudley, told them recently that Dumore isn't able to give raises right now. The three employees handle the news differently. Rosina is passive, Lucy becomes aggressive, and Ivan chooses the assertive path.

Before each of the following sentences, indicate which employee would be most likely to have made the statement. Use R (Rosina), L (Lucy), or I (Ivan).

_____ 1. I quit.

_____ 2. I will stay because I probably won't get a good recommendation if I don't.

_____ 3. I'll make an appointment with Mr. Dudley and remind him what I've done for Dumore.

_____ 4. It's Dudley's fault Dumore is losing money.

_____ 5. I hope I didn't look disappointed in front of Mr. Dudley.

_____ 6. I like it at Dumore. I'll get a part-time job to supplement my income and ask for a raise in three months.

_____ 7. I'm going to go in there and tell Dudley what he can do with Dumore.

_____ 8. Maybe I didn't work enough overtime.

_____ 9. I'll ask Mr. Dudley if I'm eligible to apply for Clarence's job. I hear he's leaving.

_____ 10. I'll tell Mr. Dudley I want to apply for Clarence's job and ask him what my chances are.

_____ 11. If Mr. Dudley says he's not replacing Clarence, I'll tell him I could handle his responsibilities too, but I will need a pay increase.

_____ 12. I'll stick around awhile, but I'll be sick a lot next year.

_____ 13. I feel sick.

_____ 14. I hate it here.

_____ 15. I'll take a day off next week and figure out my next moves.

_____ 16. Dudley is such a jerk.

_____ 17. I don't like the situation, I need a raise, and I plan to get one.

_____ 18. Wait until I tell everyone they won't be getting raises this year.

Take the statements you like, add five of your own in the space provided, and put them together to form a strategic plan to get the raise in the next few months.

Your statements:

1. _____
2. _____
3. _____
4. _____
5. _____

Your strategic plan:

_____
_____
_____
_____
_____

If you incorporated the ideas in 3, 6, 10, 11, 15, or 17, you get the raise—and so does Ivan.

6.4 Your Communication PALs

Circle your communication strengths, and indicate any weakness you want to begin to correct.

Assertive	Is up-front and direct in a polite way.
Truthful	Is honest and straightforward.
Thoughtful	Takes time to think things through before acting or passing judgment.
Interactive	Works well with others.
Tactful	Thinks things through; acts and speaks with politeness and awareness.
Understanding	Has perspective on the needs of, and situations that affect, self and others.

Discreet	Reveals only what is necessary for clear expression; keeps confidences.
Expressive	Communicates completely, promptly, openly, and freely.
Sincere	Says what is meant, means what is said.

I will develop my ability to be: _____

Add the quality that you want to develop to your collection of reinforcement cards or Post-It® notes.

Take a moment to go back and look at your other cards and positive attitude lists to determine your progress. You're over halfway through the program. Are your positive attitudes keeping up with the pace?

Take New Tools on the Road

6.5

Look over the New In Your Tool Kit list at the beginning of this chapter. Choose and write here the three most important tools you gained from reading this chapter.

1. _____

2. _____

3. _____

For each tool listed, write one example of how you will apply that tool to achieve success in school and in your future career. Include changes you plan to make, as well as how you will continue or reinforce existing behavior.

1. _____

_____

_____

2. _____

_____

_____

3. _____

_____

MOVING ON

III

Be willing to take a risk,

don't be afraid to fail. If you

go the extra mile, things will

start happening. I think if you

put yourself out there you try

that much harder.

KAREN MITCHELL, SALES MANAGER

7 Tools That Create Opportunity

RESOURCES TO POWER YOUR JOB SEARCH

NEW IN YOUR TOOL KIT

Networking

Mentors

Resource building

Job hunting

So far our focus has been on you: If you've been paying attention, you've had the chance to work on becoming more self-aware; you've put together some important goals and sorted through your priorities; you've learned how to manage your resources, communicate and negotiate, make decisions, and take care of yourself. In short, you've become a more confident and knowledgeable person. You are becoming a hot commodity—a more marketable package. Once you've done all this, you are ready to start preparing for the next step—putting it all to the test in the real world.

However, that doesn't mean that opportunities will start breaking down your door. Uh huh. You've got to learn how to find—and create—opportunities. That's what this chapter is all about. It will show you how to seek help from libraries, school sources, and other people. It will describe the choices and challenges you will face when you begin your job search and how to develop the street smarts to deal with them. Finally, the chapter will suggest ideas for tracking down future career leads.

Take time to find out now about some of the opportunities that will await you. Ask questions and find answers. Prepare yourself to make the most of your future.

Help: Inside and Outside Your School

People have different attitudes about getting help. Some welcome all the assistance they can get and use it to build their strengths and skills. Others try to tough things out on their own with no outside aid. Still others would like help but have no idea where to get it.

Our advice? The more help you get, the better. No man—rather, no person—is an island! These are big decisions that you will be facing, decisions that will make a huge difference in the rest of your life. Getting advice, using connections, and taking advantage of outside resources are ways to make the most of every future opportunity. It will also give you an edge over the competition. Informed, on-purpose decisions are always better than a "get stuck with whatever comes your way" approach to life.

In this chapter, we'll explore many of the resources that can help you identify good future career choices for you. These same resources may also be the ones you will use to track down actual jobs in your future chosen profession. Some of the resources we'll look at include:

- Networking with family, friends, teachers, alumni and alumni associations, and business contacts
- Mentors
- School placement and career counselors
- Libraries
- Unions
- Newspapers and magazines
- Employment agencies and commissions
- Bulletin boards
- The Internet

NETWORKING: THE PEOPLE CONNECTION

People helping people make the entire business world go 'round. People help each other learn on the job; find jobs by providing connections, references, advice, and recommendations; and make contacts and boost business by associating with each other's companies. The whole basis of commerce is exchange. Without people, there is no business, period.

The process of developing and maintaining contacts in the workforce is often referred to as *networking*. Networking means staying in touch and helping each other whenever you can.

This doesn't mean that every individual you meet in your school or working life will help you (although many of them will). But smart businesspersons know that the success of their business depends on the networks they build with others, just as your success depends on your connections and cooperation. Open yourself up to the information on the outside. The more you open up, the more you will connect with others on your future job. Networking starts now. You will find people with whom to network both inside and outside of school, as illustrated in Figure 7.1.

Make sure you understand what networking really is. To do that, you need to know what networking isn't. Networking is not asking people for a favor. It's not something you do only when you need something. It's also not something you do only when you want to find a new job. All of these concepts are wrong.

Networking is about people. We don't live in isolation, we don't go to school in isolation, and we don't work in isolation. We need each other. Networking is about enjoying people, building friendships, helping each other. Networking means showing that you care about someone enough to stay in contact and share ideas, experiences, and yourself. Networking means living life by the Golden Rule: treating others the way you like to be treated. Networking is a lifelong process of nurturing relationships, caring for people.

Network, *noun.*

A group or system of interconnected or cooperating individuals.

verb.

To develop contacts and exchange information with others, as to further a career.

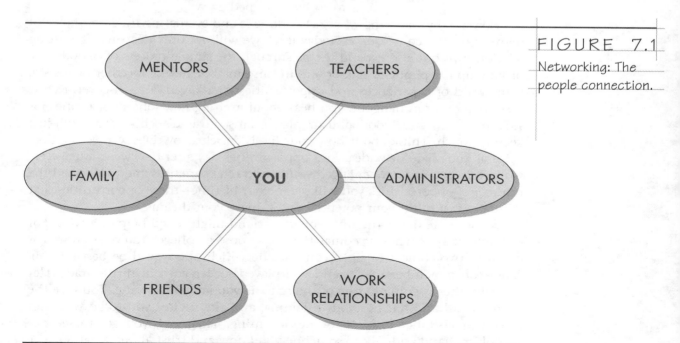

FIGURE 7.1

Networking: The people connection.

Networking is not about using people. Networking is not a one-way street. And, networking is not momentary. It is a long-term commitment to a friendship, the development of a strong relationship.

Clearly all relationships are different, and the depth of our relationships will vary from person to person. However, you might be surprised at how many acquaintances can develop into mutually rewarding relationships simply by staying in touch. Sharing ideas or seeking to help each other transforms casual or professional relationships into lifelong friendships.

You already do some networking. You have lunch with a friend. You talk with a relative. You strike up a conversation with someone sitting next to you in class. Think about the various stages and places in your life and the people who were important. There are various levels of schooling—grammar school, middle school, high school. Maybe you've already had a part-time job or two. Think about any community organizations you enjoyed—Girl or Boy Scouts, sports teams, youth groups, etc.

Now think of how many of these people you can contact by phone or mail, and how many with whom you are in regular communication. If you are like most of us, you have lost contact with a great many of these people. We regret "losing" these friends and these relationships, but somehow they seem to have slipped away.

Food for Thought

As you meet more and more people, keeping track of names, addresses, and phone numbers becomes increasingly difficult. Organize this information in an address book, a Rolodex® card file, or better yet, on your computer using your word processor, your electronic calendar program (e.g., Schedule+), or a label program (e.g., Avery LabelPro). And if you use e-mail, you might also consider putting this information into your e-mail address book.

However, by clarifying what networking is and evaluating the importance of networking at a conscious, everyday level, we will not only deepen our existing relationships but also expand them. Through the simple process of periodically picking up the phone to talk or sending an e-mail or getting together for a soda, your world of experiences and opportunities is enlarged. You discover a great new shop or a fun hangout. You hear about exciting new job opportunities for students. Your school football team plays against a friend's school team. You just keep in touch. Think about how your life is enriched by these valued relationships as you share new ideas and opportunities day after day, week after week, year after year. You have enlarged your world of experiences and multiplied the number of opportunities you will see in your lifetime—those opportunities that will help you fulfill your potential and achieve your dreams.

Somewhere down the line, you or a friend might need help or advice. For example, maybe when it comes time to choose a college. You've narrowed it down to two choices but just can't decide which one would be best for you. Then you remember that friend you played soccer with in ninth grade. Her older brother is going to one of the schools you are considering. You give the friend a call and tell her your dilemma, and she invites you to go with her family to visit her brother for homecoming. That way, you get to see the school firsthand and talk to someone you know and trust about what it's really like. It sure beats thumbing through a college catalog! All of this is made possible because you've nurtured a friendship. Of course, friends are glad to lend you a hand when you need one. Just make sure to be there for them when they need you to return the favor!

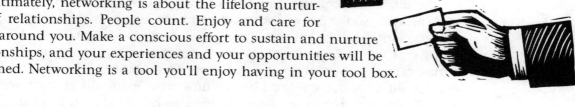

Ultimately, networking is about the lifelong nurturing of relationships. People count. Enjoy and care for those around you. Make a conscious effort to sustain and nurture relationships, and your experiences and your opportunities will be deepened. Networking is a tool you'll enjoy having in your tool box.

At School

Your school is not only the classes that you attend. It is also a network of people who can give you all kinds of practical advice about your career path. We'll talk about the guidance and placement counselors in a minute; they are a special case because it is their job to help you choose future schooling and employment. The other people available to you at school can help you broaden your network in many different directions. Who are they?

TEACHERS. Your teachers often have been, or occasionally still are, working in the fields that they teach. They have had their own experiences and have learned valuable lessons that they can pass on to you. Their advice can help you clear a few hurdles that you may have stumbled over on your own. If you feel like you need extra help in your preparation for the job world, they may tutor as well.

Teachers also have their network of friends and business associates to whom they can refer you. By getting to know your teachers well, you may be able to hook into the network that they have already established. Ask teachers when they have some free time to talk, and make yourself available.

ADMINISTRATORS. Most school administrators are where they are because they have worked their way up through the ranks and demonstrated outstanding knowledge in the fields for which their school offers programs. Because their decisions about the school's direction strongly influence its success, they have up-to-the-minute knowledge of the business world. You would be wise to take advantage of any chance to benefit from their knowledge. They are there to serve you.

Like teachers, administrators have an extensive network of contacts in place. If you have a particular kind of future job in mind, don't be afraid to ask them if they could recommend to you any companies to contact. You have nothing to lose and everything to gain if you just get the nerve up and ask. Contact the school office, and make an appointment to see an administrator. When you go to your appointment, don't forget to dress for success!

ALUMNI. Some private schools have an alumni (former graduates of the school) association that continues to provide support, information, and even job leads to its graduates and former students. If yours does, make a point to involve yourself when you eventually move into the working world. It may be a free service or may require a small yearly fee to become a member. Alumni associations often hold regular meetings, and some send newsletters to members. They may hold workshops or other informational meetings.

An alumni association can give you continued information as you work and provide you with a ready-made support group with whom to share achievements and difficulties. Plus, it is a network of contacts and relationships that can help you embark on a new job search at any time in your future career. If your school does not have an alumni association, it may still have a list of successful working alumni who maintain contact with the school. Some of them may make an effort to hire graduates from the school and will want to see recent graduates come in to interview. Alumni are a bridge between inside and outside because they have experienced both sides.

What kinds of information should you seek from your contacts? Think about what you learn in class. You learn skills and information. But you don't necessarily get the "real story" about what it's like to win a job and earn a living after you get out of school. That's what you can find out from the people who have "been there, done that." Here are some questions to ask:

- How did you get started in your field?
- What are the most interesting and challenging aspects of the job?
- What is a typical day like?
- What kind of salary can I expect at the entry level in my field?
- Are jobs readily available in this area, or will I need to commute or relocate?

The people around you at school can help you sort through tons of questions that may not come in class. Do you already have people with whom you feel comfortable enough to ask for help? Keep yourself open to their advice and know-how. You will never regret it.

On the Outside

One of the best ways to find out what a particular job or profession is really like is to network with someone currently doing that kind of work. They can supply the inside story, providing a picture of what they do each day: the tough realities they encounter, the benefits of the job, the way they are treated, and what the pay is like.

Who can you network with? Broaden your thinking. How about your family? Neighbors? Friends? Friends of friends? There may be quite a few people in your circle of acquaintances who work in a field that interests you. Ask around and find out what people do for a living.

You may actually be surprised to discover that the people you know do such interesting work. It's often amazing how little we know about the people closest to us. Have you ever spent a day on the job with your parents or grandparents? Do you even know what they really do? Now is a great chance to find out. Talk to them. Visit their worksites, if you can. Find out what made them choose their professions. They'll appreciate the interest you take in their lives, and you'll learn something valuable for yours.

Same thing goes for other relatives and friends. Ask around; take an interest in their work. You never know who might know someone who knows someone who knows just the right future career path for you!

If you have no friends or family who work in areas that you want to find out about, ask around to see if your friends and family have other friends who could help you. Ask everyone; the more people you ask, the wider your network will become. If you ask ten family members for help, and each one of them has another ten people they know, you are greatly increasing your chances of finding someone who can help answer your questions.

Once you find a few people, talk to your contacts in a deliberate, organized, and focused manner. Set up times where you can sit down with each one, and spend half an hour or so asking about their work. Have a pen and paper handy to write down names, phone numbers, or other notes (for sample questions, refer to the previous list in this chapter). Find out as much as you can—facts, stories, and opinions—about the profession.

Be careful about taking negative information at face value. In other words, be skeptical; take everything with a grain of salt. Not everything we hear would be true for us. Negative information is one person's subjective view of events and not necessarily what is really happening. Listen to what people have to say, process the information, and continue to investigate for yourself.

MENTORS

The wisdom or advice that you can get from the people in your life is some of the best training you'll ever get. If you feel comfortable with one or more of the people that you get to know, and they seem open to giving you advice and lending a listening ear, you might want to continue the relationship. Someone you turn to for advice—for example, a teacher, a business contact, or a more experienced relative, could become a good friend and mentor.

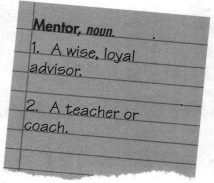

Mentor, *noun.*
1. A wise, loyal advisor.
2. A teacher or coach.

We hope there will be many people who will help you and give you advice. But mentors go one step further to develop a special interest in you and in your success, and they go out of their way to help you along your path. A mentor keeps watch over your progress and offers advice and support, often over a long period of time. Above all, a mentor is there for you when you reach out and has your best interests at heart. Mentors may not see how you are doing every second, but when you need them, they provide the assistance that gets you through a particular situation.

You may already have a mentor, or a few, in your life. Your mentor may be a parent, an older brother or sister, a friend, or another family member. Your mentor may be a teacher or coach or a current or former employer that you know.

Food for Thought

Think about the people you go to when you are upset, confused, or at a dead end. These are the people whose words make you feel comforted, who always seem to give you a different perspective and a way to make a change in your situation. These are your mentors! Most often they are older individuals. Part of the reason why you seek them out is because their experience has given them knowledge that you need. Do you always call a parent? an old teacher? or the father of a friend? Think about how they make you feel. Look for that feeling when you begin to get to know people at school or at work. Trust your gut instincts, and it will lead you to mentors that you can trust.

Everyone needs a little guidance! A mentor—someone who knows you well—can be one of the best sources of that guidance. No matter who you are, there are people in your life who know more than you do and have had more experiences. You need to respect that knowledge and be open to learning from it.

It's often hard to take advice from others. Having a mentor takes some courage; it requires the listener to be open to new ideas. A person becomes a mentor when the person to whom they give advice receives that advice openly and respectfully, shows appreciation for it, and tries it out. It's an exchange: The mentor gives the words of wisdom and educational stories, and the recipient gives respect and a willing ear (fertile ground for the growth of new knowledge). Can you think of a time when advice from a more experienced person helped you choose the right path?

Remember, you don't have to follow all advice. A true mentor would not expect you to do so. The most a mentor can expect is that you will listen respectfully and consider the ideas offered. If you can recognize that someone else may have more knowledge and experience than you and that you might be able to learn from that knowledge and experience, you are showing a great sign of maturity. None of us know it all! Listen and learn!

Don't force the issue with anyone if you don't yet have a mentor. Mentoring relationships sprout on their own when you least expect them. Your most important role with your mentor, or potential mentor, is to seek advice and be open to what you receive. You may develop a friendship that will be part of your life for many years to come. Your mentor may learn from you as well. You will be able to grow and develop together.

PLACEMENT AND CAREER COUNSELORS

Beyond your personal network, a number of career resources exist that can help you, as noted in Figure 7.2.

FIGURE 7.2
Career resources.

- Your network
- Guidance/placement/career counselors
- Work-study programs
- Internships
- Internet
- Newspapers/magazines
- Libraries
- Unions
- Employment agencies
- Bulletin boards

Real People, Real Stories

Make an appointment to talk with a favorite teacher, coach, or counselor. Tell this person about your efforts to prepare yourself for a future career and that you've been reading about how important finding mentors can be in that process. Ask this person to tell you about important people who have helped shape his or her careers. Listen to any advice about how you can find a mentor to help you reach your professional aspirations. Record your discoveries on a separate sheet of paper.

At School

Unlike your teachers, who are hired to teach you and can choose to give advice on their spare time, your guidance or placement counselors work specifically to advise you about the working world. A counselor's full-time job is to keep informed about all kinds of career opportunities and to pass that information on to you. Most schools employ one or more guidance or placement counselors full time. Meeting with them may even be part of your classwork.

Your counselor can provide vocational aptitude and other types of career assessments to help direct your future career path and can also supply a people connection, with sources of contacts and jobs in the community when you finally apply for work. Make an appointment to speak with your school guidance counselor soon. Help the school help you by seeking out these services.

On the Outside

More often today, people are making their way in the world as independent contractors—people who are not connected with a business, who look for work on their own, and who do it independently. Some of these people are career counselors. They have studied the systems and psychology of the business world as well as the skills and personal characteristics that different jobs and careers require. Their knowledge can help you choose a future job wisely.

Food for Thought

Sometimes the most confusing issues are personal ones that don't seem related to your career. But you may find, as most people do, that they can easily interfere. Are there personal issues getting in your way? Let your guidance counselor, career counselor, your placement counselor, or a favorite teacher help you sort through them. Do you need a job that allows you to take care of a child? Do you have a parent who has a problem with your chosen career? Do you have an addiction that you are worried will get in the way of work? You don't have to face it all alone.

You will also find businesses that focus solely on career planning. Such a business will employ several career counselors and may offer more services than an independent counselor. You should check into both kinds of opportunities when you search for advice on the outside.

Those of you with solid guidance or career placement services in your school may not need to seek outside career counseling. School services are accessible and convenient and cost nothing. If you check with your school first, you will be sure that you haven't missed anything. For those who don't have those in-school resources or those who would like another perspective, independent career counselors can be a valuable source of information.

"Let your fingers do the walking!" You can find listings of career counselors and counseling programs in your Yellow Pages under Career and Vocational Counseling. Services offered will vary and may include:

- Career counseling
- Vocational testing and assessment
- Resume development and preparation
- Job search training
- Interview coaching
- Support groups
- Practical and emotional support

The drawback is that most of these programs and individuals will cost you money—but not all of them. Talk with your parents about what kinds of resources are available for assistance like this. Some programs may offer discounted or free services, so be sure to ask about these options. Then, look for a person or program that suits you best, and get the help you need to get your future career started on the right track.

YOUR LIBRARY

You will find a wide range of materials at your school or public library or resource center that can help you build your storehouse of information. Schedule some time to spend there so that you can find out what's available to you.

What can you find that can help you? Here are some ideas to get you started:

- Trade magazines published by people in the fields of which you may have an interest

- Newspapers and magazines with listings of jobs offered in the classifieds (you might only get one newspaper at home; the library will have a wide variety)

- Books about various professions

- Materials about the general job market found in periodicals that chronicle the nation's employment rates, jobs in decline or on the rise, developments in education, rights of employees, and laws regarding employment (for example, see *Time*, *Newsweek*, or *U.S. News & World Report*)

- Books that give you information about companies (for example, *Standard & Poor's Register of Corporations, Directors, and Executives*)

- Books on personality types as they relate to career choices

You may not know where to start looking for these materials, so ask a librarian. Take advantage of the librarian's expertise. This person spends all day cataloguing and keeping track of everything that is available to you. The librarian can point you in the direction that will help you most.

Borrow what you can take home, and read reference materials during your visit. Don't forget a pad and pen to write down useful information. Then let all those bits and pieces of information sink into your brain—they will come in handy.

At School

Many schools will have some sort of library or resource center. It can range from a little room with specific career-oriented materials to a full-size, full-service library. Ask for help, as you need it, to find materials on careers of interest to you.

On the Outside

Even if your school has a library, you should also check out the public library or a local university library. Chances are it is much bigger and has a greater range and supply of resources. It might not seem as user-friendly as your school library, but take the time to enlist the help of an experienced librarian. Because you may have a lot of looking to do, plan your visit so that you have time in which to explore everything available to you at the library.

Food for Thought

Try using the Internet to do research on a career or a specific job opportunity. Online services such as America Online have made career and job search easier. You can find information on career strategies to tips on resume writing to specific job opportunities. Among other topics, subjects listed on one online service included career guidance, resume writing, job listings, America's Job Bank, company research, job strategies for the 2000s, and career resources.

UNIONS

Unions are formally organized groups of workers who work for the benefit of the other workers in the same trade. They negotiate for good work standards as well as wages and benefits for their members. They have a lot of knowledge about the trade and the job market because they are directly involved. And they monitor job conditions and take action when trouble arises.

First, find out if the trade you are interested in has a union. Not every trade does. (Your teachers, your counselors, or even your librarian should be able to help you answer that question.) If there is none, then there's not much you can do in this category. If there is, the next piece of information you need is whether there is a local union chapter in your area. Ask at your school, or call the union's main office to find out. Most unions have their national offices in Washington, D.C. If you know the exact name of the union, you can call information and get the number.

The following is a list of the kinds of information and/or services a union can provide:

- Information about being a member—meetings, dues, rules, and benefits
- Names of companies that are registered with the union and/or hire union workers (an assurance that they are safe and follow union regulations)
- Where to find such places and how to apply for work there
- What you will need to apply (papers, equipment, skills, dress requirements)
- Additional training programs—including apprenticeship and internship opportunities

When you have found the location and phone number of the union you are interested in, take the initiative—call them and ask to be transferred to the membership or education department. Tell them about your interest in this particular trade, and ask them if they have any information that they can send or if there is someone you might talk to for more information.

Choices and Challenges

All of us would love to have work that brings us joy, makes the most of our talents, and fulfills our needs. But finding that ideal work situation will take a lot of time and energy. After you choose and train in a career field, the next step will be to track down and pursue job leads, as illustrated in Figure 7.3.

You will find this both an exciting time and a scary time. You will want to be on the positive end of the decisions that employers make, of course. But, as many people in all kinds of jobs can tell you, that doesn't always happen right away. You may hit on the perfect situation quickly, but more than likely you will follow leads and interview for a few months before something you can live with comes along. Gear up by preparing yourself ahead of time.

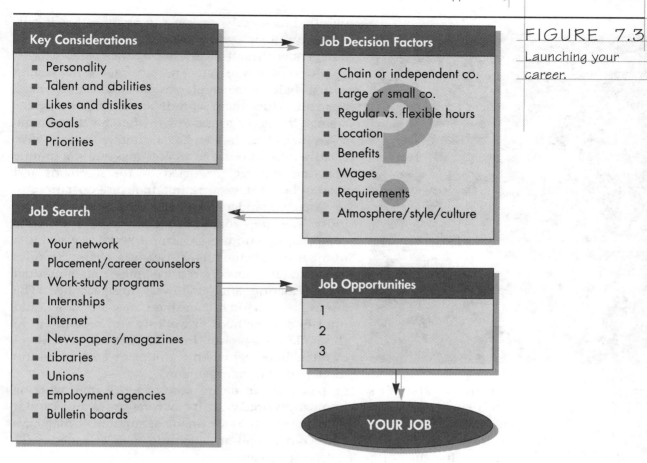

FIGURE 7.3
Launching your career.

CHOICES

There are many factors to consider when you are ready to search for a job. Take time to do it now, before you start the job hunt. If you think things through now, you won't waste time pursuing jobs that won't suit your lifestyle. You will have a chance at the end of the chapter to indicate your preferences in these areas.

When we assign different characteristics to different kinds of companies, we speak in general terms. Some companies may prove exceptions to the rule. Take it all in, but remember that you may discover lots of variety in the real world. This is only a general map to guide your exploration.

Chain/Franchise or Independent Company

Each has its good points and bad points. Chains usually have well-organized workforces; established rules about conduct, duties, and employee treatment; and consistent and reliable pay systems. The fact that many branches of a company exist shows that the company has enjoyed a certain degree of pop-

Food for Thought

Keep current by reading news-oriented magazines or a local newspaper on a regular basis. It will provide you with a knowledge base that will help you understand important trends and better identify and evaluate future employment opportunities. If you focus on yourself and allow your world to consist of only your family, school, and part-time work, you will have a much more difficult time identifying and evaluating employment in a future new field or industry. Stay in touch with your world!

ularity and success, so you can assume that it will stick around for a while. Chains are more likely than independent small businesses to offer benefits.

Conversely, you can sense an impersonal feeling with a chain. Some employees may not feel that management values them as individuals with particular talents. It's easier to get lost in the crowd as a franchise employee. If you are a unique person with creative ideas and like to work things out in a unique way, you may feel restricted by the standards and rules of how things work in a franchise operation.

An independent company can offer more flexibility. The rules come down from those within the company, not from a governing board overseeing a number of different franchises of a chain. So rules and standards more often can take the individual work situation and employees into account. The atmosphere in such a business may be looser, and unorthodox methods of working and moving up in the ranks may prevail. Independent small businesses often have tighter-knit groups of employees and more personal management.

But working for such a business can mean more of a risk than working for a chain. Because the company works with its own revenues and cannot rely on a higher management organization for financial support, it may have a shakier financial situation. Looser rules and attitudes may at times result in less efficiency or preferential treatment.

Large or Small Company

In comparison, large and small companies are much like the chain and independent businesses. A large company may have financial strength, hiring power, job opportunities, and locations. The jobs available at a large company may cover a greater range of possibilities. You may have more mobility, a greater chance to move up through positions. You are more likely to enjoy benefits at such a company. You should have more job security, although in recent years even the largest, most successful companies have been downsizing because of a struggling economy or new technology.

There are potential drawbacks of working at a large company as well. You may not get as much personal attention and/or guidance from your superiors. You might feel like just another Social Security number on the payroll. Some workers' personalities may not jive with the kind of structured system of rules and duties that a large company will most likely use. If you don't like working around a lot of other people, you may feel a bit overwhelmed.

Working at a small company offers you a more personal, comfortable environment with fewer employees. Your work may have less structure and your duties more flexibility. Even work time and schedules may be more flexible. If you deal with customers or clients, you may find it easier to develop personal relationships with them. Personal relationships with your manager(s) may grow more easily.

Some of you, though, may find a small company environment stifling. You may prefer working with a lot of people. If you dislike the people with whom you work at a small company, you will still have to deal with them day after day—you cannot get lost in the cubicles too easily. Small companies may offer small benefit packages or, in some cases, none at all. And you may feel like your opportunities to move up are limited.

Regular or Flexible Schedule

Different jobs offer different levels of flexibility. You will need to decide how much you need. Some people like a rigid, regular schedule to help them keep their lives organized. If you don't require much flexibility, you may have an easier time finding a job that suits you. Look for one with a steady schedule. If your personality or other factors in your life lead you to seek flexibility, find out when you eventually interview how much flexibility the job will allow.

Some situations that might require a more flexible schedule are:

- A preference for working out of the home
- A preference for working odd hours (evenings 5 to 12, or graveyard, 12 to 8), perhaps in order to accommodate an outside interest or hobby
- A desire to coordinate work with other independent projects such as schooling
- A need to balance family and child care responsibilities

Flexible jobs do exist. Many people work unconventional hours, but often there is a downside. They may lose out in job security and/or in salary because some employers will pay more for a full-time, steady employee than they will for someone who may not be around all the time or who may leave on short notice. Also, if a company has to downsize (cut down on the number of employees), those on more flexible schedules seem more expendable and may lose their jobs first.

Location

Will location matter to you? If you have a reliable car or a fairly comprehensive public transit system and don't mind a commute, you may not put location high on your priority list. If getting around will be more of a problem for you, or if you want to spend as little time traveling as possible, then you will probably choose to pay more attention to location.

You will have various choices to consider. Of course, your choices will differ depending on the job you seek. Will you want to work in the city or the suburbs? Will you need a good parking facility, or will you need to work near a major transit stop? Will you want your workplace convenient to your other needs such as food, gasoline, or housing? Would you care if you worked in a lower-class neighborhood? You may not find a job that suits all your location needs, but if you keep them in mind, you will certainly end up with a few.

Benefits

Some jobs will offer benefits—health insurance, pension plan, paid vacation time—but some won't. You will need to decide first if benefits are crucial to you. They certainly are to most people. If so, you should consider more seriously the jobs that offer them. Benefits can make life much easier for you. Having guaranteed health care will ease your mind, and a pension or investment plan will help you save for the future. In addition, someone else takes care of the bulk of the paperwork! Unfortunately, fewer and fewer companies are offering such comprehensive benefits to employees. For example, today's employees may be asked to pay for a certain portion of their health insurance premium.

You may find when you interview that some jobs that do not give benefits will offer a higher salary. A little extra money might look good, but remain cautious. If you take a job with no benefits, you might need to purchase your health insurance independently (and probably at a higher price than a company group rate would offer). You may end up spending all the extra money you would make on the benefits that another lower-paying job would have given you automatically.

For example, suppose you will have to make a choice between two possible jobs. One will pay you $12 per hour and offers health care. The other offers $14.25 per hour without benefits. Working forty hours a week, in a year these jobs would give you (before taxes):

$24,960 at $12 per hour
$29,640 at $14.25 per hour

At first glance, the second one certainly looks better—$4,680 better—until you realize that if you have to purchase health insurance, it would probably cost you more than $3,000 per year. Now things look different. As it turns out, you will probably save money by taking the lower-paying job because of the benefits you will receive.

Many different situations can occur. You will need to examine your particular situation carefully to make sure that you don't miss out on a bargain. Look at where the money goes, and compare prices of benefits so that you end up with the best deal.

Wages

In some vocations, different jobs will have fairly comparable wages (for example, if a trade has a union, the union may regulate the pay scale). Others may have a wide range depending on the individual businesses, local cost of living, and job descriptions. Finding a job that pays well is a priority for almost everyone. If you are offered a job with a good salary, you will need to consider the trade-offs. Will you have to give up other priorities in exchange for the high wages? Will the salary be worth it to you if you have to travel out of your way, if you have no flexible time, or if you dislike the atmosphere? Make your choices carefully.

Although most workers will be paid regularly every two weeks, with taxes already taken out, some may have opportunities to work in a freelance position, for example, doing design work or creating Internet Web pages. Freelancing, or working as an independent contractor, means that you will receive payment only when you work and that you may not have taxes taken out. Sometimes freelancing will help you get your foot in the door at a company that may later hire you as a full-timer. Some trades lend themselves to freelancing, so find out if the one you are interested in does. Then if you should have trouble finding a full-time position, you could look into doing some freelance work. It may help you move up later.

Requirements

Some jobs have a lot of requirements, others only a few. Make choices about which ones you can fulfill to apply for the jobs you want. Typical requirements include degrees or certain kinds of training, certifications, previous experience, certain skills, or dress code. If you don't meet a certain requirement, you may lose the chance for a job. Does the job mean that much to you? If so, you could choose to work toward fulfilling that requirement. If a requirement seems like too much trouble, look for jobs that won't ask for it.

Atmosphere/Style/Culture

It usually takes a visit or interview for you to determine the atmosphere of a business and the style that its managers use, unless you know someone who works there. Some people prefer a relaxed atmosphere and a loose style of management. They like feeling trusted to accomplish their tasks without having to follow strict rules.

Others don't work well in a relaxed environment because they need structure to keep them on track. Some people like rules about how to work, and they appreciate someone keeping an eye on them and pushing them to accomplish a task. These folks would do well in a more controlled and tightly managed atmosphere.

Have you ever visited a business where you could see and feel the enthusiasm and energy of the employees? Or have you ever visited a business where it felt cold and sterile and the employees seemed afraid to even smile or ask a supervisor a question?

Businesses not only produce a wide range of products and services, but they also have their own personalities, their own "feeling," or their own cul-

ture. Would you rather work for an open and energetic company where you are encouraged to take risks, where hearing laughter in the background is the norm rather than the exception? Would you expect productivity, loyalty, and employee commitment to be higher in a company "run by the numbers" or in a firm where objectives and results are developed and evaluated in a collaborative manner and where people really count? Or would you rather shop in a department store where a salesperson is happy to help you as you move from casual clothes to the shoe department or in a store where you have difficulty finding someone to simply ring up your purchase?

Culture is a set of values, standards of conduct, and beliefs that guide behavior in an organization. By guiding behavior, an organization's culture directly and powerfully affects the environment that we sense—what we feel, what we see, what we hear, and what we do.

Although values might be stated in a company's mission, credo, or employee handbook, an organization's culture is typically undocumented and is usually left for an individual to figure out. And despite the potential challenge of figuring out an organization's culture, it is well worth the effort. An organization's culture directly affects how comfortable and effective we are at work, just as we individually contribute to and affect the culture.

Your fit with an organization's culture will affect how comfortable you will feel at work as well as the viability of a longer-term employment relationship. Maybe you have visited places where you felt immediately at home. People were accepted for who they are, and it appeared everyone was having fun. Clearly, it would be nice to be a part of this environment and contribute in some way. And surely you have also visited job sites where you immediately felt uncomfortable and knew you probably wouldn't fit in.

A reaction to an organization's culture is very similar. People can feel comfortable and want to contribute or feel like they don't belong and want to leave—or worse, be asked to leave. As a consequence, understanding a company's culture is particularly important for someone looking for a job. Yet all too often, when we are exploring employment opportunities, our focus is on compensation and benefits, functional requirements, and location, without much thought about potential fit or compatibility with an organization's culture.

You can find out this information on organizational culture from talking to employees at the company or even from questions you will ask in the interview. Go back to what you know about yourself. Do you slack off when no one keeps a strict eye on you, or do you thrive on being able to push yourself and progress on your own? Are you happier and more productive when your activities are tightly structured and observed by a supervisor? Then prepare specific questions to ask any employees or prospective employers you will meet. The following questions will help you to determine if a company's atmosphere and management style will suit you.

FOR AN EMPLOYEE

- How often does your supervisor check up on your work?

- Are you formally evaluated? How often—after each project, quarterly, weekly? Are evaluations general or focused on specific tasks?

- Do you feel over- or undermanaged? What is your personal preference? (If the interviewee's personal preference is similar to yours, you can determine that you might feel the same way about the management style.)

- How would you describe the atmosphere?

- What kinds of breaks can you comfortably take during your workday? What relaxation is acceptable?

- How are deviations from plans or structure received? Are new ideas welcomed and used right away or shelved until they can be coordinated with the existing structure?

FOR A PROSPECTIVE EMPLOYER

- How would you describe the management style at this company?

- How often do employees report to supervisors?

- What kinds of systems of evaluation do supervisors use, and how often do they evaluate employees?

Food for Thought

How do you do in school? Do you have more success when a teacher keeps you on task, or do you work better when you focus on independent projects? Your learning style reveals a lot about your ideal working atmosphere. Be honest—even if you don't necessarily like a teacher watching you and keeping your classwork structured, you may make more progress in that atmosphere. If you were on your own, you might not accomplish much! But, some people really do thrive when working alone. Some have the discipline to act as their own teacher and push themselves. Knowing your own work style will help you find a job.

CHALLENGES

We've looked at some of the choices that you have ahead of you. Now, you have four challenges to address—issues that call for special effort, thought, and dedication.

One: Find an Employer Who Respects You

An employer should respect you, treat you well, and not take advantage of you. No matter how many benefits a job offers or how high a salary you will receive, you should never have to put up with disrespect or mistreatment. No amount of money justifies that kind of situation. You must respect yourself first, and then you must expect the same respect from others. If you should allow yourself to linger in a job that hurts you in any way, you would show yourself tremendous disrespect. Stand up for yourself! Look for a situation where you will feel valued.

There are different levels of disrespect, and what you can tolerate depends on your personality. Also, what one person finds to be an unacceptable situation may seem normal to another. If you know yourself well, you can determine when a situation will be detrimental to your well-being. When might you feel mistreated? Here is a range of possible future situations:

- You constantly endure angry criticism from a supervisor, regardless of whether the problem was your fault.
- You have worked hard and are up for a promotion, but someone who has not shown as much dedication is promoted over you because of his or her relationship with the manager.
- You often receive last-minute, time-sensitive work to complete, and you work many hours of overtime without being adequately compensated.
- Your ideas are flatly rejected if they deviate at all from the normal structure.
- Your supervisor expects you to perform personal duties outside of your job description that seem servile to you.
- You receive some indication that you are inappropriately valued for something other than your competence and skills.
- You feel that your talents are underused and ignored.
- You are rarely or never complimented, thanked, or rewarded for your hard work.

These examples differ in their levels of seriousness, and they may inspire different reactions in different people. Use them to become aware of the kinds of disrespect that may appear in the workplace. Of course, you cannot always sense how things will go just from an interview. If you do have doubts, listen to your gut feelings. If you have heard stories from people you trust, keep them in mind when you explore the opportunity. But if you end up taking a job and find out later that you have made a mistake, don't worry about the time you've lost. Just make the break politely before you become too miserable. You're better off having worked there a little while and learned something than not to have tried at all. Take the lesson you learn with you, and move ahead to greener pastures.

Two: Prioritize

In choosing what factors will mean the most to you on the job, you are setting your priorities. Prioritize the big factors, and make the decision at the start about what you must have, no matter what. Put the important points in order, and keep them in mind when you make the other decisions that we have discussed here. Your priority list will guide you in those directions.

For example if you should list your priorities as (1) salary and benefits, (2) easy transportation, and (3) nice people to work with, you would first take the wages and benefits package into consideration. You would keep the transportation situation in mind, and maybe you would turn down a job that has pretty good wages but no convenient transportation available. You would probably reject a job that has nice people and good availability if the wages were awful. Prioritizing will help you balance your options.

Three: Know When to Compromise

It's important to know when to compromise or look at the trade-offs. Not many people ever find a job that suits all their priorities, at least not right away. You will probably find a position that will match with some of them, but you need to know when to make a compromise. Even though a job will not fulfill an important priority, you might have to make a few sacrifices.

Suppose you eventually find a job that fits your top two, but it scores zero on your third and fourth priorities. What should you do? You might want to compromise and take the job anyway. Trade the lesser priorities for the privilege of having the most important ones. Or, you could keep looking. You might even take a job that will require you to perform duties that you don't really like because it has everything else that you seek!

Four: Keep Your Personality in Mind

Remember the topics covered in Chapter 3. Knowing your personality will point you in the direction of the right job for you. When you eventually do actual job hunting, look for situations that will make the most of your own special abilities.

People often forget about their special talents and needs when they encounter the reality of searching for a niche in the workplace. The job hunt can sometimes make anyone feel stressed, tired, and insecure. You will need to work hard to not let your important priorities fall by the wayside when you get ready to hunt for a job. Keep who you are in the forefront of your mind. Remember, when you find a job that suits your personality, it will make you happy, and a happy person is a more efficient and successful employee.

Using Your Street Smarts

What are street smarts? What do they have to do with the job hunt?

Street smarts are a specific kind of common sense—the kind that tells you what to do, where to go, to whom to talk, and how to talk. Originally, the term street smarts referred to the resourcefulness that someone who actually lived on the streets had to use to stay warm, hide, and find food. In this book, we will use the term to mean a basic sense of the right way to get around and get things done.

How do street smarts differ from the other resources you will use for your search? Street smarts involve the use of the following:

- Quiet observation over direct inquiry

- Gut feelings over thinking
- An unwritten code of conduct rather than well-known behavior guidelines

Through that kind of subtle observation and attention to intuition, you will develop the street smarts that clue you in to systems of relationships, acceptable behavior and dress, and the most sought-after personal qualities.

When you use street smarts, you will take note of details such as how the personnel supervisor treats the secretary when you visit the company. You will notice the most common style of dress at the company. You will find out what kinds of qualities a certain company values most by observing what kinds of people work there. When you get ready to hunt for a job, your street smarts will get you noticed in a favorable way, which can often lead to getting hired.

As a high school student, you have been through many different experiences and hopefully have learned lessons from them all. You build street smarts as you incorporate what you learn from those lessons, for example, how to get around school confidently, how to deal with teammates at an important championship game, or how to dress for certain events. Your career compass—your experience, intelligence, and intuition—helps you to compile that information and make sense out of it. You can develop even more specific street smarts, which are the specific tools you need for the particular job you will seek.

> **Street smarts, noun.**
>
> 1. A practical knowledge of how things work or how to get something done.
> 2. A capacity to be creative in the face of obstacles.

Every career field has its individual requirements, its style of operation, and its own particular personality. Individual businesses or firms within each field may differ. One plant may require uniforms whereas another will require only that clothing fit the safety standard without regard to color or style. Different offices may have different rules about hours, coffee breaks, and office etiquette. Every situation is unique. The following is a list of things to look for when researching jobs, checking out actual businesses, or eventually interviewing:

- How people dress on the job—casual or business, uniforms or not
- Behavior toward one another—formal or informal, first names or titles
- Power structure—who is at the top of the pile, who is next in importance, and who is important to please
- Operational structure—who answers to whom, who takes orders from whom, who reports to whom
- Manners—big or small emphasis
- Credentials—what kinds of experience, schooling, degrees, or certificates you need
- Skills—which are necessary, which are icing on the cake

There are more things you'll learn as you explore, but use these to get your mind focused on the kind of information you are seeking. Your aim is to discover the particular street smarts you will need for what you want to do. Once you have begun to narrow your course of study, you can start to find answers to your questions. You have a few avenues of exploration. Some involve people; some may take you on solitary searching and researching. Overall, the key is to observe and make good mental notes (even written notes, if you like) about your observations. Talk to people in the trade you are interested in. Visit prospective companies, stores, offices, plants, or salons.

Talking to people is one of the best ways of developing your specific street smarts. Ask a few people who have had experience to share information from their own valuable store of knowledge. Even if they learned the hard way, they may have received the most reliable lessons.

Take in all the advice you receive, and give yourself time to think it over. Be an attentive but selective listener! Opinions may differ. One person may advise you to pursue a certain job while another may tell you to avoid it. People may have different ideas about traits to emphasize or people to meet. They all have their reasons. Consider them, but don't let a negative person convince you that bad experiences will automatically apply to you. Evaluate the information, and that will help you make the decision that will be right for you. Your street smarts come from paying attention to what remains unsaid—body language, implied ideas, your overall impression—as much as from the specific advice you hear.

One way to gather a lot of information about a prospective employer is by making a visit. Call the personnel department or secretary, and ask if you can make an appointment for a tour. Of course, this method of discovery won't work for every trade or position. Some companies won't offer this option, and others don't have the type of work environment that would make a tour a worthwhile process. If all you'll see is three offices with desks and filing cabinets, you'll want to focus on the other methods we have talked about instead.

Food for Thought

Think back for a moment to the chapter about discovering your personality (Chapter 3). Make sure to keep all that you have learned about yourself in mind when developing your street smarts. Part of street smarts is knowing what is best for you and keeping away from what isn't. Because you know yourself, you are very capable of doing just that. For example, you may find what looks like a great job in a field that interests you. When you talk with someone there, however, you discover that you clash with that particular person. You wonder if the other employees behave similarly. Don't judge right away; explore further before you make any decisions. But it is important to trust your instincts. If you feel strongly that you would be unhappy, keep looking because something even better for you will come along.

When you have built a solid base of street smarts, put it to work when you eventually search for a job. If you have learned that a certain mode of dress is the way to go, set yourself up with a nice version of it. (Not necessarily new, just nice!) If you are interested in a certain company, try to meet someone influential there. If you discover that you and an employee went to the same school, use that information to start a conversation. Make yourself as noticeable and as desirable as possible, using your street smarts.

You can also use your street smarts to guide you away from situations that would make you unhappy or would not suit your personality and talents. If you end up taking a look at a trade, job, or company that for any reason turns you off, think it over before you put energy into applying and interviewing. Don't waste your time pursuing work that wouldn't be right for you.

Tracking Down Career Leads

How will you start to find jobs for which you could apply? Turn again to the tools you already have. Think about the resources and personal contacts available to you. Most of the same sources that helped you gather information about the working world and the trade you are interested in will have information about where to find available jobs. If you have worked or are working part-time now, you have already used some kind of resource to find that job, and you may want to use it again. Several additional resources beyond the ones we have already discussed include:

- Newspapers and magazines
- Employment agencies and commissions
- Bulletin boards
- The Internet

Newspapers and Magazines

There are two ways to find information about available jobs in newspapers and magazines. The first, and most obvious, is to read the Help Wanted listings in the classified advertising section. Many companies will post ads for specific positions they need to fill. You would respond with a phone call or a letter with resume attached, depending on the specifications mentioned in the ad.

Set aside plenty of time for looking through the Help Wanted sections. Sit down with a big empty pad and a pen. Mark ads that interest you, and jot down notes about them, taking special note of the people to call and their phone numbers. Then take your list and call to make inquiries. Weed out any positions that don't suit you, for whatever reason, and then pursue the others.

The other, less obvious, method for using newspapers and magazines to find a job involves reading between the lines. For instance, you may come across an article in the business section about a company that talks about how fast the company is growing. Hmmm . . . It stands to reason that growing companies need more employees. Do some digging for information about the company, and see if you can find out if there is a match between your skills and the skills they need.

The same process works if you read about a company that sounds a lot like the kind of company you'd most like to work for. You really like the kind of product or service that they provide. The leadership seems progressive and creative. The work environment is friendly. It seems to match many of the items on your priority list. So what would you do? Take some initiative. Make some phone calls, read more about the company, and find out all you can about the kinds of positions that will be available. Then use your street smarts to find a way to get your foot in the door for an interview!

Employment Agencies and Commissions

As a high school student, you may be able to find leads about jobs through your high school guidance counselor's office or, if your community has one, a youth employment service. Later, if you go on for advanced training at a community college, university, or vocational school, the school should have a placement office to help its graduates find jobs. The services at these types of offices should be free.

Once you've gained some experience and training, you might find the services of a professional employment agency helpful. Some of these agencies specialize in placing people with specific types of skills such as high-tech or medical expertise. Others provide temporary jobs at more entry-level positions. Although most agencies will only charge the companies that list openings, some may also charge you a fee for the information that they provide you. Check with individual agencies to find one that best meets your needs.

Employment commissions are state and city offices that can help you find job openings. To take advantage of their listings, you may have to take a test to evaluate your skill areas. Using the test results, they will give you an employment classification (administrative assistant, data entry operator) that will help them locate a position for you. Their services are free.

Bulletin Boards

When you can find them, bulletin boards will have all kinds of different job listings. Bulletin boards may appear in the following locations:

- Schools
- Neighborhood shopping centers
- Bus stops
- Community-oriented cafes or diners
- Career centers or offices of independent career counselors
- Libraries

Take time to go through the jumble of posters and leaflets, and you may find some good future job possibilities. And if, in the future, you are looking to move up within the company or agency that currently employs you, you may find a bulletin board in the personnel office or elsewhere that lists job openings and opportunities right there. Some companies may also provide job hotlines available by phone.

Food for Thought

Think about family businesses, people you know who work with friends or family, or even famous people who take advantage of a family connection. If someone in a position to hire already knows and likes you, it can work to your advantage. People like to hire other people that they know they can trust; as a friend or family member, you have already built a base of trust, respect, and affection. It makes sense that you would have a jump on the competition. Make the most of such a situation if it comes your way.

The Internet

Your generation has an edge over all the generations that have come before. It's the Internet, and it is fast becoming an incredible resource for information about careers in general and specific jobs in particular. Use a search engine to find information about a specific type of career or for online classified ads.

MAKING THE CONTACTS

After you establish your range of job possibilities, you would lay out your plan for pursuing them. Before you begin thinking about what you will say at your interview, you will need to make contact with the companies and earn the opportunity to be interviewed.

Think about your future job search. Organize your approach. Would you make three phone calls a day? Will you send out ten resumes a week for a month? Will your school set you up with contacts? However you eventually do it, keep a record of the following:

- People you contact
- Companies to which you apply or send resumes
- Jobs you rule out (jobs that become unavailable or don't suit you after all)
- Interviews—company names, contact people, dates, and times

Records such as these will enable you to easily chart your progress. You can record information in a specific notebook, on the computer, or on index cards. List everything that happens with each job possibility. Include names, addresses, and phone numbers that you will need to know. Even if something doesn't pan out right away, you never know what may happen; sometimes a company will have a different job opening a few months later, remember you, pull your number from the files, and call you to interview again.

Into the Job World

You now know how to combine a number of your skills to effectively prepare yourself for your future job search: your interpersonal skills for networking, your basic information skills for seeking and evaluating job market information, your basic skills (listening, writing, speaking, reading) for gathering advice, and your thinking skills for making smart decisions. When you clear your path in this manner, you will give yourself the best chance for a great opportunity. You will be ready to handle the search, the mailings, and the outcomes with style and grace. And you will stay confident throughout the process that you will eventually succeed.

Your Tool Kit at Work

Career Choices and Priorities

7.1

Imagine yourself a couple of years from now. Decide which of the following conditions and responsibilities you prefer. Your career compass—your intelligence, experience, and intuition all working together—will help you. Your compass will lead you toward the environment in which you will feel the most comfortable, and that is the place where you will do your best and most productive work.

Put your career compass to work by answering the following questions. They are a guide to discovering your most ideal working conditions and atmosphere. Try to see yourself in each different situation. Which ones feel right to you?

1. What size workplace do I prefer?
   _____ small (under 25 employees)
   _____ medium (up to 100 employees)
   _____ large (over 100 employees in one location)
   _____ Parent company (many locations)
   _____ Multinational

2. What environment is my favorite?
   _____ working indoors
   _____ working outdoors
   _____ traveling/field work
   _____ working at my home
   _____ a combination

3. What schedule(s) fits my lifestyle?
   _____ nine to five/conventional
   _____ flex-time
   _____ part-time
   _____ rotating shifts
   _____ evening shift
   _____ early morning start
   _____ independent contract (set own hours)

4. What kind of job structure do I prefer?
   _____ permanent position
   _____ temporary jobs
   _____ self-employed/entrepreneur
   _____ seasonal work

5. a. What are my favorite courses in school? _____

    b. What skills am I learning in these courses? _____

    c. What are my least favorite courses? _____

    d. What about these courses do I dislike? _____

    e. What are my favorite responsibilities in the jobs I've had? _____

    f. Based on my answers to a through e, what skills would I like to use the most in my career/job? _____

    _____

    _____

    g. What responsibilities would I like to be given? _____

    _____

    _____

6. I prefer my work to center around

    _____ a few tasks I perform well.

    _____ responsibilities that change from day to day.

    _____ meeting customers and clients.

    _____ very little personal contact.

    _____ new duties for which I'll receive training.

7. I would like my workplace to offer (check all that apply)

    _____ convenient location/less than one-half hour from home.

    _____ public transportation.

    _____ indoor parking.

    _____ parking close by.

    _____ attractive offices/well decorated with pleasing colors.

    _____ individual workstations.

    _____ individual offices.

    _____ windows/natural light.

    _____ up-to-date equipment.

    _____ state-of-the-art equipment.

    _____ environmental safety.

    _____ friendly, compatible co-workers.

    _____ cafeteria.

    _____ fitness center.

    _____ childcare facilities.

    _____ orderly, professional atmosphere.

    _____ casual, laid-back atmosphere.

    _____ other _____

8. How do I want to be paid?

——— hourly wage (may be higher but might involve fewer benefits)

——— yearly salary

——— weekly

——— biweekly

——— bimonthly

9. What benefits do I need and want? (Larger companies usually can afford to offer better benefits.)

——— educational/training opportunities

——— medical/dental insurance

——— life/disability insurance

——— paid vacation/holidays

——— maternity/paternity leave

——— personal day(s)

——— overtime pay

——— retirement plan

——— savings plan

No job will have every one of your preferred conditions. As with planning your to-do list or your budget, you need to set priorities. Go over your choices and give them an *A*, *B*, or *C* priority.

- *A* is for the essentials you need to have to be productive and successful.
- *B* is for the conditions that aren't quite as crucial but will make your job a special experience.
- *C* is for the extras that will be great if they are offered but aren't necessary for your job satisfaction.

As you prioritize, let your self-knowledge and your career compass be your guide.

Professional Pals—Looking for Faces in All the Right Places

7.2

Professional pals are the people who can help you find the right job. Be specific and include names of people you know in each group. Circle one pal in every category you will contact to talk about your future career plans. Write the name of the pal you will contact first.

People at your school

Anyone you know who works in your field of interest

Leads from placement office and/or newspaper

Supportive friends and relatives

I will contact: _____

For help in thinking of people who may not have occurred to you, fill in the first of the following two charts. Next to each person's name, write what you intend to ask that person to do for you; for example, answer questions about your career field, write a letter of recommendation, or act as one of your references on your resume or application.

Person	Name	What I Will Ask
Former employers		
Former coworkers		
Present employer		
Present coworkers		
Friends		
Relatives		
Religious group members		
Union members you know		
Counselors		
Teachers		
Clergy		
Neighbors		
Classmates		
Attorneys		
Members of community (police, small business owners)		

As you receive all this advice and help, why not think about how you can help others? Remember, what goes around comes around! Think of a few friends or family members who could benefit from your knowledge or connections, and write in the next chart their names and what you could do for them. Maybe you could provide information about your school contacts that may bring job opportunities. You will remember those who help you along your path to success—and likewise, those you help will remember you, and they may be able to return the favor someday.

Who I May Be Able to Help	What I Have to Offer
1.	
2.	
3.	
4.	
5.	

What Am I Going to Say?

7.3

You wrote down the name of the pal you're going to contact first. Before you do anything, think about what you said you were planning to ask. Different people can help you in different ways. What can this one give you to aid in your job search? Check one or more.

_____ Information on a job or career

_____ Connections to people who may have jobs available

_____ Advice on job-hunting strategies, resumes, and/or interviews

_____ Moral support and life-planning help

Eventually, you will make that first phone call. If the person doesn't know you, introduce yourself by stating your name, how you heard about the person, what subjects you're studying, when you'll graduate, and what part-time job experience you have. If the person is acquainted with you, you can be brief.

Write your introductory information here.

_____

_____

_____

State the purpose of your call. Tell the person what information you seek and politely ask what might be a convenient time to meet so that you can talk in detail about this information.

Purpose _____

Describe how you will ask for a meeting _____

_____

Go from there. Most pals are flattered by the request to share their expertise. Unless their schedules are full, you will get a yes. Remember to arrive a few minutes early. Give the pal the same courtesy you will give interviewers. After all, this person may turn out to be a prospective employer.

What do you say at the meeting? In a small notebook, write specific questions, and leave plenty of space between them to scribble the information that you receive. Take the notebook and a pen to the meeting. This is a situation, unlike the interview, where you can read your questions from the notebook and write the answers as you hear them. Use the questions from the Networking section of this chapter as a guide.

Look at the A and B priorities you listed when focusing your career compass. Based on those priorities, define and list here the questions you will ask.

1. _____

_____

2. _____

3. _____

4. _____

5. _____

6. _____

Write your pal a thank-you note within twenty-four hours, just as you would do after an interview. Get ready for an interview by practicing now.

7.4 Looking for Jobs in All the Right Places

As you look for job search advisors in all the right places, you will need to do the same with job opportunities. A job search plan will set you on the right path. Plot your job plan right now while you have time left in your school program.
    Complete these sentences.

During the time remaining in school, I will concentrate on the following skills:

_____

_____

I will make an appointment at the school guidance office by _____ (date).

I will read the employment section every Sunday to get specific information about jobs. From those ads, I want to learn: _____

_____

_____

I will talk to my pal by _____ (date).

I will talk to two other pals, _____ and _____, by _____ (date).

I will ask two pals, _____ and _____, about job opportunities in their companies by _____ (date).

I will go to the library and find _____ books, _____ journals, or _____ trade publications in the field I am interested in by _____ (date).

I will read those materials by _____ (date).

Plug Your Knowledge Into Real Life

7.5

Popular street smarts say, "It's not what you know; it's who you know." Your career compass street smarts, based on your intelligence, experience, and intuition, will tell you that it's both who and what you know. You may find out, possibly the hard way, that you will need a wide variety of skills to get the career you want. So did Rosie, but then she forgot her compass. See what you can suggest to get her back on track:

Rosie enrolled in the two-year electronics program at Taylor Tech. The first month she attended every day and earned mostly A's on her assignments and quizzes. But Rosie and her husband had been having problems for a while, and he decided to move out. Rosie, without his income to help with the bills, had to find a job. Her attendance and her grades dropped. She didn't tell her family about her predicament. Her friends weren't aware of the situation or her troubled state of mind. She didn't talk with her teachers at Taylor. After three months of trying to help her through offers of tutoring and counseling, Rosie's advisor at Taylor asked her to leave. She became angry and yelled at the administrators.

When she went out to look for a job in the electronics field, she discovered that she wasn't qualified. Rosie wants to go back to Taylor, but she is afraid to call because of the scene she created.

What advice do you have for Rosie? How can she use some street smarts to balance her life and get back in good graces at Taylor? As you think about your answer, consider how Rosie might use the following tools:

- Understanding social and organizational (school and company) systems
- Communicating thoughts effectively
- Problem solving and decision making
- Integrity and honesty
- Responsibility and commitment
- Self-knowledge and self-esteem

_____

_____

_____

_____

_____

_____

_____

_____

_____

_____

If she does succeed in reentering the school, what kinds of opportunities will she have given herself for tracking down job leads?

_____

_____

_____

_____

_____

Based on some of the ideas you explored for Rosie, which part of this advice can you give to yourself? Employers hire people who are flexible, are responsible, have excellent attendance and good grades, learn technical knowledge in school, and communicate well with peers at all levels of authority. Rosie didn't exhibit these credentials at first. Employers do consider improvement, however, so it's not too late for Rosie. You are in a good position. You are still a student and have the opportunity to make immediate improvements in a supportive atmosphere. What will you do differently in the time you have left in school that will show employers you know how to improve?

What advice do you have for yourself?

_____

_____

_____

_____

_____

_____

_____

7.6 Take New Tools on the Road

Look over the New In Your Tool Kit list at the beginning of this chapter. Choose and write the three most important tools you gained from reading this chapter.

1. _____

2. _____

3. _____

For each of the tools you listed, write one example of how you will apply that tool to achieve success in your future career. Include changes you plan to make as well as how you will continue or reinforce existing behavior.

1. _____

   _____

   _____

2. _____

   _____

   _____

3. _____

   _____

   _____

8 Putting Your Tools to Good Use

ENTERING THE WORKING WORLD

NEW
IN YOUR TOOL KIT

Filling out
 applications

Putting together
 resumes

Writing a cover letter

Researching
 companies

Dressing for the
 interview

Interview techniques

Following up

You have thought, talked, studied, prepared. You have explored your inner self and your outside world, looking for the options that will fit you the best. Eventually, it will be time to get out there and do it. If you do something that you enjoy, that you do well, and that even inspires you to learn more and grow, then your exploring or doing will be meaningful . . . and as Jean de La Fontaine wrote, your work will reflect this meaning.

You won't have much trouble telling when the time comes to take your tool kit on the road. Perhaps your courses end soon, or if you have been working toward a certificate or diploma, you will graduate soon. Maybe you've decided to work during the summer instead of taking classes. Maybe you'll need to work to help pay your way through college. Or maybe you are just tucking away all these skills for later use. All kinds of deadlines may come up. Recognize yours, and dive into the job search when the time is right for you.

Food for Thought

Throwing together your materials and interview clothing in a rush would be like a runner ambling up to the starting block and taking off with a casual stroll. With the lunge and crouch before the start, a runner can coil his energy and release it in the all-out burst that makes a winning race possible. Without that preparation, a clean start won't happen, the runner's energy will scatter and weaken, and potential will fade into the dust of the road. But if you prepare yourself, you will make a fast and focused exit from the gate.

Get ready, get set—but don't go until you have created and pulled together all your tools. Prepare yourself adequately for this future task by taking time to package yourself professionally. Create a neat, complete, and professional-looking resume and application. Clarify your prior employment record, if you have one, so that it will speak well of you. Establish reliable references. Become fluent in interview etiquette, from what you will wear to what you will say. And learn the secrets of handling failure and success. Give yourself the best possible opportunity to succeed by using all the skills you have mastered.

You will soon have a new beginning in your life—a chance to start fresh and pursue your goals in earnest. Each step of preparation, if done well, takes a fair amount of time, as shown in Figure 8.1. Plan ahead, and spend as much time as you need to get it right. The standard you set for yourself will determine the pace that you move ahead in the workplace. It will also determine the opinions others will form of you. Now is your chance to shine!

FIGURE 8.1

Getting that interview!

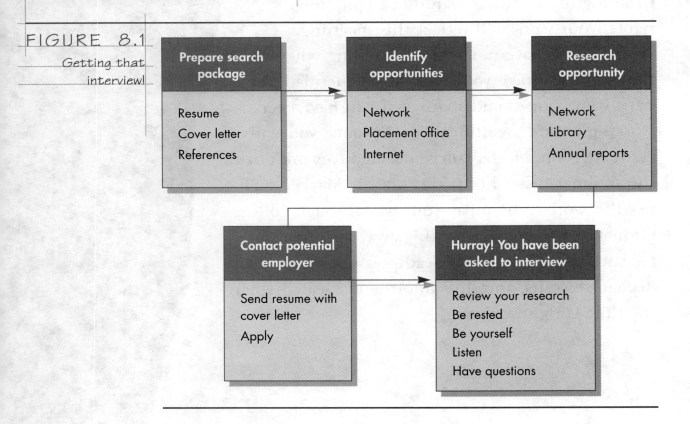

Prepare search package
- Resume
- Cover letter
- References

Identify opportunities
- Network
- Placement office
- Internet

Research opportunity
- Network
- Library
- Annual reports

Contact potential employer
- Send resume with cover letter
- Apply

Hurray! You have been asked to interview
- Review your research
- Be rested
- Be yourself
- Listen
- Have questions

Resumes

The purpose of a resume is to get an interview. Most employers will require a resume, so you will need to have one ready to submit with your application. When you write a resume, condense your information onto one page, which should be easy if you are just beginning your work life. Take a look at the sample chronological resumes in Figures 8.2 and 8.3. These styles are proper, although other acceptable variations exist. Consider the following guidelines for putting a resume together, which are for a resume in standard chronological order.

BE NEAT, CLEAN, AND CONCISE. Resumes must be typed. Try to fit everything onto one page. Many employers won't have time to read two pages; you also risk the danger of your pages becoming separated. If you have too much information, evaluate it and prioritize. Knock off the least important pieces. Remember, this is a summary of your major accomplishments, not a chronicle of your life's story!

USE STANDARD FORM. Refer to the sample resume (see Figure 8.2). A standard resume has the following features:

- Name, address, phone number, and e-mail address (if available)
- Applicable work skills
- Work experience (company name, job title, and duties performed)
- Education experience (from high school on)
- Awards or honors that further illustrate your positive attributes
- "References available upon request"

USE NICE PAPER. You don't need fancy paper, just clean, neat paper with a little weight to it in a white, off-white, or light gray. Photocopying service centers or printers will tell you which papers work well for resumes. Remember, the resume will say something about you before you ever get anywhere near the company. Appearances count, and not only in how you dress! The appearance of anything representing you will also say something about you. You will want your resume to make a good impression.

BE ACCURATE. Pay attention to details when you compile your resume. Check your educational facts and dates. Make sure you have the right years and

Food for Thought

Let's say you have worked part-time in the past with an auto technician and an electrician. Put both on your resume, but adjust your cover letter depending on the kind of job for which you apply. If you apply for a job in the electrical field, mention your employment with the electrician in the cover letter. If you seek something in auto repair, emphasize the assistant mechanic job you held. Your prospective employer wants to see immediately what qualifications you have that will make you the right person for the job. Help out by making the most important items perfectly clear in your cover letter.

FIGURE 8.2 Sample chronological resume.

THOMAS M. ZETLMEISEL

4757 Cragsmoor Court #9E
Tucson, AZ 85719

602/555-8055
tzetlmeisel@earthlink.net

OBJECTIVE:	Seeking a position that utilizes my new and updated skills as a computer operator.
SKILLS:	Word; Excel; dBase; Data entry; Windows; Typing, certified 58 wpm.

EXPERIENCE:

Wolfe Industries, Tucson, AZ
Inventory Control Clerk, February 1999 to present.
–Enter inventory data into computer system
–Enter new items into warehouse locations; enter locations onto database
–Update database and eliminate out-of-date items
–Receive returned items and place them back into inventory

TGIFriday's Restaurant, Tucson, AZ
Manager, September 1998 to January 1999.
–Interviewed, hired, and evaluated employees
–Managed activity on the restaurant floor
–Coordinated employee scheduling

TUSD Summer High School
Assistant Secretary, summer 1998.
–Entered student and class data onto database
–Provided class lists and schedules from database
–Maintained and updated class schedules

TUSD Summer High School
Intern, summer 1997.
–Organized files and made photocopies
–Assisted the secretary with telephones and distribution of materials to teachers

EDUCATION:

Killingworth Business School, Tucson, AZ
Microcomputer Software Operations Program
Graduation November 2000

HONORS:

Killingworth Business School
Dean's List
Perfect Attendance Certificates
Student Representative

REFERENCES AVAILABLE UPON REQUEST

MORGAN L. ASHLEY

237 Smith St., Fort Collins, CO 80527   (970) 555-3975 • morganash@mailto.com

OBJECTIVE: Seeking challenging employment that combines skills in graphic design, computer user interface, and software development, with opportunities for future advancement.

SKILLS: AutoCAD; Gif Animation; HTML 3.0; JAVA; JavaScript; PageMaker; Quark; Strata Studio Pro; Typing, certified 70 wpm.

EXPERIENCE: **Neotech,** Fort Collins, CO
Lead Designer/Project Director, August 1999 to December 1999
- Directed project, including graphic interface and design, site architecture, animation, and HTML

World Design, Austin, TX
Intern, Summer 1998
- Worked with clients to develop graphic design and information structure of corporate Internet Websites
- Used HTML 3.0, Photoshop, Illustrator, JAVA, and image mapping

Office Max, Fort Collins, CO
Electronics Sales Manager, June 1995 to August 1996
- Managed activity in electronics department
- Assisted customers with personal computer purchases
- Answered questions and supplied information about computers

EDUCATION: **Colorado State University,** Fort Collins, CO
Degree in Bachelor of Arts, Graphic Design
Graduation May 1999
- course concentration in Computer Science, Computer Programming, Calculus, Technical Writing, and Painting

Rocky Mountain High School, Fort Collins, CO
Diploma May 1995

HONORS: Colorado State University
- Dean's Recognition of Outstanding Students, April 1999
- WebAward for most advanced web site design, December 1998

REFERENCES AVAILABLE UPON REQUEST

Food for Thought

Why is a cover letter named a cover letter? So your resume will not be naked. Don't send a naked resume to an employer. Always cover your resume with a letter. Don't miss an opportunity to tell a prospective employer your interest in the company as well as to emphasize a relevant skill or key qualification.

months for when you held different jobs. Accurately report your duties and accomplishments at those jobs. As with a job application, any untruths or inaccuracies can surface and cause you trouble. Should your prospective employer call a former supervisor of yours, you want that former supervisor to confirm everything that you wrote.

PROOFREAD. After you have finished and feel comfortable about the accuracy of your resume, activate your proofreading skills. Check carefully for mistakes, spelling problems, inconsistent spacing, or strange sentences. A picture-perfect resume will show that you care about how you present yourself, that you take time to do the job right, and that you take pride in your work. Conversely, a misspelled word on your resume could eliminate you from consideration. To be safe, have someone else proofread as well.

INCLUDE A COVER LETTER. Even though your resume describes you, it doesn't directly address the person who will read it. A cover letter will give you the chance to introduce yourself more personally and warm the cold facts of the resume. You don't need to write more than a couple of short paragraphs. Use nice paper and type the letter, making sure to sign it afterward. See our sample cover letter in Figure 8.4 to get you started. Use a basic three-paragraph structure as follows:

- In the first paragraph, identify what kind of job you seek, what has led you to become qualified, and how you came to find out about the job (newspaper listing, personal reference, school referral).

- In the second paragraph, talk about why you want the job and explain in more detail what you have to offer (specific skills and experiences). It can be hard to decide exactly what to talk about because you want to be brief. Think about yourself. What would you want a prospective employer to know first about your skills and qualities? What seems to fit best with the requirements of this specific job? Choose facts that can make the reader want to continue on to your resume.

- In the third paragraph, mention any enclosure, express your desire for an interview, and politely request a response.

Applications

Many employers, even if they require a resume, will ask you to fill out a standard application. An application provides factual information about you that will help employers determine whether you will fit their needs. Ask the

THOMAS M. ZETLMEISEL

4757 Cragsmoor Court #9E
Tucson, AZ 85719

520/555-8055
tzetlmeisel@earthlink.net

Ms. Melinda Mayotte
Personnel Director
Tassian Communications, Inc.
93 Avery Drive Suite #800
Tucson, AZ 85719

5 October 2000

Dear Ms. Mayotte:

I am a student of computer operations at the Killingworth Business School and will be graduating next month. I made the decision some time ago to pursue a career in computers and am looking forward to a full-time position in this field. I found out about your job opening from a notice posted here at the school's placement office.

I am interested in speaking with you regarding this job because I have spent the past nine months perfecting the same skills that the notice indicates you require. Also during that time, I have worked part time as a computer operator at Wolfe Industries where I have received valuable hands-on information and experience. I am currently still employed part time at Wolfe. Furthermore, I have a particular interest in your company because a neighbor of mine who is employed there has given consistent good reviews about the atmosphere and personnel.

Enclosed is my resume, which details my work experience and my education. If you would like to interview me in person, I can be reached at 520/555-8055. If I don't hear from you by 31 October, I will call you. Thank you for your kind consideration, and I look forward to hearing from you soon.

Best regards,

Thomas M. Zetlmeisel

employer to mail you one; if you live or work nearby, you can probably pick one up. Here is some advice for you when you fill out your application.

BE LEGIBLE. Whether you type your application or write it, your prospective employer must be able to read it! No one can begin to consider you for a job if your application is unclear. If you type, make sure that you have set your typewriter so that it types on the lines and in the boxes. If you don't have access to a typewriter or don't like to type, make sure you print clearly and neatly. Printing is usually easier to read than cursive.

BE COMPLETE. Applications can sometimes be long and involved. Even if you think you've filled out everything, you might have missed a section, box, line, or signature. Give yourself time to fill it out slowly, and then go back and proofread your work. Make sure that every part designated for you to fill out has been completed. Sometimes a section will stump you—you won't know how to complete it, or you won't know if you have anything to write. Ask a teacher or counselor for help. You may want to call someone at the company and ask for clarification.

BE HONEST. Applications may ask questions about your education, previous employment, and even criminal convictions. Honesty is definitely the best policy. Messing around with the truth will come back to haunt you. Employers can verify any of the information you will give them, and they often do (for their own protection). They want to make sure they're hiring a person of integrity. Even if something in your past wouldn't look good on an application, an employer would rather hear it from you than from an outside source. Lying on an application can disqualify you from a hiring pool immediately. Honesty just might keep you there, despite any questionable history.

BE QUICK. When many people apply for a job, the ones who return their applications promptly have a better chance of getting an interview. Make completing the application a priority! The more quickly you can complete and return your application, the sooner the employer can consider it and give you an answer either way. If you eventually get an interview, your speed may have put you ahead of a number of other applicants. If you don't get an interview, you can move on to other job applications without wasting any more time. See Figure 8.5 for a look at a sample application.

Your Prior Employment Record

Those of you who have no previous employment truly start with a clean slate! That has good points and bad points. To your benefit, you have no black marks to discredit you to potential employers to whom you submit applications—no firings, bad references, or difficult experiences to discuss. On the other hand, you also have no proof of your value as an employee—no recom-

FIGURE 8.5

Sample application for employment.

APPLICATION FOR EMPLOYMENT
(PRE-EMPLOYMENT QUESTIONNAIRE)   (AN EQUAL OPPORTUNITY EMPLOYER)

Personal Information

Date _____

Name _____ Soc. Sec. # _____
Last   First   Middle

Present Address _____
Street   City   State

Permanent Address _____
Street   City   State

Phone No. _____ Are You 18 Years Or Older ☐ Yes ☐ No

SPECIAL QUESTIONS

Do not answer **any** of the questions in this framed area unless the employer has **checked** a box **preceding** a question, thereby indicating that the information is required for a bona fide occupational qualification, or dictated by national security laws, or is needed for other legally permissible reasons.

☐ Height _____ feet _____ inches   ☐ Citizen of U.S. Yes _____ No _____

☐ Weight _____ lbs.   ☐ Date of Birth* _____

☐ What Foreign Languages do you speak fluently? _____ Read _____ Write _____

☐ _____

* The Age Discrimination in Employment Act of 1967 prohibits discrimination on the basis of age with respect to individuals who are at least 40 but less than 70 years of age.

EMPLOYMENT DESIRED

Position _____   Date You Can Start _____   Salary Desired _____

Are You Employed Now? _____   If So May We Inquire Of Your Present Employer? _____

Ever Applied To This Company Before? _____ Where? _____ When? _____

EDUCATION	Name and Location of School	*No. of Years Attended	*Did You Graduate?	Subjects Studied
Grammar School				
High School				
College				
Trade, Business or Correspondence School				

* The Age Discrimination in Employment Act of 1967 prohibits discrimination on the basis of age with respect to individuals who are at least 4 but less than 70 years of age.

GENERAL

Subject of Special Study or Research Work _____

U.S. Military or Naval Service _____   Present Membership in National Guard or Reserves _____

77 105   (continued on other side)

---

mendations from supervisors, list of duties and accomplishments, awards, or promotions to present. You have only the raw good, which is yourself, so concentrate on putting your "package" in the best shape possible.

What kind of experience will you describe to a potential employer if you have had no formal job? You probably have learned skills from various situations in your life that did not involve being employed per se. Those skills can have as much value as skills learned on the job. What kinds of situations will give you marketable qualifications? Following are some examples:

FIGURE 8.5
Continued

FORMER EMPLOYERS (List below last four employers, starting with last one first).

Date Month & Year	Name and Address of Employer	Salary	Position	Reason for Leaving
From To				
From To				
From To				
From To				

REFERENCES Give the names of three persons not related to you, whom you have known at least one year.

	Name	Address	Business	Years Acquainted
1				
2				
3				

PHYSICAL RECORD
Do you have any physical limitations that preclude you from performing any work for which you are being considered? ☐ Yes ☐ No

Please Describe _____

In Case Of
Emergency Notify _____
　　　　　　　　　　Name　　　　　　　Address　　　　　　Phone No.

"I certify that the facts contained in this application are true and complete to the best of my knowledge and understand that, if employed, falsified statements on this application shall be grounds for dismissal.

I authorize investigation of all statements contained herein and the references listed above to give you any and all information concerning my previous employment and any pertinent information they may have, personal or otherwise, and release all parties from all liability for any damage that may result from furnishing same to you.

I understand and agree that, if hired, my employment is for no definite period and may, regardless of the date of payment of my wages and salary, be terminated at any time without prior notice."

Date _____ Signature _____

Do Not Write Below This Line

_____ Date _____

_____

_____

Hired: ☐ Yes ☐ No _____ Position _____ Dept. _____

Salary/Wage _____ Date reporting to work _____

Approved: 1. _____ 2. _____ 3. _____
　　　　　　Employment Manager　　　Dept. Head　　　General Manager

This form has been designed to strictly comply with State and Federal fair employment practice laws prohibiting employment discrimination. This Application for Employment Form is sold for general use throughout the United States. Gussco assumes no responsibility for the inclusion and said form of any questions which, when asked by the Employer of the Job Applicant, may violate State and/or Federal Law.

77 105

- Helping out a friend or family member at work —doing work similar to that of an intern position
- Taking on special responsibilities at school —heading up a committee, organizing any gathering or group effort, acting as a teacher liaison or aide
- Long-term child care —taking care of a child (your niece or little brother, for example) during the day on a fairly regular basis
- Volunteer work —spending time tutoring young emotionally disturbed children

■ Special duties at home—taking care of the bills each month and budgeting

What other experiences have helped you develop valuable skills and personal qualities? Brainstorm for a while, and you may think of more examples when your life experience has given you qualifications a potential employer desires.

What qualities and specific skills would the above-mentioned experiences show that you have?

■ **Working at a friend's or family's business without pay shows dedication and loyalty.** Did you take phone calls? You communicate well and have good telephone skills. Did you help re-sort and clean up files or equipment? You may be skilled at organizing data and company assets. Did you take in money, count money, or keep the books? You might be a whiz at money management, records, and accounts.

■ **Performing special duties at school shows responsibility, dedication, dependability, and energy.** Were you a representative for your class at school, administration, or alumni meetings? You show leadership qualities and skill in working with others. Were you a teacher's aide? You may be good at taking initiative, cooperating, and listening.

■ **Child care shows responsibility, flexibility, and a caring nature.** Did you care for children who have schedules full of school, sports practices, play dates, and other appointments? You have good time management skills. Did you care for a baby? You probably have a good working knowledge of basic first aid and medical care. Did you care for more than one child at a time? You may be especially efficient and capable of handling multiple tasks.

■ **Volunteer work shows caring, values, and good time management skills.** Sometimes it's hard to fit volunteering into a busy day! Did you help out at a center for children who are emotionally disturbed? You may have a talent for creative thinking and decision making, as you might never know what might happen next. Did you spend time socializing with residents at a home for the elderly? You may have a solid command of social systems, communication, and listening. Did you help to rebuild and repaint a dilapidated school? You show command of the equipment and technology you used as well as a good sense of cooperation and self-management.

■ **Helping out at home with budgeting and planning shows many skills.** You may know a lot about organizing and evaluating information as well as maintaining a budget.

When you have evaluated your nonprofessional experiences and named the skills that you developed, how will you organize and present this information to a prospective employer? You could use a form called a skill-based resume. Unlike a chronological resume, this form does not list jobs and their respective duties; rather, it focuses on your skills, grouping specific duties and skills under general headings. You could also include skills you have developed in classes under your headings.

This form is not only for those of you who have no job experience. Anyone who wants to emphasize skills over specific job experience may use it, although the chronological form is the most universally recognized and accepted. You can even have a resume in combination form, in which one part lists your skills in the skill-based form and another part lists your jobs in the chronological form. Figure 8.6 is an example of how Thomas Zetlmeisel might construct a combination resume.

As you build your skill-based resume, think back to the SCANS list of skills in Chapter 1. Remember that these are the skills most crucial to your future success in the workplace. Looking at the categories and their specific items can help you define how your skills will be marketable. Choose skills that you feel would have value in the workplace, and word them in such a way that they reflect your command of the SCANS skills. Here are examples of headings you might use in your skill-based resume (you can see how some of them are used as you look at the top half of the sample resume in Figure 8.6):

- Planning
- Problem solving
- Writing
- Reading
- Communicating
- Using information processing
- Managing
- Organizing
- Evaluating

Remember, your resume is only part of how you will sell your "package." You will have other ways of emphasizing your marketability. To supplement a skill-based resume, you could talk to your prospective employer about your skills during the interview. You should also emphasize them in a cover letter that will be sent with your resume or application. For example:

> Dear X:
>
> I have had a lifelong interest in health care, and my health care administration certificate from Y School reflects this interest. I have had substantial experience working at several doctor's offices to help pay for my schooling; in addition, I have worked as a volunteer at Z Hospital. My responsibilities were [describe them here]. I feel that the skills I acquired from these experiences give me additional qualifications for the office administrative position at your medical clinic.

You have already read about how to detail your prior work experience on a resume, and how to highlight the experience that best relates to the particular job for which you write that letter. A few more thoughts about how to evaluate, organize, and prioritize that information are provided here:

THOMAS M. ZETLMEISEL

4757 Cragsmoor Court #9E
Tucson, AZ 85719

520/555-8055
tzetlmeisel@aol.com

OBJECTIVE: Seeking a position that utilizes my new and updated skills as a computer operator.

SKILLS: **Technology**—WordPerfect; Lotus; dBase; Data entry; Windows; Typing, certified 58 wpm.

Management—Interviewed, hired, and evaluated employees; handled operations on restaurant floor.

Information processing—Entered warehouse locations into database and inventory items into locations; updated database and eliminated out-of-date items; entered student and class data onto school database; maintained and updated class schedules.

Organization—Kept files and made photocopies; organized and distributed materials to teachers; coordinated restaurant employee schedules.

Communication—Handled telephone calls, both incoming and outgoing; reported to teachers as student representative to the school administration.

EXPERIENCE: *Wolfe Industries,* Tucson, AZ. Inventory Control Clerk, February 1999 to present.

TGIFriday's Restaurant, Tucson, AZ. Manager, September 1998 to January 1999.

TUSD Summer High School. Assistant Secretary, summer 1998.

TUSD Summer High School. Intern, summer 1997.

EDUCATION: *Killingworth Business School,* Tucson, AZ
Microcomputer Software Operations Program, Graduation November 2000
Dean's List, Perfect Attendance Certificates, Student Representative

Magruder High School, Tucson, AZ
Diploma May 1997
Honor Roll, FBLA Vice-President, Varsity Letter

REFERENCES AVAILABLE UPON REQUEST

BE SELECTIVE IF NECESSARY. If you have had many assorted jobs—too many to include on your resume—list only the ones that gave you the most responsibility and the ones that will relate to your future career path. A very important job at which you held a respectable position, even if it doesn't seem to fit the kind of job you now want, shows personal qualities that apply to any line of work.

BE PREPARED. You should be able to talk honestly about any job that you list on a resume or an application. By listing it, you indicate to any prospective employer that you agree to reveal details about your experience at that job. If you don't offer enough information, anyone considering you for a job can simply contact your previous employer. You don't have to volunteer any information, but if the question arises, answer it. If you were fired, be honest about it; explain the situation clearly. If you feel you made mistakes, talk about what you learned from them. If you feel you were wrongly dismissed, take a moment to calmly justify your side of the story.

BE TACTFUL. Never bad-mouth a former employer, fellow employee, or place of employment. If you have negative feelings, don't go into detail about them. If you spend time in an interview talking about what a nightmare you had at that other job, your interviewer might wonder what you would say about this job in the future. Plus, you never know when your interviewer might have a close or friendly connection with someone you dislike! Play it safe—if you can't say something nice, hold back.

Your prior employment record is part of you. Learn from the good parts and the bad parts. Present the best of what you learned to the people you hope will hire you!

References

Most job applications will require you to list at least references the prospective employer can call or write to ask questions about you. In addition to their names, you may need to provide addresses and telephone numbers. You may also have to indicate your relationship with that person (former supervisor, former teacher, present coworker, etc.). Your resume, of course, will say that you can provide details about your references if someone requests them.

An interviewer may ask you about your references. Don't refer to them unless you are asked for more information. Most prospective employers will contact your references in the interest of their company. Employers don't want to make hiring mistakes. To stay on the safe side, assume that anyone you list or discuss will be contacted.

Follow these four steps as you consider candidates for references.

FIRST, THINK OF PEOPLE WHO WILL DESCRIBE YOU FAVORABLY. They don't have to be the highest-ranking folks you know. Perhaps the people with the most impressive titles at your former jobs—manager, director—don't know you well enough to discuss you. If they do, great! Include them. If not, someone who knows you better will do more good than a person with a big title who has no opinion of you.

SECOND, THINK OF PEOPLE WHO WOULD BE ABLE TO TALK ABOUT YOUR SKILLS AND YOUR INTEGRITY. Include as many professional references as possible. Even though your father and your cousin may have a high opinion of you, they might not know any specifics about your job qualifications or other special abilities that will make you marketable, and their opinions would be perceived as biased.

THIRD, ASK PEOPLE FOR PERMISSION TO USE THEM AS REFERENCES! Someone who receives a surprise phone call may not feel prepared to talk about you or might not say what you would like to have said about you. Sometimes when people agree to act as references, they will ask you what qualities you would prefer them to emphasize if they receive a phone call. Know in advance what you want to focus on, and have an answer to that question if it arises.

FOURTH, DOUBLE-CHECK THE CONTACT INFORMATION FOR EACH REFERENCE. You can easily do this when you call to ask about a person acting as a reference. Verify the spelling of each name, and make sure you have correct addresses and phone numbers. Have a few more names ready if you have to go into a second interview!

Interviews

Although your resume can attract the attention of your potential employer, it is the interview that will really give you the chance to open the door to career success. All jobs will require an interview. Even when you are being considered for a promotion or a different job within the same company later on, you will have to interview with your potential supervisor.

If your application or resume goes over well with any of the companies to which it was sent, someone will ask you in for an appointment. Follow these tips when you schedule the interview:

- Ask the person who calls you for the name and position of the interviewer, the exact address and office location, and the expected duration of the interview.
- Schedule the interview when you know you can make it on time comfortably (and stay for a while) without throwing the rest of your life (school, sports, job) into a tailspin.

- Ask the caller for detailed directions to the interview location if you have never been there before. Ask for public transportation information if you need it.

- Write the date and time where you will notice it—on your calendar, on a bulletin board, in your date book, on a note pasted to your bathroom mirror, or whatever works. Write the name of your contact person and the phone number next to the time and date, in case you need to reach that person for any reason.

RESEARCH ABOUT THE EMPLOYER

It's smart to know about the company before you interview. If you have done research and can ask knowledgeable questions about people, structure, activities, money, and your role in the company, your interviewer will take notice. Your effort will display intelligence, resourcefulness, and diligence. Plus, you will benefit more from the interview because you know more of the basics and will be able to go into depth.

A number of different sources potentially hold information for you when you set out to research a company. Seek out one or more of the following until you feel like you have the information that you need.

THE PERSONNEL DEPARTMENT OF THE COMPANY. People who supervise interviewing and hiring know that potential employees will be looking for information. They may be able to answer your questions or send information regarding company structure, activity, size, and scope.

PEOPLE YOU KNOW WHO WORK THERE. Talk to any friends, family, or fellow students you know who currently are employed by the company. They will have more insider information regarding salary potential, how people get along at the company, what the power hierarchy is like, and what the rules and regulations are.

THE COMPANY'S INTERNET WEB SITE. More and more companies are doing business on the Web these days. There's a good chance you'll find up-to-the-minute information about the company by using a search engine to find the company's Web site and any other related information.

ANNUAL REPORTS. You can request these from any publicly held company (any company traded on the stock exchange). They contain the basic facts about the company and offer details about how well it did in its last fiscal year.

LIBRARY. Annual reports can be found here. Your library may also have access to newspaper articles or periodicals about the company. Check the business directories such as *Standard & Poor's* for basic data such as address, size, income, and profit.

THE BETTER BUSINESS BUREAU. It will be able to tell you the company's legal track record and can inform you of any violations, investigations, or claims of bad business practices.

THE DAY OF YOUR INTERVIEW

You have worked hard to develop your skills and to get this interview. What should be your primary goal on your future interview day? To be there! Strangely enough, people often neglect to show up for their interview appointments. Keep in mind that this is your chance to show off, get a start in your career, and begin a new life. You can't even start to take advantage of a job opportunity unless you appear in person to show that you deserve it. So be there, and let your interviewer know that you mean to make something of your life.

You can do yourself two favors to help yourself out when your interview day comes. First, allow more than enough time to get where you need to go. You never know what may happen—traffic, late train, car breakdown. Unexpected delays can take up valuable time. If you plan ahead and give yourself extra time, you will be ready to handle whatever difficulties may come your way.

Second, look your best. The fact is, what you look like enters a person's mind before you speak a word. Appearance has more impact on a first impression than any other factor. So pay close attention to how you look. You never get a second chance to make a first impression! Your appearance matters in the working world, especially when you interview for a job.

For better or worse, an interviewer will make as many as ten judgments about you in the first forty seconds of your meeting, based on your appearance when you walk in the door. With only a glance, the interviewer will decide such things as:

- Your trustworthiness
- Your sophistication
- Your social position
- Your economic status
- Your educational level
- Your moral characteristics

> ## Food for Thought
>
> Prepare for your future interview. Think about the questions you might be asked and answer them aloud in front of a mirror. Evaluate your answers and delivery. Are you using the information on your resume, in your cover letter, and from your research of the job opportunity? As the saying goes, "practice makes perfect."

Perhaps people shouldn't make such snap judgments. They don't know you yet, of course, and they have very little information on which to base such decisions about your character and background. But this is the real world, and truthfully, people judge each other almost instantly and with little to no information most of the time. Your best defense will be to walk in with an appearance that says you have confidence and style, at least enough to encourage the interviewer's quick judgments to be positive ones!

Consider your own experience. What happens when you meet someone for the first time? Even before you have spoken with the person for more than two minutes, you have formed an opinion about that person based on dress, speech patterns, degree of eye contact, body language, and grooming. Making those kinds of quick judgments is human, but be sure you realize that such a fast evaluation may not be accurate. Leave room to change your opinion as you become better acquainted with this person. Although you can hope that your interviewers will be the kind of people who leave room for you to improve upon a first impression, the better choice is to look terrific from the start; that way, you won't have to worry.

A neat, clean, healthy appearance will tell an employer that you care about yourself, that you know how to take care of your health and appearance, and that you understand that looking good makes a difference on the job. It also makes a difference because it tells customers and clients, subtly, that you will care about their needs as you care about your own.

Make sure your clothes are clean and neat. Stick with something relatively neutral in color and style. You want your interviewer to focus on the real you, not on an outrageous outfit or on something else that you are wearing.

If you get an interview for an office job, dress in office attire. Females should wear a dress or business suit. Males should wear a suit with tie, jacket, and slacks (nice shoes, too). For other jobs, more informal (but attractive, neat, and clean) clothing may work, although interview attire should always be more on the formal side. Even if you would dress in a uniform and get dirty on this job, wear something nice for the interview so that you make a good impression. Styles and degrees of formality also differ in different parts of the country. Use your street smarts to do a little research, and find out what makes the grade in your area (ask people you know in the workplace). Something that is proper in Chicago might make you look overdressed in Boise. Play the game—wear what they want to see!

THE INTERVIEW ITSELF

You look nice, you arrive comfortably early, and you have with you a pen and a pad of paper to make any notes that you will need. You have brought a copy of your cover letter and resume so that you can review the key points you want to make in the interview. You also have something fun to read just in case you have to wait for a while. Here are some guidelines for that future interview.

Be Yourself

This is the first and most important piece of advice! Your interviewer knows about your skills and qualifications from reading the material you sent. It must have gone over well because you made it to the interview stage. Now the interviewer wants to get to know the real you—your personality, your ability to react to a new situation, and your thoughts on your goals and skills. Don't disappoint anyone by clamming up or trying to be someone else. You are the best at being yourself.

You may worry that interviewers will hire you only if they see you as a perfect fit. However, that is rarely true. They have a general idea of the skills and qualities they are looking for in a potential employee, and they are waiting for someone to come in and clarify the image for them, someone to embody the perfect person for the job. You might be that person. The more you remain faithful to the unique qualities that are you, and the more clearly the interviewer can see the image you create, the more chance there is for that image to answer this hiring dilemma.

Lots of people get nervous when it comes to interviews. Don't feel bad if you find yourself nervous—you will not be alone. Do your best to relax. Read something to take your mind off your nervousness. Take deep breaths; realize that you can make the most of this chance to shine.

Listen

See how your tools will come in handy. Listening closely to what your interviewer says will make you a better interviewee. For one thing, you can answer questions completely only if you have heard the whole question clearly. Listen, let the question sink in, and give yourself time to answer. That way, you will be more likely to say what the interviewer wants to hear. If you don't understand a question, feel free to ask for clarification; you can even rephrase the question to see if you have the right idea.

Don't forget, both you and the interviewer will be making decisions. You need to decide if this company will be right for you. Your interviewer will spend time telling you about the job and about the company. If you listen well, you will have a clear picture of what will await you at this job, and you will make an informed decision. For a sneak peek at some of the questions an interviewer is likely to ask, see Figure 8.7.

What experience qualifies you for this kind of work?

Be specific. The interviewer can read the rundown of your education and work experience on your resume. Think of examples that point to your ability to perform the types of duties required by this job.

Tell me about yourself.

Forget the life story. Give a brief overview of your training and your experience, schools you have attended, any related jobs you have held, any awards or commendations you have received, and any other facts about you that will convey your fitness for this job.

I see you just came out of X program. How did you like it?

This is your chance to talk about how your training prepared you for work. Keep your response positive and to the point.

FIGURE 8.7

Tips for answering common interview questions.

(continued)

FIGURE 8.7

Continued.

Talk to me about what you did at your last job.

Emphasize any tasks or responsibilities that may have prepared you to take on this new position. If the previous job was so different from this one that you cannot do that, talk about personal qualities that you possess that will serve you well in any job: promptness, attitude, willingness to learn, dependability, flexibility. Again, keep things on a positive note, and avoid saying anything negative about your former employer.

What interests you about this job or our company?

This is where your homework could pay off big time. Use the research you have done, and combine it with your own needs and interests. Instead of saying something vague such as, "I heard this is a successful company," get specific by saying something like, "I have always wanted to work with X type of equipment, and I understand that is your specialty."

How would a previous employer describe you?

Keep it honest, but stay with the positive points you feel certain your former employer might emphasize. Think about what qualities a previous employer has specifically praised about you. If that is hard to do, try to remember a specific work success you had that your employer recognized. What did you do well?

Where do you see yourself in three, five, or ten years?

Your interviewer wants to know three things: (1) Have you thought about your long-term goals? (2) What are those goals? (3) How do they fit with this company's needs? You will answer all three of these questions at the same time if you answer completely and honestly. Simply having thought about it shows that you have the vision to be able to plan ahead.

What kinds of interests do you pursue in your personal time?

Let your uniqueness shine through on this one! Try to subtly emphasize personal qualities that they value. For example, talking about a weekly volunteer position may express your concern for others. Talking about your jogging, volleyball, or aerobics shows your efforts to stay fit and healthy. Expressing a love for reading and the arts shows a desire to continue to learn and explore.

Why did you leave your last job?

If the circumstances were positive—if you left to go to school or moved—just say so. If they were negative—you quit because of trouble on the job or were fired—explain the situation in the most positive terms possible.

Why do you feel you would be an asset to our company?

Take this opportunity to outline those skills and qualities that would best fulfill the company's needs. Emphasize your interpersonal skills, and tell them why they would benefit from having you on the job.

What are your most important values?

There are no right or wrong answers here; there is only one answer—the honest answer. Don't worry about trying to figure out what they want to hear. Tell them about what you value most in life. It's a good way to find out if your values mesh with the company's.

What are your career goals?

Talk about goals you have that you feel you would be able to achieve with this company.

Question

Take your role as a decision maker one step further. Use this opportunity to find out what you want to know about this company and this job. You may want to wait until the latter part of the interview. Often, after an interviewer has asked several questions, he will say, "Do you have any questions for me?" Even if you don't receive that obvious invitation, make sure to ask for a chance to turn the tables. You have the right to ask questions.

You may want to prepare some questions ahead of time. Your interviewer may answer some of them during the interview. Then you can address whatever doesn't come up. Ask questions politely and sincerely. What might you want to know?

- Benefits (This can be a good way to get on the general topic of money in case you want to lead into the salary question.)
- Hours
- Dress style/uniforms
- Opportunities for moving up
- Duties
- Salary (Don't be too hasty with this one. Ask if the interviewer brings it up, or perhaps save it until the end of the interview. Ask only if you have a feeling that your chances of a job offer are pretty good or if you have actually received an offer.)
- Company policies or history
- Other requirements

Other questions may come to mind. Ask whatever you would like to know, within reason. Make sure you don't walk out of the interview without important information that might help you make your decision.

Be Confident

Remember, they want to like you. It's true! If a company takes the time to advertise for a job, read resumes, and interview candidates, it wants to fill the position as soon as it can with the best candidate for the job. The quicker a company finds a qualified person, the sooner it can get on with integrating that person into the company. When you come in, it makes sense that the company hopes you are the person it needs. Time is money, and the company won't waste its time. You have reasons to be confident, as evidenced in Figure 8.8. If this company is the one you want, make it happy—be the one it wants!

Be Wary of Illegal Questions

There are quite a few questions that a potential employer cannot require you to answer. Such questions have been designated as unfair questions by law. They are not permitted because they solicit information that

FIGURE 8.8
Interview attitude.

Confident but not arrogant

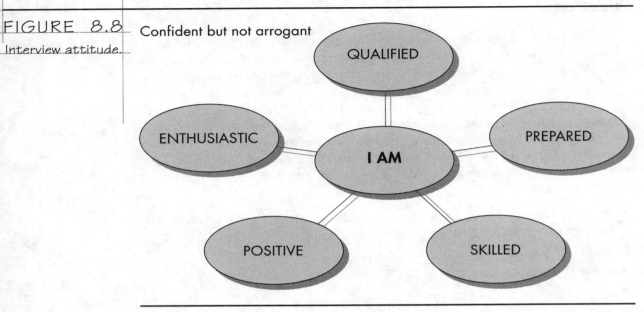

should not come into play when employers make hiring decisions. Of course, that doesn't keep everyone from asking them. Figure 8.9 contains a list of such illegal questions. Review them, and then we can talk about how to handle them.

Some employers may require certain kinds of information that will fall within the categories listed in Figure 8.9. For example, if you were interviewing to be a bartender, you would need to be of legal drinking age; even if the interviewer cannot ask how old you are, he can certainly ask if you are twenty-one or over. Asking about arrests is illegal because you may not have committed the crime for which you were arrested; asking about convictions is legal because your involvement in the crime is much more certain.

Here are some ways these questions can be asked legally:

- **Age:** Are you over the age of eighteen/twenty-one?
- **Criminal record:** Have you ever been convicted of a crime?
- **Disability:** Do you have any physical disability that would hinder you from performing the duties of this job?
- **Citizenship/residence:** Are you a citizen of the United States? If not, do you intend to become a citizen? If not, have you the legal right to remain in the United States permanently? Do you intend to remain permanently in the United States? What is your place of residence? How long have you been a resident of this city or state?
- **Organizations:** Which memberships in organizations that you have indicated are relevant to these job skills?
- **Military service:** Did you serve in any branch of the U.S. armed forces?

FIGURE 8.9
Samples of
illegal interview
questions.

Note: This is a general list. Some minor differences may occur from state to state. If you want to know your state's specific laws, check with your high school, or write to your state's human rights organization. It will be able to send you a copy of the human rights law rulings relating to race, creed, color, national origin, sex, age, disability, marital status, and arrest records.

- **Age:** How old are you? What is your date of birth? Can I see your birth certificate? These are all off limits.
- **Criminal record:** Have you ever been arrested? This is off limits.
- **Birth control:** Questions about birth control or family planning (children that you have or plan to have and whether you are pregnant) are off limits.
- **Disability:** Questions about whether you have a disability, the nature of a disability, whether you have a disease and the treatment of any disease are off limits.
- **Marital status:** Any question is off limits.
- **Nationality:** Any question is off limits.
- **Race/color:** Any question is off limits.
- **Religion:** Any question is off limits.
- **Organizations:** Any question about your membership in organizations that you have not mentioned and/or are not listed on your resume as relevant to your ability to perform the job are off limits.
- **Sex/gender:** Any question is off limits.
- **Birthplace:** Any question is off limits.
- **Citizenship:** Are you a naturalized or native-born citizen? Of what country are you a citizen? Can I see naturalization papers? Are your parents naturalized or native-born citizens? All of these are off limits.
- **Military service:** Any question regarding your service in any militia other than that of the United States is off limits.
- **Education:** During what years did you attend? What was your graduation date? These are off limits.
- **Language:** What is your native language? How did you learn to speak [any] language? Both are off limits.
- **Names:** What is your original name (if name has been changed by court order, marriage, or otherwise)? Have you worked under another name? These are off limits.
- **Photograph:** Any request for a photograph before hiring is off limits.
- **Relatives:** Any request for names, addresses, phone numbers, and ages of relatives not employed by the company that is hiring is off limits.

- **Education:** What schools have you attended? What education have you received?
- **Language:** What languages do you speak/write? Are you fluent?
- **Name:** Have you ever worked for this company under a different name? Do we need to have information regarding a change of name to check into your work history?
- **Relatives:** Please list the names of relatives who are already employed by this company.

Be Realistic

Most employers know that they are not supposed to ask certain questions, and they follow the rules. We hope that you encounter these people in your future interviews. But some employers ask illegal questions even though they are aware they cannot do so by law. Then there are poorly informed people who just don't realize when they have asked an illegal question. In the course of your career, you might run into some questions you will not be legally bound to answer. What should you do?

It's easy to say, "Don't ever answer an illegal question. Tell the interviewer that you are not required to answer that question. Politely refuse to respond." In some cases, that behavior will be extremely appropriate and necessary, and we encourage you to do so when possible.

Sometimes, however, you may feel that refusing to answer will make you seem haughty, self-righteous, or uncooperative. You might feel more comfortable simply answering the question honestly and trying to move ahead from there. That information may be of little value anyway. You might feel that increasing your chances of getting the job will be worth answering an illegal question. The decision is up to you! How can you weigh your options carefully before you decide?

- **Think about what this interview will mean to you.** If you don't have a good feeling about the job anyway, it may not hurt to politely refuse to answer a question. If this job would be important to you, you may make some concessions to stay in the running.
- **Size up the interviewer.** Does it seem like an honest mistake, or do you think the person is trying to entrap you?
- **Consider the question itself.** Would you feel comfortable sharing this information with the interviewer or not?
- **Think about how you might feel later.** You don't want to sacrifice your integrity and say something you'll regret later.

If you do decide to answer the question and are afraid that your answer might disappoint the interviewer, think about how you might turn the potential negative into a positive. What if your interviewer asks you about your apparently Latino background? Someone who chooses to answer might say, "Yes, I am Puerto Rican, and I speak three languages. I think my language skills would serve me well in this job because your clients seem to come from a wide range of backgrounds." Find a way to emphasize a trait of yours that may unexpectedly impress the interviewer.

A FEW MORE PIECES OF ADVICE

- Make eye contact. It shows that you are direct, sincere, and honest and that you mean business.
- Use a firm handshake, and introduce yourself using your first and last names.
- As stated, bring an extra copy of your resume. That way, you can refer to it as you speak, and you will also be able to point items out to the interviewer if the copy you sent isn't at hand.
- Speak clearly and distinctly, in full sentences. Use proper grammar. And don't chew gum or smoke!
- If you do discuss the salary question, be realistic about how much to expect. Be honest about how much you need, but respect the salary range and limit that the interviewer may convey to you.
- Emphasize the positive. Discuss your good points, and put a positive spin on your weaknesses instead of apologizing for them. Express how willing you are to learn and improve.
- Focus on action. The company wants to know what you can do for it more than anything else. Emphasize your qualifications and experience in terms of what you have done and what you now are able to do.
- Know the interviewer's name and use it in the interview. It will make you seem prepared and warmly conversational. Ask the secretary's name, too; use it when you arrive or when you talk to the secretary on the phone. Sometimes a good impression made on a secretary will give you a boost with a boss.
- We said it before and we'll say it again: Don't ever speak badly about a former employer or coworker. It shows a poor attitude and an inclination to speak ill of the present interviewer and interviewing company in the future.
- Use your pen and paper after the interview, when you will have time to write down everything you remember. If you write during the interview, it may disturb the conversation and will break the eye contact you make with the interviewer.
- Thank the interviewer for the time spent and the opportunity to meet.

Food for Thought

Suppose a just-married, 22 year old woman encounters illegal questions while being interviewed for a job. The interviewer asks her age and inquires about her marital status and family. She doesn't have a problem with the interviewer knowing her age because she doesn't feel that her age will affect the interviewer's opinion about her ability to do this job. So she reveals her age. But the marital status and family question is a different story. She feels that if the interviewer knows that she is married and has no children, the assumption could be made that she is planning to start a family soon. That assumption can give an interviewer pause because it may mean losing the employee to maternity leave and, in some cases, having to pay medical benefits for a family instead of an individual. If she feels strongly enough, she may choose to not respond to that question, knowing that her very lack of response may answer the question anyway.

Real People, Real Stories

Grab a friend and take turns interviewing each other for your dream jobs. Use the questions and tips included in this chapter—try sneaking some illegal questions in to test each other's quick response skills. Write a summary of the process, including your career choices on a separate sheet of paper.

AFTER THE INTERVIEW

Write the interviewer a courteous note on good paper or a simple card (typed is better, but you can write if your handwriting is clear) to thank him for taking the time to see you. If you have a sincere interest in working there, you can add a note of hope. "I look forward to hearing from you" is one example. If you don't want to pursue the job, just say thank you. Keeping in touch will remind the company of you; if it is having trouble making a decision, it could give you an edge.

Handling Failure and Success

In job hunting, as in most things, there are no guarantees. You'll win some and you'll lose some. A lucky few get their dream job right away. More likely, though, it will take some time to find a situation that will make you happy.

FIGURE 8.9
Your job will happen.

Finding a job takes effort.	Plan and work your plan.
It will take time.	Perhaps it will take weeks or maybe several months.
You will have emotional highs.	You get an interview.
You will have emotional lows.	You get turned down for a job.
Learn to deal with success and rejection.	Constructively channel your emotions.

You need to prepare yourself for whatever will come your way. As Figure 8.10 notes, many different possibilities exist.

DEALING WITH FAILURE

Failure can take so many forms! It depends on how each individual defines it. What you consider a failure might seem like a step in the right direction to someone else. Maybe you will get some job offers but not your favorite one. Maybe you will get none. Maybe you will only apply for one and won't get it. Maybe it will take three months to get a job offer. How will you deal with your version of failure?

You will need to stay aware of the fact that you are a capable, valuable person. Dig down to the tools from earlier chapters—your self-knowledge, positive attitude, motivation, commitment, patience. If you believe in yourself, you will persevere through the emotional roller coaster of the job hunt. You will be able to accept the way the process unfolds for you, and you will be able to stay confident that the job you were meant to have will arrive in due time.

Share your thoughts and your disappointments, and you will discover that failure to secure the right job right away happens to all sorts of people, all the time. You are not alone. Trading stories with others can bring you peace and comfort. It will be a relief to see that others have made it through a challenge like yours, and it will give you confidence that you can, too.

You will need to look on the bright side as much as you can. Sometimes you'll find the wait worthwhile because you'll end up with a better opportunity later than you had at the beginning. Other times, you'll find out something about a company that didn't hire you that will make you glad that it didn't.

Realize that you won't always know exactly why you did not receive an offer. Maybe someone already at the company wanted to move up, and the company went with a sure thing. Maybe economic difficulties forced the company to downsize. Maybe the interviewer had a bad day or didn't feel well when interviewing you and ended up hiring someone who came in on a better day. You cannot assume that you did not have enough talent and skill for the job!

Do what you can to learn from each interviewing experience. Maybe you will need to think out better responses to interview questions. Maybe you will need to spruce up your interview outfit. Maybe you will need to have someone else drive you to interviews so you won't get rattled by traffic. Take a close look, and give yourself the best chance by making any improvements you think you need.

Some of the best lessons you will ever learn will be learned the hard way. Everyone fails—failure is part of the human experience. But not everyone uses failure to their advantage. Learn from your mistakes, and use that knowledge to move ahead. That way, you'll turn your failures into success.

DEALING WITH SUCCESS

You might not think that success needs "dealing with," but it could go to your head if you are not careful. Try to take as much care and spend as much time considering your successes as you do your failures.

Eventually, when you receive a job offer that you plan to take, don't forget that this big moment is just the beginning! Now you will have to prove yourself on the job. Your future employer has indicated confidence that you have what it takes. The company has given you a terrific vote of confidence as well. Remember this point when you begin working and show that the confidence is well founded. You will have only just begun the route to success on the job.

Stay sensitive to others around you who may not enjoy success right away. You probably know many people in your school and in your circle of friends and family who are in a job hunt. Try to remain supportive of them as they ride the roller coaster. No one knows what the future will bring. Remember that you may encounter a disappointing time down the road when you will want to turn to them for help. If you have been kind to them, they will be there for you as well. Support is a two-way street.

When you start that future new job, celebrate! And then get to work! You definitely owe yourself a little pat on the back. Go out, have a little party, treat yourself to something special (just like when you experience a failure!), and then start your job with a clear head.

The Job Will Happen

Maybe you will get that job right away, or maybe you will have to slug through several months of applications and interviews. Either way, you will achieve your goal. Finding a job is an end and a beginning. The end of a particular job search will be the beginning of your experience as a working person in a new environment. You will probably undergo a few more job searches in your life, or you might stick with one job for a long time, but that's in the future. For now, this will be your new beginning.

As an employed person, you will have cleared one of your biggest hurdles—entering the working world. You will probably stay there in one capacity or another for a long time! Do what you can to make your stay pleasant and beneficial for both you and those with whom you work.

Your Tool Kit at Work

Notes for Applications, Resumes, and Job Interviews

8.1

Sometimes getting started is the hardest part. Before you become overwhelmed by the idea of writing your resume, completing applications, or representing yourself accurately in an interview, fill out this form. It will help you organize the information in your resume.

1. Personal Information

   a. Name _____

   b. Address _____

   _____

   _____

   c. Phone _____

   d. Email _____

2. Education

	Name of School	Month/Year of Graduation
a.		
_____ High school	_____	_____
_____ College—2 or 4 yr	_____	_____
_____ GED	_____	_____
_____ Technical/vocational/ career school	_____	_____

   b. Skills learned:

   _____

   _____

   _____

   _____

   c. Extracurricular activities:

   _____

   _____

   _____

d. Honors/awards:

_____

_____

_____

3. Work Experience

Paid jobs (start with most recent, work backward in time)

Company_____

Location (city/state) _____

Dates of employment _____

Supervisor _____

Responsibilities _____

_____

_____

Skills (specific skills you used to perform your responsibilities)

_____

Company_____

Location (city/state) _____

Dates of employment _____

Supervisor _____

Responsibilities _____

_____

_____

Skills (specific skills you used to perform your responsibilities)

_____

Company_____

Location (city/state) _____

Dates of employment _____

Supervisor _____

Responsibilities _____

_____

_____

Skills (specific skills you used to perform your responsibilities)

_____

Military _____

Rank _____

Branch _____

Date of discharge _____

Skills learned _____

Volunteer _____

Job title _____

Organization _____

Year(s) _____

Skills transferable to the workplace _____

4. Specific Skills I Have/Equipment I Can Use

_____

_____

_____

_____

5. Hobbies/Interests (list if they indicate skills that relate to your chosen field and/or would enhance your employability)

_____

_____

6. Licenses/Certificates

_____ Driver's license   Name _____

Expiration date _____

Type of license/trade _____

_____ Certificates of   Type _____

proficiency   Date received _____

Level of proficiency indicated _____

7. Memberships

_____ Union   Organization/Title _____

_____ Professional   Organization/Title _____

_____ Community   Organization/Title _____

_____ Club   Organization/Title _____

Now you have a comprehensive listing of your vital information. For an application, transfer what you need. For a resume, choose the appropriate information, put it into proper resume form, and print it on quality paper. For an interview, study the information so that you are able to communicate it to a prospective employer.

8.2 Technology at Work

Use a word processing or a resume writing program to create your resume using the information you wrote above. By putting your resume on a word processor or resume writing program, you can easily customize it to better highlight the particular skills or experiences that are relevant to the different employment openings in which you will have an interest.

8.3 Your PAL

Interviewing is time consuming for employers! When you interview, the employer hopes that you will be the one with the qualities that fit the bill. If you are, then everyone, including you, can get back on task. Your job will be to send the message that you are the most qualified candidate. Knowing the traits that employers want will help you do just that.

The following are some key traits that employers seek. If you possess every one of these traits, you are the kind of employable person companies want to hire. If you are missing a few, write them in the space provided. Work on developing them before you interview.

Accepts responsibility—commits to duties and completes them promptly and efficiently.

Takes direction—carries out directives without a fuss.

Technical skills—shows and uses competent skill with technology.

Integrity/honesty—works and speaks honestly, can be trusted.

Takes initiative—comes up with ideas/performs extra duties without always needing direction.

Understands how to work with others—cooperates consistently as a team member.

Dependable—can be counted on to work hard and to be flexible and efficient.

Energetic—stays upbeat and on schedule.

Speaks and listens well—is a good communicator.

I will develop my ability to: _____

File or post what you wrote with your other attitude cards.

Of course you always need your positive attitude. That's what PAL stands for.

The Secret of the Winning Interview

You might be offered an interview because your resume or application is interesting and shows that you have the required <u>skills. When you meet your</u> interviewer, you will have the opportunity to demonstrate that you also have the required qualities. Preparation is the secret of the winning interview. We're all a little nervous before an interview, but preparation will give you the confidence you need to overcome a bad case of nerves.

The following exercise shows you how to use preparation as a tool. Put a check mark in the first box by the steps you've taken, and complete the open-ended sentences. Write a date in the second box to show when you will accomplish the other steps. Check those steps when you complete them.

Task/Question	I have accomplished	I will accomplish by (date)
I have information on the company.		
I got the information from:		
The product or service is:		
The market is:		
The approximate number of employees is:		
The number of locations is:		
The company has been in business for:		
Other information I have on the company is:		
I know the directions to the interview.		
I took a test transportation run.		
My outfit is ready. I will wear:		
I tried everything on recently.		
I have worn the outfit for at least an hour.		
The outfit is clean and mended.		
My shoes are heeled and polished.		
My appearance is professional.		
I am wearing conservative makeup (women).		
My nails are clean and manicured.		
My accessories are conservative:		
I have practiced questions I may be asked. Three are:		
1.		
2.		
3.		

(continued)

Task/Question	I have accomplished	I will accomplish by (date)
My answers to these questions are:		
1. _____		
2. _____		
3. _____		
I have questions ready to ask the interviewer. Three are:		
1. _____		
2. _____		
3. _____		
I have prepared everything I need to take to the interview. I am taking:		
_____		
I know the interviewer's name and how to pronounce it, the interviewer's position, and the interviewer's gender.		
Name: _____		
Position: _____		
Gender: _____		

Before the interview, look over the exercise again. Make sure you have checks in all the boxes. You're ready, you're set, go!

8.5 Assess Your Interview Quotient (IQ)

Complete the following sentences with "will" or "won't." After you finish, you'll discover your level of interview expertise.

1. I _____ arrive fifteen minutes early.
2. I _____ shake hands firmly.
3. I _____ smile.
4. I _____ say both my first and last names clearly.
5. I _____ maintain good posture sitting and standing.
6. I _____ take a pen and small notebook.
7. I _____ take notes during the interview.
8. I _____ smoke or chew gum.
9. I _____ fidget.
10. I _____ speak in complete sentences using good grammar.
11. I _____ emphasize what I can do over what my interests are.
12. I _____ say so if I don't know how to answer a question.

13. I_____ exaggerate my employment record.

14. I_____ speak frankly about any negative experiences at former jobs.

15. I_____ ask the interviewer to repeat a question.

16. I_____ ask about the salary and benefits at the beginning of the interview.

17. I_____ ask about the duties and the hours of the job.

18. I_____ show interest and enthusiasm.

19. I_____ show self-confidence.

20. I_____ say I'm interested in the job if I am.

21. I_____ say I'm interested in the job if I am not sure.

22. I_____ say I'm interested in the job if I am not.

23. I_____ write a thank-you note within twenty-four hours.

Check your answers with your instructor.

If you scored from 20–23, you have a high interview quotient.

17–19 means you need to review your interviewing skills and pump up your drive to succeed.

Below 17 indicates that you may sabotage your own interview success. Go back and think through your interviewing skills again, and consider what you will have to do to give a successful interview.

After you complete an interview role-play during class time, take a moment to evaluate your performance. Do you think that you lived up to, or even exceeded, your interview quotient? Go back to the previous exercise and check the statements that you feel you fulfilled in your role-play. If there are any that you did not fulfill, highlight or circle them. This will help you see if you reached your potential.

Don't be hard on yourself for the points you missed. No one has a perfect interview, and you may have done better than you think. Two things are certain: you learned a lot, and you will eventually have a chance to put your knowledge to work in a real interview.

Plug Your Knowledge Into Real Life

8.6

You don't need a crystal ball to see the future. You can shape your own future with a positive self-image. Too often people focus on their pitfalls and failures. Turn that around and think about your successes. Here's an example of how one person did it, to help you begin to figure out how to do it for yourself:

Sam had prepared for his interview with MBS Heating and Refrigeration. Two days before, he rehearsed the questions he wanted to ask, made a test run to the company location during rush hour, and picked up his jacket from the cleaners.

Then, the night before the interview, Sam sat in his living room and took the last important step of his preparation. He thought about the times in the past when he remained calm and achieved his goals. He remembered the homecoming game in his senior year when he carried the ball for the winning touchdown; the A he earned at Columbia Tech in English, his most difficult subject; and the time he rescued his two-year-old cousin from drowning at the community pool. He let himself relive the feelings of accomplishment and exhilaration he experienced after each success, and he thought about the state of mind and the specific actions that brought him those successes. He didn't spoil his positive thinking with thoughts of the games he sat on the bench, the low English grades he got in high school, or the job from which he was let go. As he visualized his successes, Sam wrote the following comments in the notebook he'd carry to the interview:

- I am a team player.
- I am a star.
- I am a good student.
- I think and act quickly.
- I make good decisions.

Then Sam took another step. He imagined how he would feel and behave if he were offered the job. He visualized happily shaking his interviewer's hand, imagined the excitement he would feel on the drive home, and pictured the look his wife would have on her face when he told her he was offered the job. Give yourself the same opportunity. Think quietly for a few minutes and then write down three of your past successes and how you felt about each. List the skills you used in each situation and write affirmations that fit your accomplishments. Finally, imagine the hour after a successful job interview. What will it be like?

I was successful when I did the following:

1. _____

   _____

   _____

2. _____

   _____

   _____

3. _____

   _____

   _____

After each success I felt:

1. _____

   _____

   _____

2. _____
   _____
   _____

3. _____
   _____
   _____

I used the following skills/took the following actions to achieve my success:

1. _____
   _____
   _____

2. _____
   _____
   _____

3. _____
   _____
   _____

From thinking about my successes, I affirm that I have the following positive qualities and abilities:

1. _____
   _____
   _____

2. _____
   _____
   _____

3. _____
   _____
   _____

After these skills lead me through a successful interview, I will:

1. _____
   _____
   _____

2. _____
   _____

3. _____
_____
_____

8.7 Take New Tools on the Road

Look over the New In Your Tool Kit list at the beginning of this chapter. Choose and write here the three most important tools you gained from reading this chapter.

1. _____
2. _____
3. _____

For each tool you just listed, write one example of how you will apply that tool to achieve success in your career. Include changes you plan to make as well as how you will continue or reinforce existing behavior.

1. _____
_____
_____

2. _____
_____
_____

3. _____
_____
_____

9
Packing Up Your Tool Kit

STANDING OUT ON THE JOB

NEW IN YOUR TOOL KIT

Independence	Brainstorming	Empowerment
Responsibility	skills	Leadership
Personal best	Promptness	Self-evaluation
Problem solving	Loyalty	Volunteering
skills	Dependability	Embracing change
Decision making	Pleasantness	
skills	Innovation	

Y ou're on the launch pad. You
have given yourself the invaluable gift of a formal education. You have carefully chosen and
honed a collection of tools that will serve
you faithfully for years to come. Now you will
soon begin your new life. You may stick with
your first career for a long time, or you may
come to new conclusions about yourself and
switch gears one or more times. Whatever lies
ahead, you have prepared yourself well.

Now you will complete your tool kit with
hints about taking advantage of your fresh start
and making the transition to the workplace.
You will learn how to give your best on the job
and also what your rights are as an employee. We
will talk about handling layoffs, firings, and resignations; going for the promotion; and changing
jobs. Finally, we will send you off with some ideas
about staying aware through self-evaluation and
contributing to the health of your world.

It's a Fresh Start

You weren't a kid when you started this course of study. You were already a mature person with ideas and emotions stemming from the experiences you have had thus far in your life. All this remains with you; it is part of who you are. But that doesn't mean you can't make changes. You can close the door on some experiences and actively steer your future course. You can change what you present to the world. Now that you know yourself better, you can be truer to the real you and be more aware of which road to the future is yours.

Right now is the perfect time to make those kinds of changes. Your studies and your entry into the workplace can give you the opportunity to approach your new working life with a positive state of mind. Following are a few different ways to make change a positive force in your life.

YOU CAN CHANGE YOUR ATTITUDE

There is nothing like a new environment to give your attitude a lift. If you have been dissatisfied with some aspect of your life, you now have the opportunity to seek a new direction.

But think about what you have accomplished. As a result, you will enter the workforce as a trained, prepared, and well-rounded person. You will have a new environment, new coworkers, and new duties. You have every reason to move ahead with a positive attitude about your future.

YOU CAN CHANGE YOUR FOCUS

Maybe you had once been pegged as someone who excelled at one specific task or had one specific ability. Perhaps the feeling that you had more to offer inspired you to take additional courses. Now you can switch your focus to something new and present yourself as proficient in that new area. For instance, if you've been completely absorbed in sports, you can certainly use what you've learned about being a team player but change the focus to a new area of expertise such as sales or management.

YOU CAN CHANGE YOUR HABITS

You know yourself fairly well by now, and you know which habits help you to succeed and which ones

Food for Thought

Have you ever run a footrace? Remember how hard it was to not glance to your left or right to see if anyone was gaining on you or about to pass you? It's hard to not look, but the instant you do, you lose a tiny bit of your energy, fall slightly out of step, and lose sight of your goal—the finish line. Losing your concentration for that one split second gives someone else a chance to pull ahead. Apply this rule to your life. Try to not look too closely at what everyone else is doing because it steals energy that you could put toward your own unique goals. It robs you of a little bit of your own strength. By keeping your focus and ignoring the competition, you will achieve your personal best.

weigh you down. It's incredibly tough to adjust those habits, but sometimes a big change of scene can give you the boost you need.

YOU CAN ERASE "COMMON" KNOWLEDGE

Many aspects of your experience—your actions, the events in your past—combine to influence how other people perceive you. Often, even though you would like to erase some of them, other people's perceptions stick with you and can act as roadblocks on the career path. Even if you've made mistakes in the past, this is your chance for a fresh start. Learn from your mistakes, of course, but use this opportunity to draw a whole new picture of yourself.

Keep in mind that our abilities might not be fully recognized in certain circumstances and that we all develop at different rates. Did you know that when Thomas Edison was a child, his teachers told his parents to keep him home from school because he'd never learn anything or amount to anything; that Albert Einstein could not read or write until the age of ten and was considered a slow learner; and that Michael Jordan was cut from his high school basketball team?

YOU CAN CHANGE YOUR APPEARANCE

This may seem superficial. But we aren't talking plastic surgery here. We mean for you to consider expanding the fresh start to your grooming and wardrobe. Besides uplifting your mood, a well-kept appearance will enhance the positive impression you will want to make at your new job.

Consider extending your fresh start to your physical and mental health. Take the opportunity to weave regular workouts into your newly constructed schedule. Resolve to improve your eating habits—maybe make your own lunch every day. Take mental health breaks. A new start somehow makes these other changes easier to incorporate into your life.

Making the Transition to the Workplace

You may not think that starting a job and living on your own after being in school and living with your parents will be any big deal. Many of you who have held part-time jobs know what to expect of a job. And, you've been doing chores and helping fix the family's meals for ages now. So what's the big deal? Believe us on this one. It's a different world out there! Give yourself some time to adjust to the change.

One of the changes in store for you will include greater independence to structure your time. You will also need to take more responsibility for your actions. And you will need to adjust your focus to fit the workplace.

INDEPENDENCE

While you are still a student, you don't make all the decisions about how you spend your days. Someone else tells you when to attend which classes. Sports practice, appointments, your curfew—it's all laid out for you by other people.

When you move into the working world, you will be, for the most part, in charge of your time, although others may tell you when you need to be at work and when you can leave. You will have a job to do, and you will decide how to do it. You will have deadlines to meet and will decide how to meet them. No one will monitor your every move and word. You will have to learn to make the most of your time.

It will be tough to use your independence wisely. When you get a lot done, you deserve the credit and the satisfaction. When you make mistakes, you get the blame, and rightly so. It can take some getting used to, even if you've been there before! Take time to think through your schedule and make efficient decisions. Don't worry about miscalculations—they will happen. Try to remember the lessons they teach. You will have the power to order your own time, so make it a positive power.

RESPONSIBILITY

You've already learned something of responsibility in school. The teacher gives you an assignment, and you take responsibility for completing it on time. The difference is that, as a student, you don't have to create, choose, or structure your tasks—that's your teacher's job.

As a working person, your level of responsibility will move up to this next level. You'll be responsible for completing tasks at work, and you'll take more of a role in deciding how you will approach them. Once you know how things operate in the new environment, your manager or supervisor will expect you to take care of your responsibilities efficiently.

It's one of those situations with pros and cons. You will gain more freedom, with its apparent pleasures. But freedom always carries the burden of responsibilities for decisions. Consequences will also change as responsibility grows.

If you miss a day of school, your teachers are there to help you catch up. If you miss a day of work, you might miss out on a day of pay. Miss often enough, and you might lose your job! Sure your boss will make some effort to help you find a better way to work or will take it easy on you if you could not have prevented your absences, but—bottom line—the majority of the responsibility will rest

Food for Thought

Have you ever changed jobs or schools or moved to a new town or state? Do you remember how you felt? It was probably difficult to make new friends, but you may have secretly relished the chance to remake yourself. Because no one really knew you yet, no one could judge or label you. Maybe at your old job or school or location, everyone thought you were a nerd, and you wanted to be more athletic or sophisticated. Or maybe they considered you a partygoer, and you wanted to be taken more seriously. At your new spot, you have a good chance to redefine yourself.

with you. That's where the pressure of freedom will come in! You have the power to take this responsibility and work it to your advantage.

AN ADJUSTED FOCUS

When an Olympic runner prepares for a race, she spends much time and energy focusing on her goal. The runner establishes a training plan for the months before the race. She coordinates daily obligations so that training fits into each day's schedule. She sets a goal for a fast time and works toward it steadily with each training session. So that the goal seems more real, the runner focuses on the thought of winning or at least achieving a personal best time. When the race ends and the times flash on the scoreboard, the runner begins almost immediately to think about how to improve on technique and speed for the next race.

Most of us aren't Olympic athletes, but the same spirit of striving for success is a must in the workplace. If you focus your thoughts on each goal, devise a plan of action, devote time and energy toward reaching the goal, imagine yourself achieving success, and treat each goal achieved as a stepping stone to further achievement, you will prime your mind for success on the job. The single-minded focus, determination, and dedication of an athlete make sense as you pursue career dreams. You could get by on the bare minimum of others' expectations, but if you play to win, you will fly ahead in the race to continually improve yourself and beat your own personal best.

What is "personal best"? When you move into the workplace, no one will paste a letter grade on your every action. No one will give you a numerical rank in the group of employees. Test scores won't put you on a curve above some employees and below others. Now you will have the best perspective on your own progress, and you will be your own best competition. Your personal best isn't what you do better than anyone else; it is the best you can do at any given time. The focus is on you rather than on where you stand in the pack.

If your best isn't as developed as someone else's, no matter—you progress at your own rate. Every person has unique goals, talents, and weaknesses. If you try to compete with others, you will trip yourself up because you will measure yourself against their standards instead of your own. That's like trying to look good in clothing that doesn't fit you at all. You

Food for Thought

Taking on greater responsibility and independence after leaving school will be a lot like growing up. When you are young, someone else makes all the big decisions, and most of the little ones, too! Later, you begin to make decisions and take responsibility for what happens as a result of those decisions. Finally, that first time you live on your own, you will find you are in charge. Some parts of that will be a kick, such as doing what you want to do, when you want to do it, without having to answer to anyone else. Some parts will be hard, such as finding out that no one pays the rent, does the laundry, or helps you say no to things that may cause you harm. Eventually, through trial and error, you will figure out what you have to do, and you will find success on your own.

know yourself better than anyone else. You know the goals you have set and the rough spots you need to smooth. Keep striving to set new personal bests for yourself, and you will continue to grow and succeed. Remember, success is motion, process, and progress—not the finish line.

Giving Your Best—For Yourself and Your Employer

Everything you have studied so far is aimed at helping you succeed on your future job. Employers value these tools that you have acquired:

- Good attitude
- Positive self-image
  - Motivation
    - Commitment
      - Good habits
      - Patience
      - Integrity and honesty
      - Tolerance and acceptance
      - Self-understanding
    - Goal setting and prioritizing
  - Resource management (time and money)
- Reading, writing, listening, and other basic skills
- Interpersonal skills (communication, dealing with conflict, handling criticism)
- Speaking
- Stress management
- Mental and physical health

The workplace strategies that we will now address come from using those tools in combinations. They will help you to stand out on the job and make the most of your opportunities to succeed.

ON-THE-JOB TRAINING

Your education and training don't end when you leave high school and accept a job, as illustrated in Figure 9.1. They will continue in general terms as you learn from your ever-increasing experience. They will continue specifically with any initial training that your company might provide when you begin your new tasks.

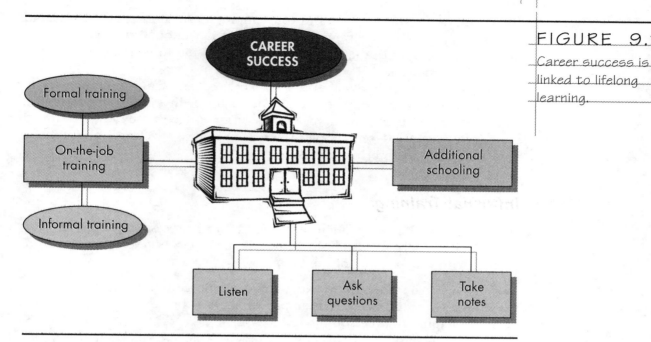

FIGURE 9.1
Career success is linked to lifelong learning.

On-the-job training cannot, and does not, replace what you learn in high school or training programs. On-the-job training concerns the specifics of a particular job, the ins and outs of procedure and getting along, and the information to which people refer when they say they are "learning the ropes." Your essential conceptual tools, confidence in your abilities, and skills and techniques all come from your studies. When you bring those to a new job, your on-the-job training will help you learn how to use them in that particular environment.

Most companies will give you some type of on-the-job training when you begin your employment, in either a formal or informal format. Your boss will determine which is necessary, based on the situation.

Formal Training

Some businesses will have a few days or even longer set aside for you to train when you first start. Every employer should give you time to get used to the surroundings and to figure out your duties. Some employers have a formal, structured training session lasting a day, a week, or longer. Such training is standard for all employees on certain levels performing certain jobs. If you are hired with another employee, you probably will go through the training together.

Your on-the-job training will require the same attention, energy, and commitment that you are now giving to your studies. Avoid the temptation to slack off and think you are "home free." The more attentive and hardworking you are during training, the more your employer will notice, and the better impression you will make from the start. What a great opportunity for you to make your employer think, "I made the right decision in hiring that person!" This will be your chance!

It's hard to describe what you will experience in training because each job differs, even within the same field. You might be in a group, or you might go one-on-one with your manager or supervisor. But because formal training sometimes resembles school (with writing, reading, lectures, and taking notes), don't forget to bring your tool kit.

Informal Training

Some of you will go through an informal training process as you begin your new job. Every job or business differs in its methods, but you can count on dealing with one or more of the following elements:

- Shadowing another, more experienced employee (following that person around, watching what that employee does in the course of the day, perhaps helping that person)
- Discussion of the particular rules and regulations of the company
- Tour of the facilities you will be using
- Lessons on any equipment you will have to operate
- Introductions to others who will be working with you

You will find that this experience is a lot like learning about a new town or a new school. But because it is a job and you are being paid to learn, it will demand special concentration. Below are some suggestions for getting the most out of your informal training. You will be able to apply the skills of note taking, listening, asking questions, and using nonverbal language that you have been learning in previous chapters.

TAKE NOTES WHEN POSSIBLE. Bring a notebook and pen with you during the first few days to use when you receive training or are given any other information you will need to know. Write down everything you must know. That way, you will have it for reference, and you won't have to bother your supervisor or your fellow employees with repetitive questions. Your notebook will become your homemade training manual. Even if it is only a sheet of important phone numbers, phone extensions, or prices, you will be glad you have it with you.

LISTEN, LISTEN, LISTEN. Sometimes informal training is sandwiched in between lots of other work, and it can go fast. The person talking with you or giving you a tour will have a lot to say and little time to say it. There will be a lot of information coming your way. Only by concentrated listening can you pick up everything you will need to know.

ASK QUESTIONS. No question is stupid. Don't be afraid to ask anything that comes into your head. You will be new, so no one will expect you to know exactly how the place runs. Only by asking questions will you become informed and begin to feel comfortable in your new job. Speak up and, of course, listen carefully to the answers.

PEOPLE ARE WATCHING. Be aware that people will be evaluating you during training. They will be looking for signs that indicate how well you work with others and whether you are a team player, show initiative, or have a good attitude. You will come through with flying colors if you also remember that your posture, eye contact, and facial expressions are a large part of the positive impression you will make.

Strategies for Success

Everything in your tool kit will make your life easier and more productive in the workplace. But your managers and supervisors will look to see if you have a few more specific skills that show you can contribute to the success of a company or business. These skills are effective work habits, critical thinking, teamwork, innovation, and initiative, culminating in the goal of excellence, as shown in Figure 9.2. If you show mastery of these skills, you will increase your chances of job longevity and/or promotion within the company.

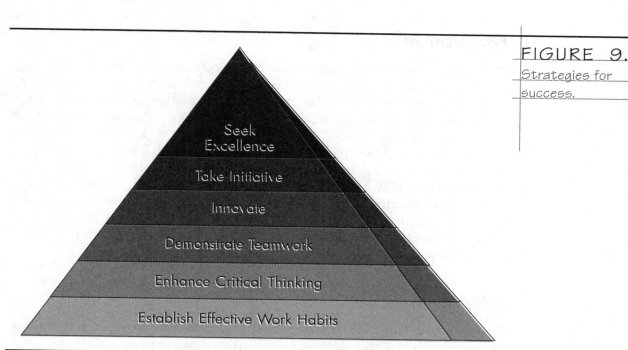

FIGURE 9.2
Strategies for success.

Seek Excellence
Take Initiative
Innovate
Demonstrate Teamwork
Enhance Critical Thinking
Establish Effective Work Habits

EFFECTIVE WORK HABITS

Loyalty and Dependability

Two prized qualities in an employee—loyalty and dependability—often carry more weight than skill level because it's easier to teach someone additional skills than to create loyalty and dependability where there is none. Although the two qualities are related, they differ slightly. *Loyalty* refers to your faithfulness; a loyal employee is faithful to the ideals, rules, and integrity of the company, as well as to fellow employees. *Dependability* refers to how trustworthy you are; a dependable employee can always be relied on to complete assigned tasks, follow directives and rules, and remain committed to the company's needs and goals. These two qualities must go together. If you are loyal without being dependable, your loyalty has no value. For example, if you believe in the company ideals and follow the rules but have trouble completing your work adequately, your employer will perceive a problem despite your loyalty.

Pleasantness

A pleasant nature, tone, and attitude are jewels in the workplace. Problems are a given. You can't control what problems will arise during the day, but you can control the attitude with which you will handle them. A pleasant nature can make problems easier to work through and brighten the day in general. Best of all, it's catching—one good-natured person can help others lighten up.

Promptness

Most companies strongly emphasize the importance of promptness. You cannot begin to accomplish your tasks until you arrive at work! You won't necessarily need to be early, and you could be forgiven an occasional tardy arrival due to unforeseen circumstances (a traffic jam, a family emergency, an illness). But plan your travel to allow for the time you know your commute will require. You shouldn't use a traffic jam as an excuse if your "traffic jam" is the regular morning rush hour! Be smart—factor in daily obstacles such as the rush-hour traffic and any regular stops you must make, and add the extra time to your commute. If it means you will have to leave your home a half-hour earlier than you have in the past, so be it. The impression you will make on your supervisors is worth the extra effort. It will show attention to detail, conscientiousness, and concern for your company.

Adaptability

No two days on a job are the same. If change is upsetting to you, you will create more stress for your coworkers and supervisors than you alleviate. But if you can roll with the punches and adapt your behavior, work schedule, and

~~tasks to the changes~~ in situations that will occur, you will prove yourself a valuable asset to the company. Adaptability involves both the ability to prioritize and a knowledge of your company's operations and social systems. You will be able to shift gears efficiently if you understand which tasks take priority over others, as well as which people have the authority to make requests that take precedence over the regular daily routine of your work. Your state of mind will also play an important role. Keeping a cool head will help you rise above the turmoil of last-minute changes and unexpected shifts.

Separation of Work and Personal Life

We talked about this crucial element of your success in the section on relationships. These two sides of your existence will only get in each other's way if you allow them to overlap. If your personal life issues show through at work, they might make you seem unprofessional and lacking in control. But if you can set boundaries and maintain the separation—addressing work issues at work and personal issues on personal time—you will impress those around you with your professionalism and maturity.

Proper Use of Work Privileges and Resources.

Don't take advantage of your workplace! Many jobs will give you special privileges, such as benefits and discounts on goods and services. You also might have access during your workday to equipment and various kinds of supplies and resources that you will need to accomplish your work-related tasks. Use only what is rightfully given to you, and only for the tasks for which those supplies or resources are designated. Any unauthorized use of supplies or discounts translates as theft.

There are gray areas, of course. When in doubt, ask. For example, if you ask permission to print out a quick private note on the computer during lunch hour and your boss allows it, that's fine. But if you spend company time, paper supplies, and postage to mail out invitations to a private party, you have gone over the line. Be honest and be reasonable with your requests.

Respect for Company Practices and Customs

Every company has its own culture, that is, its own method of operation, standard of behavior, value system, power structure, systems for completing tasks, dress code, physical surroundings, and customary ritual. As you become accustomed to a new job, trust your street smarts to help you find your way in the workplace culture.

Maybe you will have casual day on Friday and wear jeans. Perhaps a coworker will give you a comprehensive tour of where the supplies, personal belongings, and coffee break items are kept. Maybe there will be certain tasks that you will not be permitted to do even though you are capable. Maybe there will be regularly scheduled meetings that you cannot miss or snack breaks that will serve as pep rallies to psyche employees up for a big project; there might be unwritten codes of conduct and power structures among employees who are technically on the same level. Your ability to work with these systems will help you become an integral part of your company's staff.

CRITICAL THINKING

One useful strategy on any job is critical thinking. Critical thinking involves two specific skills: problem solving and decision making. Your success in the workplace will depend on your ability to think problems through and make decisions wisely. Problems that require decisions occur in an infinite variety in all job settings, for example, deciding where to transfer a call, scheduling shifts on a hospital ward, or figuring out which size bit to use on a drill.

Even if you have terrific job skills in your chosen field, you won't make the most of those skills without good problem-solving and decision-making skills. If you cannot solve a problem, you won't benefit from the skill development that comes from taking action to get past that problem. If you cannot make a decision, you won't even reach the point where you can use your skills. Knowing how to efficiently deal with problems and decisions will free you to use and develop all the skills required for your particular job.

PROBLEM SOLVING

This skill involves a rather simple sequence of steps. The hardest part is taking the time and energy to think each one through. Here are the four steps:

1. **Analyze the problem.** What's the issue? What's at stake? Where in the dilemma lies the actual problem?

2. **Brainstorm to come up with possible solutions to the problem.** Let your mind roam, and then take note of any ideas that arise, no matter how inappropriate or far-fetched they seem. Don't censor your thoughts. Also, wait until you have finished brainstorming before you begin evaluating. If you explore your ideas one by one as they arise, you may settle on an adequate choice but miss out on a better one just over the mental horizon. Also, ask others for ideas. It's amazing how different each individual's perspective on a problem can be—you might hear some terrific advice.

3. **Explore each solution.** What does each solution involve? What does each require of me? Try thinking backward from the solved problem through the solution process. Does it make sense? Is it workable?

4. **Chose and execute the solution process.** Determine the best solution for you and any others involved in the process. Don't rush into the choice, but don't wait too long, or you may lose your power or your will to decide. Strike a balance; act when you feel ready.

Real People, Real Stories

This is it. Time to get out and make it happen. You've had lots of practice talking to people you know; now it's time to try out all your new skills on someone you may not know at all. Identify either a specific person who has a job you admire (maybe you've read about this in the local newspaper) or a specific type of job you want to learn about. Use all the street smarts you can muster to land an interview with someone in either of these categories. Tell the person you are investigating career options for your future and would like to talk about their work. Come prepared with a list of questions, a notebook, and a pen, and ask away. Find out all you need to know about whether this would be a good career choice for you. Write your conclusions on a separate piece of paper.

DECISION MAKING

You make decisions almost every minute of your life. Some are significant; others are mediocre. In one day, you can decide to buy your first car and then decide to have a sparkling water instead of a soda. Naturally, some decisions are more involved than others! If you avoid making a big decision, it can create lots of other tough decisions in its wake.

Be a decision maker! Don't let life just happen to you while you accept whatever it brings your way. Choose your path. Here is a three-part system to help you make those decisions:

1. Establish the needs that must be considered in the decision—whether they belong to a person, an object, a group, or a company.

2. Name, investigate, and evaluate the available options. Be creative when thinking of options that may work. Don't censor yourself right away—you can throw away the unsuitable ideas later. Look carefully at the consequences of each option and how they will affect you and any others involved. Ask others if you want; take in their perspective and information. But remember, you are the ultimate decision maker.

3. Decide on a plan of action, and pursue it to the goal.

As you determine your needs and evaluate your options, refer back to everything you know about yourself. Self-knowledge leads you to better decisions because you are more aware of your needs. Self-awareness is the key to sound decision making.

One last step you should take each time you make a major decision is to evaluate the result. You can learn much from the results of your decision, and you can save yourself some trouble the next time you make a similar decision. Even if you use this system carefully, you won't always make a perfect decision. Your mistakes are valuable teaching tools! Take a lesson from each mishap, and try to avoid repeating mistakes.

TEAMWORK

Combine self-knowledge, communication, and cooperation, and you come up with teamwork—a crucial interpersonal skill. A manager will pay close attention to how you work with others because so often teamwork is a crucial aspect of any working environment. Nearly every job, almost without fail, involves working with other human beings. The more easily you cooperate and help, the more you will benefit your employer and your own image.

Start with self-knowledge—know what you do best. Communicate with others; let them know your strong points and where you think your talents would best benefit the group effort, and listen as they tell you theirs. Discuss the tasks at hand and who would best complete which parts of those tasks. Cooperate by pooling your resources to work together when such opportunities arise. Change tasks when new factors come into play. Use each person's contribution to create a whole.

Behind every successful group effort is efficient delegation, that is, the organized distribution of tasks. It's tough to get anything done if everyone begins working without any direction or focus. In that case, some tasks might be completed many times in different ways, and some might be ignored completely. The designated leader of the group will usually delegate the tasks to various members of the team according to factors such as each person's area of expertise, job description, time commitment, and experience. Once the team members understand their own responsibilities, the job will be completed much more efficiently.

Members of a team or group who work together to complete a task will have a number of other responsibilities to uphold. When part of a team or group, you should do the following.

AVOID NEGATIVE ATTITUDES OR APPROACHES. In group work, negativity can be contagious. One person spouting negative thoughts about the project—about the way the leader is running the operation or about one team member's failure to complete a task properly and on time—can start others griping. Soon more energy goes into growling than into fixing the problem and moving ahead with the project. As with any relationship, one must address anger or frustration immediately with those who are most directly involved. Develop a solution, and try to disturb the other team members as little as possible.

RESPECT THE OPINIONS AND CONTRIBUTIONS OF OTHERS ON THE TEAM. No two people would run the operation or complete a task in exactly the same way. Your energy will be better spent working on your own part than on criticizing or changing what others are doing. If you are the leader, or if team members are given a clear opportunity to present thoughts and ideas, then you would be within your rights if you wanted to put in your two cents. Otherwise, you will be wise to focus on your own tasks. If you foresee an especially thorny problem that has the potential for harm to the project or to a person, address the team leader or supervisor rather than going to the source of the problem.

SEE YOUR OWN TASKS THROUGH TO COMPLETION. Your primary responsibility as a team member will be to complete your assigned task. Anything else is beyond that responsibility. Even if you have the greatest ideas for other kinds of contributions or aid to other team members, those ideas will be worthless if you don't complete your basic task.

SPEAK UP IMMEDIATELY IF YOU EXPERIENCE CONFUSION OR ENCOUNTER A PROBLEM. If you hesitate out of embarrassment or out of confidence that you can figure it out on your own, you might still be in the middle of figuring it out by the time your deadline hits. Asking for help right away saves time and is the mark of an efficient worker. The sooner you ask, the sooner you will receive an answer and learn something new that you can immediately put to use.

It's true that you will feel a lot of pride about successfully completing a task on your own, but teamwork will bring a special satisfaction. There's something energizing about pitching in and achieving more together than each of you could on your own. Plus you will have the added benefit of learning from each other's talents as you work together. Everyone will come out ahead.

INNOVATION

Too many workers do just what their managers expect of them and no more. Following directives to the letter without going beyond won't lose you your job, but you might reduce your chances of promotion or the development your position to include more responsibility. You might end up feeling stuck in a holding pattern.

Innovation means coming up with new ideas, new ways of performing tasks, new structures, and new ways of cooperating. You have so much brain-

Food for Thought

Improvement comes in a variety of packages. Don't swallow your thoughts because you feel they won't make enough of a difference, or because you think they concern something insignificant. Sure, an innovation in a computer program might seem to make a big splash. But even the smallest ideas create an atmosphere for change. What if you developed a new way to organize the schedule, or you thought to install a small refrigerator so that employees could eat lunch nearby instead of taking extra time to go out? Those ideas could make people happier, and happier employees are more efficient. Every little bit counts.

power! Use it! If ideas occur to you that you think will improve your personal efficiency or the efficiency of the workplace, tell someone. Make others around you, especially your supervisors, aware of your thoughts. Remember that ideas are also tools that you could use to improve your job and your workplace.

Some ideas will work better than others. If, after some consideration, your supervisor doesn't think the idea will work, don't sweat it. You will have made an impression simply by demonstrating that you have spent time looking for innovative ways to gain efficiency. That effort itself will impress those who observe you.

If your idea should make sense to the person in charge and actually increase efficiency, you will have proved that you know how to use your brain and that you care about the efficiency of your company or business. That will work to your advantage.

LEADERSHIP

Leadership is an extension of teamwork and innovation. When someone acts in a leadership role in a team setting, that person develops ideas and pushes for them. The leader also is often in charge of distributing tasks, setting schedules, and monitoring progress. Leaders often take the initiative and move ahead without the need of direction from others.

Not everyone enjoys the leadership position! Employers need workers who will take direction and complete tasks reliably just as much as they need workers who will lead the action and guide those who cooperate on a project. Don't worry if putting your ideas in plain sight and leading others in their tasks don't appeal to you. Know yourself, and be true to yourself.

If you enjoy leading others, take the reins when the opportunity arises and be effective. If that role makes you uncomfortable, don't think a leader's achievements have more value just because they seem more visible. Focus on what you do best, and realize that those merits will seem as valuable to your supervisors as those of a leader.

STRIVING FOR EXCELLENCE

You don't have to be a leader to make a splash! If you continually work to improve your skills and your attitude, do your work well and find ways to do more, continue learning, cooperate, and make changes for the better—in other words, if you strive for excellence in all that you do—you will prove your value as an employee. More importantly, you will prove to yourself that the sky is the limit. Every time you reach a new personal best, your potential for achievement will grow. True success will lie in your own progress. If you strive for excellence in all that you do, you will achieve personal satisfaction. A large part of striving for excellence is admitting when you haven't exactly achieved it, in other words, taking responsibility for your mistakes. Everyone will make mistakes at work. A smart employer knows that and realizes that mistakes teach some of the most lasting lessons. So use the rule of admit it, fix it, prevent it. As soon as you discover your mistake, admit it to your supervisor. Consult with the person on what you can do to repair it or help lessen the damage. Take a close look at how it happened so that you can prevent it in the future.

It can be difficult to constantly strive to do excellent work. All of us have our not-so-excellent days! Sometimes it will seem much easier just to do what you have to do to get through the workday. The bare minimum may seem adequate, but if it is your standard level of work, chances are it will satisfy no one—not your supervisors, not even yourself. You might feel a vague dissatisfaction with your job, a feeling that comes from missing the pride and satisfaction you would receive from working to improve your personal best. No one has the energy to push themselves 100 percent of the time, but try 75 percent at least! You will be a much happier worker when you can be proud of your work.

What do you stand to gain from striving for excellence?

- You will continually learn more about yourself—where you have to work harder as well as where you have special talents and abilities.
- You will feel the satisfaction of rising to meet new challenges.
- You will earn the respect and admiration of those who work with you, which will make the work environment more pleasant for all concerned.
- You will help to promote the success of the company or business for which you work, which also benefits you because both your salary and job stability depend in part on that success.
- If you are destined for a job change due to a lack of challenge, you will discover your needs more quickly than if you didn't work to capacity.
- You will show a drive and dedication that will speak well for you when you are up for a promotion.

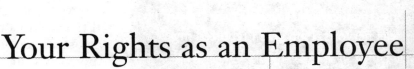

Your Rights as an Employee

You will be entitled to certain rights, privileges, and protections as an employee in this country. You should be aware of what you deserve so that you know when you should receive your entitlements. You will have a right to a contract that spells out your title, your job duties and responsibilities in general terms, your salary and pay schedule, and any perquisites ("perks" such as free parking or reduced-price lunches in the cafeteria) and/or benefits you will receive. When you take a job, you will be participating in an exchange. You will trade your services for a combination of monetary compensation and benefits from the hiring company. The company must provide you with a contract so that the details of the trade will be clear to both parties. Read your contract thoroughly before signing, and be sure to keep a copy for yourself.

Your company can not discriminate in hiring, treatment, or promotion based on race, creed, color, national origin, age, gender, marital status, arrest records, potential or actual pregnancy, or potential or actual illness or disability (unless the illness or disability prevents you from performing the required tasks). If you ever are denied a job or promotion because of any of these reasons, then your rights will have been infringed on. You could address the problem with your superiors; if that doesn't settle the issue to your satisfaction, you might consult a lawyer. Legal procedures require time, patience, and often a great deal of money. Evaluate your options and decide if it's worthwhile before you proceed.

You have a right to a workplace free of sexual harassment. Both men and women can be victims of sexual harassment, although the most common situation involves a woman subjected to harassment by a man. Sexual harassment covers a wide range of behavior that has been divided into two types. The first, quid pro quo harassment, refers to a request for some kind of sexual favor or activity in exchange for something else. It is a kind of bribe or threat.

The second, hostile environment harassment, indicates any situation in which sexually charged remarks, behavior, or items in the workplace cause discomfort for an employee. This type covers a wide range of complaints such as lewd conversation or jokes, inappropriate physical contact, or pornography kept in the office.

It is difficult to give a general definition of what constitutes sexual harassment. Mainly it is up to the individual. If you take offense or feel degraded or exploited by anything that goes on at your workplace, you have a right to speak up and address the problem. Solutions will range from a simple discussion with colleagues to clarify standards of behavior all the way to a trip to court. Start small so that you can save yourself as much trouble as possible. Approach your supervisor if you have trouble with a coworker, customer, or client, or speak with another supervisor if your supervisor is the problem. At best, the person who offended you might simply have no perspective on how the behavior was received by you and needed to understand what

Sound Bite

Don't let a situation go far. I had a male boss who continuously asked me out, and he would even call me at home. I always said no to him, but one day he brushed up against me. I thought he did it on purpose, and it made me feel uncomfortable. So I talked to someone above my boss. After he and another management person met with my boss to discuss the problem I was experiencing, the problem stopped. Even though I was nervous, I am glad I reported my feelings of being sexually harassed. I am also glad that I work for an employer that will not tolerate this type of behavior.

—L. Mercado

behavior is offensive and off limits, and why. At worst, the person might have dishonorable intentions toward you.

As with illegal questions, reporting sexual harassment is neither simple nor easy. Many people neglect to address problems at work for fear they will lose their jobs or jeopardize their chances for advancement. Some feel that others will not believe them and that revealing what has occurred will cause them to lose respect. On the other hand, victims of sexual harassment who do not report the event may damage their own self-respect, which can be extremely painful.

Think over your situation before you decide whether to report an incident of sexual harassment. How extensive was it? Do you have regular contact with this person at work? Is your job in danger? If so, is the job worth the harassment, or is losing the job worth escaping the harassment? Make a carefully considered decision and follow it through. Whether or not you report an incident, make sure that you find someone to talk with (preferably a counselor) so that you can at least work through your own feelings about it.

Leaving Your Job

No job is ever 100 percent sure. A variety of circumstances—some rather pleasant, others less so—can lead to your leaving a job. Whether you leave a job due to the good fortune of finding a better opportunity elsewhere or the misfortune of being fired or laid off, remember this rule: Always maintain your professionalism. If you handle the situation with grace, control, and tactful honesty, you will have laid the groundwork for future job searches. The respect you earn by acting in a professional manner will stay with you.

LAYOFFS

Changes happen all the time in the workplace. Companies are often in a state of flux for any number of reasons: debts, buyouts, mergers, difficult economic conditions, or a decline of interest in their products or services. In any case, you may fall victim to their troubles and be laid off.

Being laid off isn't necessarily a reflection on your performance, and you should never assume that to be true. If you choose, you could exercise your right to find out the reason you were laid off. There are many possible reasons, some of which will be beyond your control. Some companies decide whom to lay off based on seniority. Certain positions may be targeted in the event of a merger; for example, if three independent publishing companies are merged into one large company, the three people who served as editorial directors of their respective companies cannot all occupy the same position in the new company. Two of these employees will be laid off if they cannot be shifted to other jobs. Sometimes performance is a factor in a layoff. In such a case, you should be so informed.

Depending on the size of your company and on its assets, you might be offered a period of severance pay after you leave. Severance pay is a kind of salary that the company promises to pay you for a set period of time to compensate for having let you go without your consent. Severance pay can help you hang on while you interview for a new job.

Leave on the best terms possible if you are laid off. It is completely natural to be angry, hurt, or confused, but don't take it out on the people at your company. Work it all out on your own time. Express your disappointment graciously and in private to the person who has dismissed you, and part with dignity. Make sure you leave everyone with a positive impression. Don't burn your bridges—you never know when your employer might be in a position to hire you back again! Just as conditions worsen at times, so also they can improve. Keep your options open.

FIRINGS

Compared with layoffs and resignations, being fired is the least desirable situation. No one enjoys being fired! It is a tough way to find out your work hasn't made the grade. We hope that supervisors will warn employees and give them the chance to correct any problems before choosing to fire them, but it doesn't always happen that way. Sometimes a firing will come as a complete surprise.

If you choose, you might simply accept a firing and leave without question. But you have the right to know the circumstances behind your firing. In addition, you might opt to contest it, not in an angry or challenging way, but by asking for another chance. If you honestly want to stay in your job and are willing to change and make improvements, politely ask your supervisor if you can stick around and make the effort to do better. There's no harm in trying. If you get another chance, really work to improve the areas that your supervisor identified as problematic.

Again, as with a layoff, leave without causing any sort of trouble or conflict. This will be easier said than done! Be careful to control your emotions. If you are upset, you can express yourself in a nonconfrontational way. You don't have to be falsely nice, just neutral, honest, and calm. For example, here is one thought, expressed in two different ways:

NEGATIVE

I cannot believe that you never gave me the chance to work on this problem. I don't care that you fired me; I don't want to work with someone like you anyway. I'm wasting my time here as it is.

NEUTRAL

I have to say that I feel you did not give me an adequate opportunity to improve, but I have to respect your right to do what you have to do. I am disappointed that we couldn't have resolved this in some way that would have allowed me to stay on.

If you are calm, neutral, and honest as you leave, your supervisor will be more likely to retain a certain amount of respect for you and less likely to damage your reputation in conversations with those who may be in a position to hire you in the future.

RESIGNATIONS

A resignation is the most desirable way to leave a job because you are in control. You have made the decision to leave based on the evaluation of your needs. Why might you resign from a job?

- Opportunity elsewhere
- Life change (impending parenthood, illness, or relocation)
- Boredom or dissatisfaction with your job
- Trouble in the workplace (discrimination, conflict with supervisors or coworkers)

Obviously, it's much more pleasant to resign because you have found a better opportunity at another company or have a positive life change on the horizon. Other times, though, it may become necessary to extricate yourself from a job due to some problem. You know what is best for you. A troubling work environment can stifle your creativity, sap your energy, and cause dangerous levels of stress. Make your supervisor aware of any problems, and put some energy into trying to fix them before deciding to leave. If, however, you are truly unhappy and your efforts to improve the situation have had no success, then you have a right to move ahead for the sake of your mental health and your career.

If a problem at work is hindering your performance and you feel you may be fired, you could take the reins by resigning first. That way, you will have control of the situation and won't be subject to someone else's decision. With this strategy, you will avoid having a firing on your record; a resignation always looks more favorable.

If you should make the decision to resign, you have two important tasks. One is to schedule a meeting with your supervisor at which you diplomatically lay out your reasons for wanting to leave. Be as calm and kind as possible. If you are leaving because of a problem at work, don't spend time ranting about what other people on the job did to make your life miserable; concentrate on your feelings and the effect that the problem has had on you.

Food for Thought

Parting from a job can feel like ending a personal relationship or a romantic involvement. When some people want out of a relationship, they are too nervous and scared to make the break honestly and directly. Instead, they go about trying to make the other person angry so that that person will break up instead. This also happens in the workplace! Sometimes when people dislike their jobs, they will try to provoke the supervisor into firing them by behaving improperly. Don't fall into that trap! A firing remains on your record and can affect your future job searches. Make your break cleanly and honestly, and you'll have fewer regrets and a better resume for your next interview.

Your second task is to give adequate notice of your departure. A two-week notice is standard, but you may want to announce your leaving up to a month in advance, if you can plan that far ahead. Giving notice allows your employer some time to find a replacement for you before you leave. It is a courteous and proper gesture. Many companies may require your resignation in writing. If so, type up a polite letter, and give it to your supervisor.

Depending on the situation, your supervisor may try to convince you to stay. Think over any offers carefully, and make sure that your needs are being addressed if you should decide to stick around. For example, if you are leaving because you need to make more money, an offer of a salary increase might allow you to stay. On the other hand, if you want to be transferred to another department to get away from a problem coworker and that isn't possible, you might want to resist pressure to stay. If the company values your contribution, it will do whatever it can to keep you. It's up to you to decide if the company's terms are enough incentive for you.

As in the event of a layoff or firing, you will be wise to leave on the best possible terms. You never know when you will encounter these supervisors and/or coworkers again in your career. Do what you can to instill a positive impression, and it may help you in the future.

Going for the Promotion

Why might you want a promotion? And why might your company want to promote you? You might seek expansion of your responsibilities or the challenge of a change in duties that a higher position will offer. You might desire the salary increase that will usually accompany a promotion. You might anticipate the feeling of progress and achievement that will come from being promoted. Companies promote workers for their own purposes in addition to rewarding and pleasing a loyal employee. Your company might decide that your skills and talents would be more useful in a higher position. Your company might think that you are ready for more of a challenge. Or the company structure might be changing—someone may have left a position somewhere above you, and promoting you will aid in the shift of jobs and responsibilities.

There are three parts to the formula for promotion:

1. **Seniority and education.** This means how long you've been with the company and your education level. Of course, these won't help a bit if your skills and thinking aren't up to par.

2. **Job performance.** It stands to reason that you won't be considered for a better position until you've mastered a lesser one.

3. **"Above and beyond" qualities.** There are four qualities that indicate an employee's willingness to go beyond the bottom-line requirement and that have the power to propel you through the ranks. These qualities are:

- Taking initiative—originating new ideas or methods and having the ability to think and act without being urged. In a nutshell, it means being a self-starter, a person who completes tasks and pursues new ideas without being asked or guided.

- Going the extra mile—taking on extra challenges. Sure, it would be easier to just slack off when your regular assignments are done or to stop when the bare minimum requirements have been met. But, if you want to get ahead you'll have to tackle tasks beyond what is expected and wow your bosses with your energy and drive.

- Being creative—constantly seeking a better idea. Always be on the lookout for a fresh approach to your work. Find ways to improve productivity, efficiency, and effectiveness, and your creative thinking just might inspire someone to consider you for promotion.

- Having loyalty and dedication—being committed to the company for the long haul. It's another way of saying that when you go for a promotion, make sure you want it and intend to stick with it. Companies will be more willing to invest in someone who they expect will stay with them for a while.

Changing Jobs

More often these days, working people are changing jobs in the course of their careers. The instability of the economy is one factor; the downsizing and merging of companies have resulted in the shifting and reduction of job opportunities. With many two-career households, parents change jobs as their financial needs and time commitments to their children change. Increased self-awareness can lead people to seek new jobs as their needs change or as different desires and talents surface. People also change jobs not to necessarily take a different career path, but to improve their working conditions (location, salary, staff, hours, opportunity for advancement, or benefits).

Think through all the options carefully when you are considering a job change. Apply your critical thinking skills. If you seek a better salary, would you be willing to give up the great rapport you have with your current coworkers? Will the commuting money you save by working closer to home be offset by a loss of benefits? Are you sure you will have a better chance of being promoted elsewhere, or are you taking too big a chance? Weigh all the factors before making your decision.

Remember, there are advantages to staying at a job for an extended time. The longer you stay, the more likely you will be able to enjoy a stable life, increase your skills, and build your reputation as a loyal and dependable employee. Your job is like a romantic relationship—be careful not to jump ship as soon as the waters get the tiniest bit choppy. You will lose your credibility and will seem unable to make long-term commitments. This doesn't mean that you have to stay at a company ten years to establish your level of commitment, but a job applicant who has stayed at a previous job for two years might look better than someone who has had three jobs in the last year for only three or four months each time.

Conversely, pay careful attention to how you feel about your job. Do you become depressed or anxious on your way to work? Do you dread Monday and feel a weight slide from your shoulders on Friday afternoon? Are you no longer excited or moved at all at the prospect of going to work? Take a good look at these kinds of signals, and think about what's behind them. You might be able to address your negative feelings while staying on the job, or you might need to look for employment elsewhere. If job dissatisfaction causes you to lose energy and drive, you might be fired before you realize how unhappy you are. Stay in tune with your emotions so that you will be the one to make the decision.

If you decide to make a change, dust off your job hunting tools. Start asking around about opportunities (but don't solicit people at your current company until you have officially announced your departure). Update, reprint, and mail your resume to prospective companies. Rethink your interviewing skills in light of your current needs and level of experience.

Staying Aware Through Self-Evaluation

You have many things to do, tools to use, goals to set, and achievements to pursue. But how can you know how you're doing when no teacher gives you a final grade or end-of-semester evaluation? Just as you are your own best competitor, you are also your own best judge and evaluator. Sure, in many job situations, your supervisor or manager will give you a review and occasionally will talk with you about your progress, but usually not more than once every three months. You are the closest and most knowledgeable monitor. Your boss might not know about your goals on the job or in your personal life. You will need to keep an eye on all that yourself.

You can monitor your performance by doing a self-evaluation as often as you need to—once a month, upon reaching a goal, or during periods of rest in your life (weekend, holiday, vacation). How do you self-monitor? Find some time alone to think about your goals. If you have written them previously, take them out and study them. Have you moved ahead as planned? Where have you stalled? Where have you achieved a goal and moved ahead? Where have you slid back a bit? Look at both the big picture and the details, at work and at home. Give yourself ample time to ponder your current position and decide what changes you need to make.

When you complete your evaluation, take the next step and make those changes. Congratulate yourself for goals achieved. Set a new goal when you reach an old one. Visualize where you want to be, and rework how you plan to get there. If you regularly check your progress, you will have a better chance of reaching your goals.

EMBRACE CHANGE

Life equals change. By moving through life, you will find constant change in the world and inside yourself. Some of the changes you will like; others might disturb you. One thing is certain: With change comes continued learning and greater wisdom.

Two simple if not obvious observations are that the world is changing and that we need to change with it. Simple and obvious? Yes. Yet many employees do not recognize how these observations affect their employment and careers. There are a few major changes that you will need to be aware of when you prepare yourself for a career:

- **Technology is changing the world.** It seems like it's here today and new and improved tomorrow. The pace is frantic, the feats phenomenal. There is no avoiding technology's involvement in some part of virtually any career you might wish to pursue.
- **Global competition is intensifying.** Improved transportation and technology have combined to make the world a much smaller place. It's a whole new ball game out there. Be aware of how these changes will affect you.
- **Demographic shifts and fundamental changes in the ethnicity of our population pose opportunities and perils.** Businesses and employees that recognize and adapt to this change will thrive. Those that don't? They'll struggle until they realize that their customers have changed and modify their products or services accordingly.

The forces of change—including technology, global competition, shifts in demographics and ethnicity—are making it difficult not only for businesses but also for employees to maintain their effectiveness and relevance in the workplace. Impossible? No. Challenging? Yes. As an employee, the question is, "How will I create or sustain success under these circumstances?"

Although the particular approach to answering these questions will vary with the circumstances of each employee, here are three general ideas to consider as you formulate your game plan:

1. **Extend your antennas to identify the early signs of change.** Take an inward view; assess your performance and the condition of your company. Then look outside your organization; identify and monitor how technology, global competition, and shifts in demographics or ethnicity are affecting or will affect your position and your employer.

2. **Periodically take time to reflect on the forces of change so that you can better understand the effects of change on your circumstances.** We're basically talking about the WIIFM (What's in it for me?) test here. How will it affect my circumstances? What will I need to do to respond effectively to the change? Are there attitudes or actions I will need to shift in order to keep up with the change? Make sure you don't just react to the environment; instead, respond to it with thought and imagination.

3. **Be open to innovation and change.** Embrace change as good, and view change as an opportunity for personal development and an opening to help your employer in new ways.

Technology, global competition, and demographic and ethnicity shifts will continue to be driving forces of change and will likely escalate in their intensity. Adjusting to change will take awareness and effort. Learning new skills and changing old habits will require time and commitment, but the time clearly will be worthwhile. Successful employees will identify, embrace, and adapt to change. Employees who wait will put their jobs at risk until perhaps it is too late. In our world today, if it ain't broke, fix it anyway.

Stay open to change, in and out of the workplace. Look at each shift of gears, and decide what you can learn from it. Even the tough changes will have their little lessons inside, crystallized like diamonds inside black coal. Your priorities will adjust, work might become more crucial, or family time might take the lead. Your goals might fade and new ones might take their place. Your needs might flip-flop, and your life will probably take turns you could never imagine. Welcome to life! Anticipate change so that you make the most of it in your own life.

WORKING SHAPES YOUR LIFE— MAKE THE MOST OF IT

The fact is, you will spend a huge amount of time at work. Work won't be your whole life, but it sure will affect a lot of it, as illustrated in Figure 9.3. The benefits of working will go far beyond a paycheck. When you are doing something that you enjoy, it will stimulate your thoughts and interests. When you work to continually improve your skills and abilities, those good feelings will carry over into your personal life. Conversely, when you are unhappy at work, that experience will spill over into other areas of your life. A work experience that fulfills you will help to give your life meaning.

FIGURE 9.3

Success.

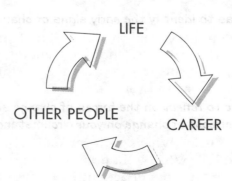

Contributing to the Health of Your World

Other than work, such things as family, friends, and hobbies make your life meaningful. But in these days of social troubles and a shrinking world—when we see problems from our own neighborhoods all the way to distant countries and understand that both kinds affect our lives just as powerfully—something else can help us understand why we're here on the earth. That something else is volunteering—making a contribution to those in need.

How can you make a contribution? Some people choose to give money, and that certainly will help. Writing a quick check to a charity can seem like an easy way to contribute; however, many of us don't have money to spare. Your time and effort are sometimes more appreciated. Though giving to charities is certainly noble and helpful, sending money off in the mail prevents you from encountering the people you might be helping. You don't have the benefit of performing an action and watching its effects, however small.

When you help someone in person, you donate time—which is your most valuable resource. When money goes, you can make more; when a minute goes, it is gone forever! The value of direct human contact is that the people you help see for themselves that you care, and you see firsthand how you have helped. When you make an effort to improve life for someone less fortunate, you derive a deep sense of satisfaction.

If you make giving your time and energy to others a priority for your life, you can weave it into both your working time and your personal time. Maybe there will be a group from your future company that tutors at a school. Maybe your future company designates a project (such as visiting a nursing home or a children's hospital or helping to clean up a neighborhood) as something in which employees can participate. Whoever organizes these activities can schedule them so that employees will use work time, personal time, or a little of both. If you volunteer on your own personal time, you could bring some of your coworkers in on the job later.

These days, companies large and small have begun to realize that they have to pitch in and do their part to improve the world, whether that means donating money, energy, or time. So whether you contribute on your own or take part in workplace-related or even company-sponsored volunteering, you (as an employee of that company) will help the company fulfill its goal of lending a helping hand or two. Believe it or not, many employers will look for community involvement and a spirit of cooperation when they evaluate potential employees. A person who volunteers displays an understanding of how caring for and helping each other can make a difference. That may impress a potential employer.

How can you go about putting your energy into making the world a better place? Many efforts need your helping hands. Some are independent; some are affiliated with religious groups, hospitals, or other national organizations. You might find an opportunity to serve food in a soup kitchen or read to disadvantaged children. You might visit elderly patients in nursing homes or work with the differently abled of many ages. You might even pitch in with cleaning or building efforts in rundown or damaged neighborhoods.

One more question arises: How will you find the time to volunteer? It isn't always easy. So many things compete for your time; however, you can make volunteering one of your priorities just like exercising, recreation, or family time. In fact, you can often combine more than one of those elements with volunteering! You might get great exercise on a cleaning or painting project. You might go with your whole family to a nursing home to sing songs and talk with some of the residents. It takes a bit of thought, but you can successfully work the gift of your time into your other activities. And for all that you give, you will get the satisfaction of knowing that you make someone else's life a little bit brighter.

Your Career Tool Kit— Don't Leave Home Without It

Although this book is coming to an end, the learning doesn't stop with the last page. We hope that it will never stop! If you take one lesson from this entire text, let it be that learning is a never-ending, lifelong process. Just as your career tools will serve you throughout your life, so too will your greatest tool—your brain—if you continue to challenge it and present it with new information and questions to contemplate.

Now when you look at the SCANS umbrellas and the skills underneath (refer back to Table 1.1), you will realize how marketable you are. You have worked, and will continue to work, to develop skills in each category that working people and employers have said are the ones most crucial to the success of employees and businesses alike. In each area—interpersonal, information, systems, technology, basic skills, thinking skills, personal qualities, and resources—you will be able to show your future employers that you have a high level of proficiency and a willingness to continue to learn and progress. The successes of conscientious workers such as yourself will together help to strengthen the economy of the entire nation. In releasing the SCANS study, the government has shown an understanding of this interdependent relationship between personal success and national success.

You have the tools now, but the tools are only means to an end. Use them to build, expand, and revise knowledge and skill. There is no limit to what you can do, learn, and know. School is not only the place where you learn and then stop learning when you walk out the door. School is also where you learn how to learn; it is a springboard to the learning that life will present in the coming years.

Think of life as a hallway, and imagine yourself walking past door after door. You open many doors as you walk past, and you explore what lies beyond them. An infinite number of doors lie ahead, and you don't know how to open them all. But if you continue to learn and grow, you will find your way. With new doors leading to fresh opportunities, a changing and growing mind will know how to use old tools to access new areas of knowledge.

You have the most important, most valuable gifts to offer the world inside and outside the workplace—yourself and everything that you do. Remember how important you are! You are part of the whole, part of all of us working together to improve life on earth. So use your tool kit to build a successful, bright future for yourself and for the world.

Your Tool Kit at Work

9.1 Knowing How to Work Productively

As you move into the workplace, take your how-to-learn skills with you. Work-place know-how makes it easy to perform effectively. The more you know how to learn, the more quickly and efficiently you will be able to adapt to the changes you encounter each day on the job; that adaptability will be one of your most valuable tools. Review your skills here and check the answer that most closely fits your present skills. Total your score at the end:

Almost always = 4 points
Often = 3 points
Sometimes = 2 points
Rarely = 1 point

	Rarely	Sometimes	Often	Almost Always
1. I have a regular place to work and store my supplies.				
2. I schedule my hardest tasks at work to correspond to when I am most alert.				
3. I plan my work time and set priorities with a to-do list.				
4. I read information about the company and my field.				
5. I read directions carefully and follow them step-by-step.				
6. When I read, I underline, highlight, or take notes.				
7. I ask myself questions on what I just read.				
8. I look up unknown words in the dictionary.				
9. I work when I am scheduled.				
10. I come to work early.				
11. I listen intently to my supervisor and co-workers.				
12. I keep a notebook for work notes.				
13. I take notes on my assignments, directions I'm given, and meetings I attend.				

(continued)

	Rarely	Sometimes	Often	Almost Always
14. I know how to determine the key points made in a meeting or by my supervisor.				
15. I take breaks and a lunch hour to relax.				
16. I write assignments in my supervisor's exact words.				
17. I review my notes as I work, to make sure I understand.				
18. I perform the priority items on my to-do list first.				
19. During a meeting or discussion, I contribute with my ideas and suggestions.				
20. I proofread.				
21. My concentration is good; I am able to focus on my work.				
22. I know and use methods to help my memory.				
23. I review my work to make sure I'm up to date.				
24. I ask questions if I don't understand.				
25. I reward myself when I complete a difficult assignment.				
26. I dress appropriately and present a well-groomed appearance.				
27. I don't spend work time gossiping and complaining about the company, the supervisors, or the coworkers.				
28. I check my work before I submit it.				
29. I spend more time working than I do worrying about the work.				
30. I am the only person responsible for how well I work.				

TOTALS   _____ _____ _____ _____

Add answers: _____ (Rarely)

             + _____ (Sometimes)

             + _____ (Often)

             + _____ (Almost always)

GRAND TOTAL: _____

110–120   Congratulations! You have excellent work skills. Keep working on making your skills even better.

100–109 You have good work skills. Look at the statements for which you checked Rarely or Sometimes, and try new hints to achieve excellence in those areas.

90–99 You have average work skills. Search for similarities in the skills indicated by your Rarely and Sometimes statements, and make changes in the habits that may hold you back in those areas. If you do so, you'll do better in school and will feel more confident in your future career.

Below 90 Your skills have weaknesses that may cause you difficulty at work. Find your potential by reviewing and building these how-to-work skills.

Take a moment to look back at your how-to-learn exercise in Chapter 5. How does what you scored back then compare with the score you earned just now? Have you improved? Stayed the same? Dropped back? Evaluate your progress and decide if you need to pay special attention to any particular skills. How-to-learn becomes how-to-work because working involves constant, continual learning; knowing how to learn enables you to work productively. When you continue to learn throughout your career, your growth and progress will bring you career success and personal satisfaction.

9.2 The Bill of Rights and Responsibilities

Currently you are a student and probably also an employee. As a student you listen to your teachers, and on the job you report to a supervisor. Your duties at work often include treating customers well. You must communicate clearly. What are your rights in these different circumstances? What are your responsibilities? And what are the rights and responsibilities of your instructors, employers, and customers?

In every situation, all the people involved—whether they are instructors, employers, customers, or employees—have both rights and responsibilities. The two R's go hand in hand. When one person has a right, the same person or another person involved has a responsibility to uphold that right. To ensure that you develop open, assertive relationships with others on the job, pay attention to the responsibility that correlates to each right.

Following is a list of key rights and their related responsibilities.

Rights	Responsibilities
1. The right to be treated with respect.	1. The responsibility to treat others with respect.
2. The right to be treated with friendliness and a smile.	2. The responsibility to treat others with friendliness and a smile.
3. The right to be heard.	3. The responsibility to listen.
4. The right to express ideas.	4. The responsibility to give freedom of expression.

(continued)

Rights	Responsibilities
5. The right to have your ideas considered.	5. The responsibility to consider the ideas of others.
6. The right to say "no" when something can't be done.	6. The responsibility to say "no" when something can't be done.
7. The right to not feel guilty about saying "no."	7. The responsibility to not let guilt get in the way of saying "no."
8. The right to make mistakes.	8. The responsibility to learn from mistakes.
9. The right to receive praise as well as criticism.	9. The responsibility to praise as well as to criticize.
10. The right to feel angry.	10. The responsibility to handle anger and resolve conflicts appropriately.

Take a look at the following four situations. For each, decide who has what responsibility and who has what right. One person can have more than one right or responsibility. Check with your instructor for possible answers.

1. Maggie's supervisor, Elise, has discovered an error that Maggie made in a report Maggie typed using Microsoft Word.

   Rights

   The right to _____ belongs to _____

   The right to _____ belongs to _____

   The right to _____ belongs to _____

   The right to _____ belongs to _____

   Responsibilities

   The responsibility to _____ belongs to _____

   The responsibility to _____ belongs to _____

   The responsibility to _____ belongs to _____

   The responsibility to _____ belongs to _____

2. Frank has a new idea about the procedure he and his coworker Henley have been following on a repair project. If they implement it, it would require some shifting of duties in midstream.

   Rights

   The right to _____ belongs to _____

   The right to _____ belongs to _____

   The right to _____ belongs to _____

   The right to _____ belongs to _____

Responsibilities

The responsibility to _____ belongs to _____

The responsibility to _____ belongs to _____

The responsibility to _____ belongs to _____

The responsibility to _____ belongs to _____

3. Doug and David are both interviewing at Damon Distributors. They have interviews scheduled during the same hour and are waiting together in the lobby. Robert, the assistant, is helping them get situated.

Rights

The right to _____ belongs to _____

The right to _____ belongs to _____

The right to _____ belongs to _____

The right to _____ belongs to _____

Responsibilities

The responsibility to _____ belongs to _____

The responsibility to _____ belongs to _____

The responsibility to _____ belongs to _____

The responsibility to _____ belongs to _____

4. Claudia has left work early four times in the last two weeks. She asks Mark, her manager, if she can do so again today. He needs to reach a certain goal by the end of today, and the task that was assigned to her is essential to that goal. She has not yet completed her task.

Rights

The right to _____ belongs to _____

The right to _____ belongs to _____

The right to _____ belongs to _____

The right to _____ belongs to _____

Responsibilities

The responsibility to _____ belongs to _____

The responsibility to _____ belongs to _____

The responsibility to _____ belongs to _____

The responsibility to _____ belongs to _____

Stylish Decisions

We all make decisions, but what's your decision-making style? Get out your career compass and apply your intelligence, experience, and intuition to the following questions. Check the column that fits your style. Then put a (+) by the ideas you'd like to develop and a (−) by those you plan to eliminate.

I Make Decisions:	Mostly	Sometimes	Rarely
1. After I look at alternatives.			
2. Quickly without looking at alternatives.			
3. By turning over the control to someone else.			
4. And blame others when the decision turns out badly.			
5. Easily.			
6. Slowly while agonizing over them.			
7. Using my feelings and intuition.			
8. That are usually disastrous.			
9. And usually view them as correct.			
10. Myself, but I ask others their opinions before making the final decision.			
11. Without anyone else's input.			
12. While considering the needs of others.			
13. After a preliminary test of my decision.			
14. And take responsibility for the outcome.			
15. And try another plan if my decision doesn't work.			

No one particular style is correct. What's right is what works for you, as long as you take responsibility for the decision, stay aware of alternatives, and change your plan if your decision doesn't work.

Here's an exercise that will guide your decision making, no matter what your style. It will help everyone from the methodical planner to the quick and intuitive decision maker.

Take a career decision you have pending. The decision may involve which part-time job to accept, how many hours you want to work, or what activities you'll have to eliminate to accept a job offer.

1. State the issue that requires making a decision:

_____

_____

_____

_____

2. The options are:

a. _____

b. _____

c. _____

d. _____

3. For each option, list the pros and cons. Number pros and cons in order of importance, with 1 as most important.

If I choose a: Pro _____ Con _____

If I choose b: Pro _____ Con _____

If I choose c: Pro _____ Con _____

If I choose d: Pro _____ Con _____

4. The result:

a. Which options have more positives than negatives, or more important positives than negatives? _____ and _____

b. Which option is the best decision right now? _____

Go ahead and act on the decision that you have so carefully made. No decision has to be final, although every decision has its consequences. Life is full of choices and changes.

9.4 Your Positive Attitude List (PAL)

You're on the last leg of the Career Tool Kit program. Review the attitudes and PALs you circled during the program (your best ones) and those you wanted to develop. Do you see a pattern in your strengths? Your weaknesses? Have you made any progress in the attitudes and PALs you listed? On the following all-inclusive list, circle the attitudes and PALs in which you feel you excel, including the ones that you have mastered in the time since you made the original circles. List the attitudes and PALs you have pledged to practice in each chapter's exercise, placing a check mark in the box that indicates their status—either "I have mastered" or "I am still working." Write in any others you're going to focus on now.

A

Ambitious — Actively seeks success.
Adaptable — Adjusts well to new situations.
Assertive — Is up-front and direct in a polite way.
Attends — . . . an exercise class.
Accepts responsibility — Commits to duties and completes them promptly and efficiently.

T

Truthful	Is honest, sincere, and straightforward.
Tolerant	Allows others to be themselves.
Takes	. . . time to sleep.
Takes direction	Carries out directives without a fuss.
Tenacious	Holds firmly to ideals and strong values; never gives up.

T

Trustworthy	Is dependable and loyal.
Thoughtful	Takes time to think things through before acting or passing judgment.
Takes	. . . time to eat three balanced meals.
Technical skills	Shows and uses competent skill with technology.

I

Imaginative	Brings creativity to the job.
Insightful	Finds ways to understand unfamiliar work practices and people.
Industrious	Works hard and steadily and completes tasks efficiently.
Interactive	Works well with others.
Involved	. . . in relaxing activities.
Integrity	Works honestly, speaks honestly, can be trusted.

T

Thorough	Is complete and comprehensive in work.
Tactful	Thinks things through; acts and speaks with politeness and awareness.
Tries	. . . to take "time outs" when needed.
Takes initiative	Comes up with ideas; performs extra duties without always needing direction.

U

Unique	Has special qualities and values them.
Unprejudiced	Accepts everyone.
Understanding	Has perspective on the needs and situations that affect self and others.
Uses	. . . appropriate birth control.
Understands cooperation	Works with others consistently as a team member.

D

Dependable	Is reliable and trustworthy.
Down-to-earth	Is realistic and practical.
Discreet	Reveals only what is necessary for clear expression; keeps confidences.
Dependable	Can be counted on to work well, work hard, and be flexible.

E

Enthusiastic	Shows a lively interest in the job and the people.
Empathetic	Can put self in another's shoes and see a situation from that perspective.
Expressive	Communicates completely, promptly, openly, and freely.
Enjoys	. . . satisfying and close relationships with friends, family, and someone special.
Energetic	Stays upbeat and on schedule.

S

Self-confident	Has confidence in abilities.
Supportive	Helps others affirm their identity and encourages individuality.
Self-controlled	Knows how to act and when to act; can defuse anger when necessary.
Sincere	Says what is meant, means what is said.
Sensibly	. . . controls drinking.
Speaks and listens well	Is a good communicator.

The following are the PALs from Chapters 5 and 7, which were listed differently than in the other chapters.

P

People at your school.
Producing good notes.

A

Anyone you know who works in your field.
Attending all classes.

L

Leads from placement office and/or newspaper.
Listening in class.

S

Supportive friends and relatives.
Studying class notes and materials.

Look closely at the attitudes and PALs you have circled. Patterns in your skill levels can indicate your areas of particular excellence and expertise. If the attitudes and PALs in which you excel tend to fall together in groups under one or more of the SCANS umbrellas, list them here with the category in which they belong. Refer back to Chapter 1 for the SCANS categories.

_____

_____

_____

_____

PALS I chose to develop	I have mastered	I am still working
Chapter 1:		
Chapter 2:		
Chapter 3:		
Chapter 4:		
Chapter 5:		
Chapter 6:		
Chapter 7:		
Chapter 8:		
Chapter 9:		

I now choose to develop the following PALs:

_____

_____

_____

_____

Congratulations on your achievements. These attitudes and PALs are yours for life.

Plug Your Knowledge Into Real Life   9.5

Read this passage and decide how to pass knowledge on to others.

Gloria is a graduate of Cutting Edge Cosmetology School. She is working at Cut-Ups in the afternoons and evenings. Her husband, Gus, works the early shift as a medical assistant at Stuart Hospital, and Gloria has time to volunteer during the morning and on Monday, her day off.

Everyone is giving Gloria advice on how to use her volunteer time. Gus is a member of Alcoholics Anonymous (AA), as is Gloria's father. A homeless shelter called her. Both the Rape Crisis Center and the Suicide Hotline could use help.

Gloria is confused because she is interested in assisting at AA, ACOA (Adult Children of Alcoholics), and the crisis center. Also, she thinks she may want to volunteer with immigrants who are learning English. Gloria's family is from Chile. She learned to read and speak English starting in the fifth grade through the ESL (English as a Second Language) program. She has quite a bit of housework to do during her time off and only has time for one activity per week.

Where would you advise Gloria to volunteer? How can she arrive at the best decision? Using the decision-making skills you've practiced in this chapter, apply the principle that we do our best volunteer work in areas where we have had personal experience.

_____
_____
_____
_____
_____
_____
_____
_____

Where are you most interested in volunteering in your locale? Where would you be of greatest help? How much time can you devote to volunteering while still maintaining the rest of your responsibilities? If you don't currently have the extra time, in what ways can you be of help to others without endangering your commitments to school, work, and your personal life?

_____
_____
_____
_____
_____
_____

9.6 Take New Tools on the Road

Look over the New In Your Tool Kit list at the beginning of this chapter. Choose and write here the three most important tools you gained from reading this chapter.

1. _____
2. _____
3. _____

For each of the tools you listed, write one example of how you will apply that tool to achieve success in your career. Include changes you plan to make as well as reinforcement of existing behavior.

1. _____

_____

_____

_____

2. _____

_____

_____

_____

3. _____

_____

_____

_____

Send Us Your Advice

This is your chance to communicate your thoughts about this book. What did you like? What could we have done better? What was new, different, and inspiring? What was outdated or not realistic? If you would like to express your opinion, take time to fill out this questionnaire.

We welcome any comments that you have. This book is about you and for you, and we want to make sure that it fits into your life as much as possible. The best way for us to know if our ideas work is to hear from you about them. If the answer to any of the following questions is no, please help us improve our next edition by explaining on a separate page what we could have done better.

	YES	NO
This book gave me a clearer focus on my career plans.	_____	_____
The ideas in this book made sense for my lifestyle and needs.	_____	_____
The material in this book took my environment into consideration.	_____	_____
I felt comfortable with the opinions, attitudes, and values expressed in this book.	_____	_____
I could relate well to the examples used to clarify the book's concepts (Food for Thought, interviews).	_____	_____
I will continue to make use of the tools in this book throughout my working career.	_____	_____
I would recommend this book to my friends.	_____	_____
I can identify situations in which the information in this book helped me to handle things more efficiently and/or positively.	_____	_____

If yes, describe briefly:

_____

_____

_____

_____

I would improve this book by adding: _____

Why? _____

_____

_____

_____

I would improve this book by removing: _____

_____

Why? _____

_____

_____

Do you have a story or an idea that you believe would illustrate an important topic? If so, please write it down on a separate sheet of paper. We will consider comments, stories, and suggestions as we revise the book for future editions.

Your name and address: Future career field: _____

_____

_____

_____

Phone: _____

	YES	NO
Do we have permission to quote you?	_____	_____
Do we have permission to contact you?	_____	_____

Sign here if you checked yes to either question:

_____

Send any comments to:

Carol Carter
Prentice Hall
1 Lake Street
Upper Saddle River, NJ 07458

Index

Key Skills for School and Work Success

SKILL	WITHOUT KEY SKILLS
Interpersonal	
Communication, Cooperating as a team member, Working with clients/customers, Leadership, Managing workplace diversity, Negotiating and resolving conflict	You have difficulties in cooperating with coworkers to complete required tasks. Everyday conflicts that are part of work can't be resolved.
Information	
Evaluating information, Organizing/interpreting information, Communicating information verbally or in writing, Processing information (as on a computer)	You don't know where or how to find data critical for an assignment. Your boss doesn't understand your report and effort.
Systems	
Social systems (human relationships), Each company's organizational system, Systems of technology—how pieces of equipment work together	You make mistakes because you don't understand your role on your team. Work and communications occur mysteriously or in code . . . you feel left out.
Technology	
Choosing equipment and/or procedures to use in a given situation, Understanding how equipment and/or procedures work, Using equipment and procedures properly	Your boss is upset with your overtime; he doesn't know you are afraid to use the new equipment. You lose your job. You didn't upgrade your skills and they became obsolete.
Basic Skills	
Reading/proofreading, Writing/taking notes, Listening, Speaking, Memory and concentration, Testing	You are confused and people don't understand you . . . everyone is frustrated. You have a difficult time getting, then keeping, a job.
Thinking Skills	
Creative thinking, Decision-making, Problem-solving, Knowing how to learn, Visualizing, Reasoning	It will be hard to grow as the job changes if you don't know how to continue to learn. Your career has stalled and you can't seem to move ahead despite how hard you try.
Personal Qualities	
Self-knowledge, Self-esteem, Integrity and honesty, Responsibility and commitment, Self-management (including self-assessment, goal-setting, motivation), Prioritizing	Despite the best technical skills, poor work habits cost you a great assignment. Your boss questions you endlessly about your work. Does she trust you?
Resources	
Managing time, Managing money, Managing material items, Managing people	Your personal financial blunders have hurt your attitude and work. You just can't seem to get to work or meetings on time. Your boss doesn't think you care.